The Federal Republic of Germany, Member of the United Nations

The Federal Republic of Germany Member of the United Nations

A Documentation

Third enlarged and revised edition

Published by Siegler & Co., Verlag für Zeitarchive GmbH,
Bonn-Vienna-Zürich, on behalf of the
Press and Information Office of the Federal Government

Overall production: Druckhaus Koblenz

Cover design: Werner Götzinger, Bonn-Bad Godesberg

ISBN 3—87748—306—2
(January 1977)

Index

Part III

Subsidiary Organs and Relief Agencies
Specialized Agencies
Intergovernmental Organizations

Part IV

Documentation

Part V

Statistics

Part I

The United Nations

1. ESTABLISHMENT

The League of Nations - the first attempt to create a world political organization — ended in failure even before the Second World War broke out, but whilst that war was still in progress Churchill and Roosevelt revived the idea of a world organization with the main task of safeguarding peace.

In 1941 they proclaimed the Atlantic Charter which embodied the beginnings of a new order of peace and co-operation and stated that the United Kingdom and the United States:

— sought no aggrandizement, territorial or other;

— desired to see no territorial changes that did not accord with the freely expressed wish of the peoples concerned;

— respected the right of all peoples to choose the form of government under which they wanted to live;

— wanted to see sovereign rights and self-government restored to those who had been forcibly deprived of them;

— wanted access to world trade for all States on equal terms;

— desired the fullest collaboration between all nations in the economic field, with the object of securing for all improved labour standards, economic advancement and social security;

— hoped to see all nations able to live in safety within their own boundaries in freedom from fear and want;

— wanted all men to be enabled to traverse the high seas and oceans without hindrance;

— believed that nations which threaten, or may threaten, aggression should be disarmed pending the establishment of a wider and permanent system of general security.

The name "United Nations" first appeared in the Allied Declaration of 1 January 1942 in which 26 states adopted the Atlantic Charter and pledged themselves to continue the struggle against the Axis Powers. By the end of the war another 25 states had acceded to the declaration.

As early as the first Conference of Foreign Ministers in Moscow in October 1943, the four nations (United States, the United Kingdom, Soviet Union, and China) declared that they "recognize the need to create as early as possible a general international organization to preserve international peace and security, to be based on the principle of the sovereign equality of all peace-loving states and to be open to accession by all states, large and small".

On 1 December 1943, the Tehran Conference (participants: Roosevelt, Stalin and Churchill) published a declaration which said, among other things: "We are sure that our accord will make it an enduring peace. We recognize fully the supreme responsibility resting upon us and all the United Nations to make a peace that will command the good will of the overwhelming masses of the peoples of the world and banish the scourge and terror of war for many generations". Representatives

3

of the United States, the Soviet Union, the United Kingdom and China drafted a United Nations Charter in the autumn of 1944. In February 1945, Churchill, Roosevelt and Stalin, meeting in Yalta, finally ended the long dispute over the question of special privileges for the Big Powers in the Security Council, with the result that each was to have a right of veto.

At the San Francisco Conference, the United Nations Charter was elaborated by representatives of the 50 nations who belonged to the Alliance. The conference began two weeks before Germany surrendered and ended more than two months after victory over Japan. By 24 October 1945, the majority of the original members had ratified the Charter. That date therefore marks the establishment of the United Nations (UN).

2. THE PATH TO UNIVERSALITY

On the day it was established more than three decades ago, the UN had 50 Members, who were joined soon afterwards by Poland as the 51st. In the meantime the number of Members has almost trebled (1976: 147). Thus the UN has developed from a limited community of victorious powers of the second world war into an almost universal organization of states. But at the same time it has acquired all the differences, tensions, and conflicts existing in the world today. The world organization is today a community of states with different political, economic and social systems.

The structure and purposes of the UN and the methods of co-operation have changed as a result of political developments since the Second World War and progress in the field of science and technology. The East-West confrontation dominated proceedings in the General Assembly into the sixties. Then, as the newly independent states of Asia and Africa joined the UN, North-South problems moved into the forefront.

More than two thirds of the present Members belong to the Third World. The work of the UN is today largely determined by this majority, their demands and their problems. To them the UN is the authoritative forum, a sounding board which they are using with increasing intensity to assert their demands for political equality and the reorganization of economic relations.

3. PRINCIPAL ORGANS OF THE UNITED NATIONS

These are the General Assembly, the Security Council, the Economic and Social Council, the Trusteeship Council, the International Court of Justice and the Secretariat (Article 7, UN Charter).

The General Assembly

The General Assembly is the central political consultative organ with the competence to deal with all matters falling within the framework of the Charter. The whole UN system, in particular the other principal organs, (e. g. ECOSOC), are under the authority of the General Assembly. Only the Security Council has a special status independent of the General Assembly, the only principal organ in which all Members are represented and have equal rights (the principle of one state, one vote, as prescribed in Article 18 of the Charter).

The General Assembly can deal with all matters of worldwide political, economic and social consequence which, as determined by the Charter, fall within the competence of the United Nations (Article 10 et seq.). The General Assembly adopts resolutions affecting the principles of international co-operation, the maintenance of peace and security, as well as disarmament and the regulation of armaments. Resolutions have the character of recommendations without binding force. If a matter is being discussed by the Security Council, the General Assembly may only take the matter up if so requested by the Council (Article 12). The General Assembly elects the non-permanent Members of the Security Council, the Members of the Economic and Social Council, and a specific number of the Members of the Trusteeship Council. Together with the Security Council it elects the judges of the International Court of Justice and appoints, on the recommendation of the Security Council, the Secretary-General.

Voting procedure

Decisions of the General Assembly on important questions are made by a two-thirds majority, on other matters with a simple majority. These questions include: recommendations with respect to the maintenance of international peace and security, the election of the members of other principal organs, the accession, or expulsion of Members, trusteeship and budgetary questions.

The General Assembly meets annually in regular session. Special sessions may only be convened at the request of the Security Council or of a majority of Members. Up to now seven special sessions of the General Assembly have been held.

The General Assembly has seven Main Committees. As in the case of the Assembly, all Members can be represented on them. The committees are:

— The First Committee, for political and security questions, including,

— The Special Political Committee, which handles more or less the same questions as the First Committee and was created to ease the burden on the latter,

- The Second Committee, for economic and financial questions,
- The Third Committee, for social, humanitarian and cultural questions,
- The Fourth Committee, originally for questions concerning the trust territories, including non-self-governing territories, now principally concerned with unresolved questions of decolonization,
- The Fifth Committee, for administrative and budgetary questions, and
- The Sixth Committee, for legal questions.

Most items on the General Assembly's agenda are first considered by the Main Committees. The Assembly then decides on the proposals submitted by the Committees. Matters not referred to one of the Main Committees are handled only by the General Assembly in plenary session.

Two other important committees of the General Assembly are:

- The General Committee, which consists of the President and the 13 Vice-Presidents of the General Assembly together with the chairmen of the seven Main Committees. It supervises the work of the General Assembly.
- The Credentials Committee, which is appointed by the President of the General Assembly at the beginning of each session and examines the credentials of delegates.

In addition to these committees, which are only appointed for the current session, there are Standing Committees, such as the Advisory Committee on Administrative and Budgetary Questions, the Committee on Contributions. Their members are appointed for a three-year term. In addition, the General Assembly appoints subcommittees and special ad hoc bodies as required.

The Security Council

The Security Council has "primary responsibility for the maintenance of international peace and security" and its decisions in this field can operate in favour of or against Members (Article 24). The Security Council is the only organ which can adopt resolutions that have binding effect on members of the UN. It has a central function among the six principal organs, its importance lying not so much in its decision-making powers as in its authority as a recognized political organ. It offers the parties to conflicts a neutral platform for the discussion and internationalization of disputes and a proven instrument for halting and settling disputes. The Security Council can help disputing parties considerably in their efforts to reach a settlement, or it can sanction or guarantee agreed solutions, especially among the Big Powers (as, for instance, when it managed the Middle East crisis of October 1973).

The functions of the Security Council are as follows:

— Safeguarding world peace by
 (a) the peaceful settlement of disputes pursuant to Chapter VI of the Charter;

— (b) coercive measures pursuant to Chapter VII.
 The Security Council determines the existence of any dispute or situation that constitutes a threat to peace (Article 39).

 Up to now the Security Council's power to impose sanctions has had only limited practical consequence. One outstanding case was the disputed action in Korea in 1951/53 (it is doubtful whether this was a genuine sanction). Then there have been the more recent sanctions against Rhodesia. Forceful measures under Chapter VII of the Charter have given way to the peace-keeping operations first introduced in 1956 (when the first peace-keeping force was sent to the Middle East). Such operations are subject to the agreement of all concerned. The Security Council plays a major role as an authorizing organ.

— Promoting a system for the regulation of armaments (Article 26). This function has had no practical significance.

— Organizational powers:
 The approval of the Security Council has to be obtained in particular for the admission of new Members, the election of candidates for important organs and offices (International Court of Justice, Secretary-General), amendments to the Charter, etc.

Structure and Composition

Unlike the General Assembly, where decisions are taken on a majority vote, the five Members with the right of veto have to come to terms so that the Security Council can act effectively. By means of the veto the Charter affords the five permanent Members a special political status which gives them considerable influence within the whole UN system over and above the Security Council. The five permanent Members are: China, France, Soviet Union, United Kingdom, United States of America. As from 1966, the number of non-permanent Members was increased from 6 to 10.

Election of Non-permanent Members of the Security Council

The ten seats for non-permanent Members of the Security Council are distributed as follows:

African and Asian states	5 seats
East European states	1 seat
Latin American states	2 seats
West European states and others (Canada, Australia, New Zealand)	2 seats

The General Assembly elects the Members of the Security Council on the strength of nominations by the regional groups. Non-permanent Members cannot be directly re-elected.

Security Council Procedure (Articles 27 et seq.)

— Procedural decisions require a majority of nine Members, irrespective of whether they are permanent or non-permanent.
— Decisions on all other matters require a majority of nine votes, including those of the five permanent Members.

On non-procedural matters any of the five Members with a veto can block Security Council resolutions, but they cannot bring about a decision by themselves. They need the assistance of the non-permanent Members. Seven non-permanent Members can prevent decisions by voting against or abstaining. Abstentions do not have the effect of a veto.

With regard to procedural decisions, the influence of non-permanent Members goes even further. In theory they can also take decisions without the approval of all five permanent Members, but in practice procedural decisions are narrowly defined. The question as to to whether the matter in hand is a substantive or a procedural decision is in itself regarded as a substantive decision, with the result that the permanent Members of the Security Council have the so-called double veto.

Since Security Council resolutions require a consensus of the five permanent and at least four non-permanent Members, the Security Council largely operates on the basis of consultation with a view to reaching agreement. Votes are usually ultima ratio where differences cannot be resolved or on practical grounds where certain Members, a veto power, say, is to be isolated.

The Role and Development of the Security Council

The Security Council, as an international organ with the power to take coercive measures, was to be a breakthrough to a new form of collective peace-keeping which would be more effective than previous attempts, particularly those of the League of Nations.

At the height of the East-West conflict the importance of the Security Council declined because it was virtually paralysed by the use of the veto. But in recent years its influence has increased and it has played an important role in containing regional conflicts, particularly in the Middle East, and to a lesser extent in Cyprus. The UN peace-keeping operations, UNEF and UNDOF, which were initiated after the Yom Kippur War of 1973, are based on Security Council resolutions.

The Economic and Social Council (ECOSOC)

In addition to the General Assembly, ECOSOC is the central UN organ for economic, social and development matters.

Membership, Meetings, Voting

ECOSOC consists of 54 Members. Every year the General Assembly elects 18 Members for a three-year term. Immediate re-election is possible. ECOSOC usually meets twice a year (spring and summer). In January a short organizational session is held. ECOSOC continues its summer session for a few days during the General Assembly. Decisions are taken by simple majority. Each Member has one vote.

Functions

ECOSOC exercises the following powers under the authority of the General Assembly:

— It makes or initiates studies and reports with respect to international economic, social, cultural, educational health and related matters and may make recommendations to the General Assembly, to Members, and to the Specialized Agencies (Article 62 [1]).

— It may make recommendations for the purpose of promoting respect for and observance of human rights and fundamental freedoms (Article 62 [2]).

— It may, with respect to matters falling within its competence, convene international conferences and prepare draft conventions for submission to the General Assembly (Article 62 [3] and [4]).

— It may enter into agreements with the Specialized Agencies (with the approval of the General Assembly) and co-ordinate their activities by means of consultations with and recommendations to them and by recommendations to the General Assembly and the Members of the UN (Article 63).

— It may consult non-governmental organizations (Article 71).

Commissions and Committees

The General Assembly and ECOSOC have set up a number of commissions and committees to cover the wide field of responsibilities in the economic and social spheres. The most important ones are:

(a) The so-called functional commissions which have a worldwide responsibility for
  — statistics
  — population
  — social development

- human rights (with various sub-commissions and a committee which submits periodic reports on human rights)
- the status of women
- narcotics.

(b) **The five regional economic commissions**

- for Europe (ECE, Geneva)
- for Western and Eastern Asia (ECWA, Baghdad, and ESCAP, Bangkok)
- For Latin America (ECLA, Santiago de Chile)
- For Africa (ECA, Addis Ababa).
- These commissions are concerned with the economic problems of their respective regions, co-ordinate regional co-operation, and advise governments and ECOSOC. They play an important role within the UN system in the field of development policy.

(c) **The Standing Committees**

- on non-governmental organizations
- on housing, building and planning
- on programmes and co-ordination (within the UN)
- on development planning
- on natural resources
- on crime prevention
- on review and assessment (of development aid)
- on science and development technology
- advisory committee on the application of science and technology to development.

Co-operation with Other UN Institutions

Other institutions reporting to the General Assembly via ECOSOC are

- the United Nations Development Programme (UNDP)
- the United Nations High Commissioner for Refugees (UNHCR)
- the United Nations Children's Fund (UNICEF).

Beyond the UN system, ECOSOC performs a co-ordinating function with regard to the Specialized Agencies, which report to the General Assembly through it (Articles 57 et seq.). ECOSOC also cooperates with non-governmental organizations.

The Trusteeship Council

The Trusteeship Council is the successor to the Mandate Committee of the League of Nations. At that time the territories taken away from the defeated powers (Germany and Turkey) were placed under the mandate of certain victorious powers under the supervision of the League of Nations (Article 22 of the Covenant of the League of Nations). The trusteeship system of the United Nations (Chapters XII and XIII of the UN Charter) was based on the mandate system and has been further developed.

The Trusteeship Council administers the trust territories together with the General Assembly and under its responsibility (Article 87). The main purpose of trusteeship is to promote the development of the inhabitants of the trust territories to such an extent that they may become independent and self-governing.

UN organs may make recommendations to the power holding a mandate but cannot enforce their application. This is one of the reasons why the trusteeship system of the United Nations has been unable to play a decisive role in the process of decolonization.

South West Africa (Namibia) was not placed under the UN trusteeship system because the South African Government refused to recognize the trusteeship of the United Nations as successor to the mandate system of the League of Nations and therefore refused to conclude a trusteeship agreement. In 1971, the International Court of Justice declared that the continued presence of South Africa in Namibia was illegal. The Trusteeship Council has from the very beginning played only a secondary role to the other principal organs, and its importance declined as the process of decolonization continued.

The International Court of Justice

The International Court of Justice with its seat in the Hague is the judicial organ of the United Nations. Only states may submit cases to it.

The Statute of the International Court of Justice forms an integral part of the United Nations Charter. All Members of the United Nations are automatically members of the Statute, though non-Members (e. g. Switzerland) may also accede to it. By and large, the Court has the same Statute as its predecessor, the Permanent International Court of Justice which operated during lifetime of the League of Nations. The Court is composed of 15 judges who are elected for 9 years by the General Assembly and the Security Council voting separately. All decisions are taken by a majority vote. Professor Mosler of Heidelberg became one of the Court's judges in January 1976.

The Court can only act if the states concerned have accepted its jurisdiction. They may do so with respect to all matters or only to certain cases pursuant to Article 36 of the Statute. If a state challenges the jurisdiction of the Court the latter determines whether it is competent to deal with the case. If its jurisdiction is established it can decide on the interpretation of treaties, any question of international law, the existence of any fact which, if established, would constitute a breach of an international obligation, the nature and extent of compensation for such breach.

Proceedings before the Court consist of a written and an oral part. The Court bases its decision on international law (i. e. pursuant to Article 38 of the Statute: international conventions, international customary law, general principles of law). If a party to a dispute does not comply with its obligations arising out of a Court decision, the other party may ask the Security Council to institute measures to ensure that the decision is implemented.

The Court may also give advisory opinions. These are made at the request of the Security Council, the General Assembly, or Specialized Agencies authorized by the General Assembly.

So far only about one third of UN Members have recognized the jurisdiction of the International Court of Justice. The Eastern bloc states, for instance, are among those who do not recognize the Court, whereas others have excluded "internal affairs" from the Court's jurisdiction. Since 1946 the Court has handed down over 30 judgments and prepared 14 advisory opinions. Apart from settling disputes, these decisions are of considerable significance for the development of international law.

Secretariat, Secretary-General

The Secretariat is the principal administrative organ of the United Nations. It consists of the Secretary-General and such staff as the organization may require. The Secretary-General is the organization's top administrative official. He is elected by the General Assembly by a secret ballot for a period of five years on the recommendation of the Security Council. Perhaps more significant are his political functions, which have been developed further within the scope of the concise provision of the Charter. His main political activities are concerned with peace-keeping measures. He can bring to the notice of the Security Council any matter which in his opinion constitutes a threat to international peace and security, and organizes and directs peace-keeping operations under the Council's supervision. He uses his good offices in the settlement of disputes and frequently undertakes missions on behalf of the Security Council or the General Assembly. But he may also take actions on his own authority.

The function of the Secretary-General ranges from that of a mere observer to that of an intermediary trying to reconcile the interests of the dominating groups in the UN, to interventions on his own responsibility. As the Secretary-General is responsible to the World Organization, i. e. its Members, he must show a large measure of skill and tact. And finally, he is concerned with humanitarian relief operations. The position of the Secretary-General vis-à-vis other organs is strengthened by the fact that he functions not only during UN sessions but holds a permanent post and has a smoothly working apparatus at his disposal. Previous Secretary-Generals were: Trygve Lie (Norway), Dag Hammarskjöld (Sweden), U Thant (Burma); the present one is Kurt Waldheim (Austria).

Secretariat staff must have the "highest standards of efficiency, competence, and integrity" (Article 101). They have to be recruited on as wide a geographical basis as possible. In the performance of their duties, the Secretary-General and his staff may not seek or receive instructions from any government or outside authority and must abstain from any behaviour which might be detrimental to their position as international officials of the United Nations.

The UN System

Within the UN system the General Assembly and the other principal organs are the political centres of numerous subsidiary organs and committees (cf. Part 3 [1]). In addition there are the Specialized Agencies which are concerned with global matters such as nuclear energy (IAEA), health (WHO), food (FAO), culture and education (UNESCO), currency (IMF), labour (ILO), posts and telecommunications (UPU), meteorology (WMO), air transport (ICAO), etc. They are based on inter-governmental treaties and in some cases are older than the UN itself. They are related to the UN by agreements (Articles 57 and 63 of the Charter) designed to secure the closest possible co-operation. Under those agreements the Agencies are obliged to report to the UN on their activities. The General Assembly may make recommendations to the Agencies with regard to their work but they act independently.

The Economic and Social Council (ECOSOC) serves as co-ordinating and information clearing agency. The Directors-General of the Specialized Agencies meet the UN Secretary-General at least twice a year under the latter's chairmanship to co-ordinate activities. A more detailed survey of the Specialized Agencies is given in Part III (2).

15

4. BUDGET, HEADQUARTERS, LANGUAGES

Budget

The regular budget of the United Nations is adopted by the General Assembly. About 80 per cent is allocated to administrative and personnel costs.

The United Nations budget has increased in volume considerably since 1946, when it was a mere 19 million dollars. By 1972 it had risen to 208.65 million dollars, and the 30th General Assembly adopted for 1976/77 a biennial budget of 745.8 million dollars. Contributions are calculated in accordance with a scale based mainly on national incomes and size of population.

However, the General Assembly has limited the maximum contribution to be paid by any one Member to 25 per cent, the minimum having been put at 0.02 per cent. In 1976, 105 countries of the Third World together accounted for only 8.1 per cent of the budget, whereas the United States and the members of the European Community together provided about 50 per cent.

In 1976 the 10 largest contributors were:

United States of America	25 %
USSR (with Ukraine and Byelorussia)	15.14 %
Japan	7.15 %
Federal Republic of Germany	7.10 %
France	5.86 %
China	5.50 %
United Kingdom	5.31 %
Italy	3.60 %
Canada	3.18 %
Australia	1.44 %

Many UN activities are financed by special voluntary contributions outside the regular budget. These include, for instance, the Development Programme (UNDP), The Children's Fund (UNICEF), and the High Commissioner for Refugees (UNHCR). The total annual volume of special contributions far exceeds the regular UN budget.

Headquarters

The Charter contains no provisions regarding the headquarters of the organization. On 14 December 1946 the General Assembly chose New York. In the early fifties, the UN moved into a spacious, modern building on the East River, but meanwhile even this has become too small for the almost 150 Members and a dozen or so observer delegations.

Members of the United Nations also have their Permanent Missions in New York. Sessions of the General Assembly are always held in New York. The other principal organs of the United Nations — with the exception of the International Court of Justice in the Hague — usually meet in New York, although in recent years the capitals of Third World countries have more frequently been chosen as the venue for international conferences. The Economic and Social Council holds its regular summer sessions in Geneva, which is also the seat of the European Office of the United Nations and several agencies. Several subsidiary organs have their seats in Third World capitals.

Languages

Rule 51 of the Rules of Procedural of the General Assembly lays down Chinese, English, French, Russian, and Spanish as the official and working languages of the General Assembly, its Committees and Sub-Committees, in addition to Arabic as an official and working language in the General Assembly and the Main Committees.

In the Security Council, Chinese, English, French, Russian and Spanish are the official and working languages (Rule 41 of the Provisional Rules of Procedure of the Security Council).

By virtue of a decision of the General Assembly of 18 December 1974 (Resolution 3555), important UN docoments are also translated into German. The translation costs are borne by the Federal Republic of Germany, Austria and the GDR.

5. MAIN AREAS OF UNITED NATIONS ACTIVITY

The founders of the United Nations were under the immediate impression of the horrors of the Second World War. Their foremost objective was to create with the United Nations an instrument intended "to save succeeding generations from the scourge of war" (preamble to the Charter).

After more than three decades, the purposes and principles laid down in Articles 1 and 2 of the Charter have acquired their full significance. Today still, the aim is to safeguard peace, to promote economic and social progress in the world by means of international co-operation, and to secure respect for human rights.

However, as the number of Members from the Third World increased the United Nations had to make allowance for their different interests and new problems. As a result, questions of decolonization, removal of racial discrimination, and world economic developments, came into prominence. Today, problems of co-operation between industrial and developing countries, the distribution of raw materials, and the development of trade relations, have become issues of central importance in the work of the United Nations.

Other new field of activity are environmental protection, a regime for the exploitation of marine resources, and the peaceful uses of outer space.

Safeguarding Peace

The Charter has declared the maintenance of international peace as the main task of the United Nations. The architects of the United Nations have created a new system of collective security built around the Security Council.

However, when the community of Victorious Powers broke up soon after the war, this plan proved largely ineffective. Above all, it could not be applied in conflicts in which the Big Powers themselves were directly involved. The Security Council was therefore for the most part paralyzed.

Upon the outbreak of the Korean War, the General Assembly adopted on 3 November 1950 resolution 377 (V), known as the "Uniting for Peace" resolution, which stated that the Assembly would assume the responsibility in cases where the Security Council was rendered incapable of action. However, some operations by UN peace-keeping forces on the strength of that resolution have not been accepted by various permanent Members of the Security Council because the General Assembly may only make recommendations to Members.

Up to now, the Security Council has never adopted military sanctions under Chapter VII of the Charter (it is a matter of dispute whether this applied in the case of Korea), and economic sanctions only in the case of Rhodesia.

Nevertheless, the United Nations has developed a system of peace-keeping operations not covered by the Charter. It presupposes the approval of the parties concerned. UN peace-keeping forces, who only use arms for self-defence, may be deployed in order to secure the application of ceasefire agreements. They also act as observers in armed conflicts.

With his preventive diplomacy, the UN Secretary-General has played a large part in avoiding crises and leading antagonists away from conflict.

Moreover, the United Nations efforts in the economic and social spheres also ultimately serve the purpose of safeguarding peace. They help to even out the disparities between nations and avoid tensions.

The world organization has not been able to do away with war and the danger of nuclear destruction, but over the years it has been instrumental in preventing crises or containing them.

Disarmament

Disarmament and arms control are a major field of activity of the United Nations and have assumed growing importance in recent years.

The development of the atom bomb made this a particularly urgent topic of discussion from the start. Even the first General Assembly, with resolution 1 (I) set up on the recommendation of the Big Powers an Atomic Energy Commission to look into the question of nuclear disarmament.

However, the United Nations has only limited scope for action in this field. The General Assembly must for the most part debate multilateral and bilateral disarmament negotiations taking place outside the Assembly and formulate guidelines for their continuation. In the annual General Assembly, the debate on disarmament takes four to six weeks. In recent years the main topic has been the proliferation of nuclear weapons, the creation of nuclear-weapon-free zones, and the reduction of military budgets with the aim of releasing additional funds for development aid. A special session of the General Assembly has been convened for 1978 to deal with disarmament questions, and it could be the precursor of a world disarmament conference.

Matters of multilateral disarmament are handled for the most part by the Geneva Disarmament Conference. One of its 30 members is the Federal Republic of Germany. (France, the 31st member, does not attend the conference). It is known as the Conference of the Committee on Disarmament (CCD). The CCD is not an organ of the United Nations but nevertheless reports annually to the General Assembly. Up to now the United Nations has been concerned with treaties or conventions on:

— the Antarctic,

— the prohibition of nuclear tests in the atmosphere,

- the ban on nuclear-weapon tests of a strength of over 150 kt,
- a ban on the putting of nuclear weapons into orbit,
- a nuclear-weapon-free zone in Latin America,
- the non-profileration of nuclear weapons,
- the prohibition of the depositing of nuclear weapons on the ocean floor,
- the prohibition of bacteriological (biological) weapons,
- peaceful nuclear explosions.

Outside the United Nations, the two superpowers are engaged in Strategic Arms Limitation Talks (SALT).

Economic Questions and Development Aid

The United Nations is devoting increasing attention to economic matters. One of its principal organs, ECOSOC, is mainly responsible for this sphere. It is the developing countries in particular who raise economic and development problems in the world forum.

Since the sixth Special Session of the General Assembly in 1974, the work of the United Nations has focused on questions concerning the new world economic order, which will consist of an attempt to reorganize economic relations between industrial and developing countries to enable the latter, with the help of the former, to develop their national economies at a faster rate and thus reduce the prosperity gap between North and South.

The United Nations Development Programme (UNDP), whose Governing Council consists of representatives of developing and industrial countries, is specifically concerned with development aid, including technical assistance, which is usually provided in co-operation with the UN Specialized Agencies. In 1964, the first UN Conference on Trade and Development (UNCTAD), was held in Geneva. Its central theme was the promotion of international trade with a view to accelerating the economic growth of the developing countries. Later the General Assembly decided to make UNCTAD one of its permanent organs, to meet every four years. UNCTAD's executive organ is the Trade and Development Board, which has 68 members, 21 Western countries, 29 Afro-Asian countries with Yugoslavia, 11 Latin American, and seven Eastern bloc countries. Since the thirty-first General Assembly, membership of the Trade and Development Board has been open to all UNCTAD members. UNCTAD is concerned with practically all aspects of economic relations between industrial and developing countries, including general questions of development policy, commodity problems, the transfer of technology, and the indebtedness of the developing countries. It also deals with problems relating to the expansion of international trade and trade with the socialist countries. UNCTAD IV, which was held in Nairobi in May 1976, elaborated further proposals for concrete steps to improve the economic situation of the developing countries. The developing countries see in UNCTAD a forum in which they can pursue their interests effectively.

The United Nations proclaimed the sixties the First Development Decade, and the seventies the Second, with the aim of increasing national incomes in developing countries through joint efforts. (For the Second Development Decade, the industrial countries were recommended to make one per cent of their gross national product available to the developing countries.) This is the object of continuous efforts to expand world trade and remove existing barriers (quantitative import restrictions, tariffs) as well as of the activities of UN Specialized Agencies in the various spheres. These include, among others, the demand for agricultural reform, which is spearheaded by the FAO. (In the spring of 1976, it was decided to set up a common fund to increase agricultural production — the IFAD — in the developing countries); measures by UNIDO (the United Nations Industrial Development Organization) to promote the industrialization of underdeveloped countries; the granting of technical assistance to developing countries, as well as a broad range of measures designed to maintain economic stability and thus achieve or maintain full employment.

At present efforts are being made to secure structural improvements and thus increase the efficiency of UN activities in the economic sphere.

Human Rights

The United Nations has been deeply involved in the problems of human rights ever since its inception, especially through the Commission of Human Rights which was set up in 1946. Numerous resolutions, declarations and conventions have been adopted relating to general human rights, the elimination of discrimination, and the status of women. Some examples are the Universal Declaration of Human Rights adopted by the General Assembly in December 1948; the Convention of 1948 on the Prevention and Punishment of Genocide; the Convention of 1953 on The Political Rights of Women; the International Convention of 1966 for the Removal of all Forms of Racial Discrimination. Of special significance are the two International Covenants on Civil and Political Rights and on Economic, Social and Cultural Rights which were adopted by the General Assembly in December 1967 after being in preparation for 30 years. They entered into force in 1976. These two covenants laid down the legal obligations of contracting parties and thus represent a further development of the principles of the Universal Declaration of 1948.

Over the years it has become increasingly clear that individual states and groups of states apply different standards in the field of human rights. This has not only made codification work within the United Nations more difficult but to a large extent been an obstacle to concrete measures for the protection of individual human rights. Whereas in Western Europe the Council of Europe was able to institutionalize a system of protection for human rights and fundamental freedoms on the basis of common values, the United Nations is still in the initial stage.

Social and Humanitarian Questions

World-wide social and humanitarian problems (Article 1, paragraph 3) are one of the main areas of activity of the United Nations. The fathers of the Charter realized that there was a close link between social and economic development.

Social and humanitarian questions are dealt with in the Economic and Social Council and in the Third Committee of the General Assembly. This Committee is responsible, inter alia, for matters concerning the application of humanitarian rights, the struggle against racial discrimination, refugees, youth and elderly people, freedom of information, and freedom of religious worship. Another important area of activity is the combating of drug abuse.

Special organs have been created for specific tasks:

— **UNICEF** was established in 1946 to alleviate the want and distress of children in the post-war era. Today, most of its work is in the developing countries. It is financed by voluntary contributions. For its outstanding efforts it was awarded the Nobel Peace Prize in 1965.

— The **UNHCR** commenced his activities on 1 January 1951. He is elected by the General Assembly and is responsible to it. He submits an annual report to the General Assembly via ECOSOC. His principal responsibilities are to give refugees international legal protection and material help and to seek permanent solutions to their problems on a purely humanitarian and non-political basis, either by securing their voluntary repatriation, resettlement in other countries, or integration in the host country.

— The **UNRWA** (UN Relief and Works Agency) for Palestinian refugees in the Middle East was established on 8 December 1949. It assists Palestinian refugees who became stateless when the State of Israel was founded in their efforts to secure a livelihood in neighbouring countries.

   The Agency is supported by voluntary contributions from about 100 countries, including the Federal Republic of Germany, and from the European Community.

— The **international control of narcotics** constitutes a permanent field of activity of the United Nations. Over 100 countries participate in the international control system. A convention adopted in 1961 in place of eight older treaties soon proved to be inadequate because such drugs as LSD and barbiturates were not covered by it. A United Nations conference held in Vienna on 19 February 1971 therefore adopted a new Convention on Psychotropical Substances which is more comprehensive and provides for strict controls.

In 1970, the Secretary-General, on the recommendation of the Economic and Social Council, set up a fund (UNFDAC) to finance practical measures of drug abuse control.

Pursuant to the 1961 convention, an International Narcotics Control Board (INCB) was created consisting of 13 experts (one of them, since 1977, a German) who are elected by the Economic and Social Council. This board has its seat in Geneva and works in co-operation with the competent national authorities.

Decolonization

No other development has changed the United Nations as much as decolonization. It was not until the newly independent states of Africa and Asia joined that the United Nations became a universal organization.

The process of decolonization began outside the United Nations (India and Pakistan). The UN Charter created a basis which has been further developed by the General Assembly. By resolution 1514 (XV) of 14 December 1960, the Assembly gave a signal of historic importance which accelerated the process of decolonization. In that resolution the General Assembly demanded independence for all colonies and dependent territories. It thus assumed a new function and developed an international responsibility in relation to dependent nations. Since then, decolonization has been one of the principal topics at the annual sessions of the General Assembly. In 1961, the General Assembly appointed a special committee which now consists of 24 members. This committee examines the extent to which resolution 1514 (XV) has been put into effect, makes proposals and recommendations, and submits progress reports to the General Assembly. The committee drafts the numerous resolutions which the General Assembly adopts on this subject every year.

The involvement of the General Assembly has greatly accelerated the process of decolonization, with the result that it has almost been completed.

Legal Questions

International law is another important area of United Nations activity. Under article 13 of the Charter, the General Assembly is required to pursue the further development of international law and to promote its codification. The Sixth Committee

(Legal Committee) of the General Assembly is responsible for codification work. It assigns mostly subordinate bodies to draft conventions — the International Law Commission, the United Nations Commission on International Trade Law, or ad hoc committees. These bodies report back to the General Assembly, which may convene an international conference or itself adopt the draft convention. There have emerged as a result such important international instruments as the four Geneva Conventions of 1958 on the Law of the Sea, the Vienna Conventions on Diplomatic and Consular Relations, the Convention on Outer Space (1967), and the Vienna Convention on the Law of Treaties (1969). In these conventions the United Nations has succeeded in finding a common denominator for the divergent standpoints and interests of the many Members, including rich and poor, strong and weak, industrial and developing countries, and that is a favourable balance.

Currently, the Legal Committee is considering, inter alia, proposals for modifications to the United Nations Charter and the problem of international terrorism. The purpose in reforming the Charter is to adapt the world organization, 30 years after its establishment, to a changed international situation (e. g. the end of decolonization and the emergence of nearly 100 new states). As regards the complex problem of international measures against the taking of hostages, the Federal Government proposed at the thirty-first General Assembly that a convention should be adopted as the first step. The Legal Committee and the International Law Commission are also working on draft conventions on the liability of states, the question of assets as regards the succession of states, and on the most-favoured-nation clause. The Commission on International Trade Law is preparing reforms in this field, for instance a new international law of purchase and a new international law on checks and bills.

Part II

Participation of the Federal Republic of Germany in the United Nations

1. THE WAY TO THE ACCESSION OF THE FEDERAL REPUBLIC OF GERMANY TO THE UNITED NATIONS

Ever since its foundation, the Federal Republic of Germany has made use of such possibilities of co-operation within the system of the UN as were open to it in a given political situation. It joined all the UN Specialized Agencies; it collaborated in UN subsidiary organizations to which it was admitted thanks to its political and economic importance. In numerous agreements it has acknowledged the competency of the International Court of Justice and submitted to it two important disputes for decision.

All the Federal Governments have been guided in their policy by the purposes and principles of the United Nations Charter — prohibition of the use of force, preservation of peace, and closer co-operation between nations.

But notwithstanding the manifold connexions and ties that the Federal Republic of Germany had long since established with the UN system, its accession to the United Nations Organization itself was not possible in view of the situation in Germany and the attitude of the Soviet Union which, as a Permanent Member of the Security Council, would have vetoed the accession of the Federal Republic of Germany without the simultaneous accession of the GDR. It was only in the course of its policy aiming at a compromise with the East and the settlement of internal German relations that the Federal Government was able to open up the way for its accession to the UN Organization. This presupposed, however, that admission was made possible at the same time for the German Democratic Republic.

Under Point 20 of the Declaration of Kassel of 21 May 1970, the Federal Government put the proposal to the GDR that the membership and co-operation of the two states in Germany in international organizations be settled on the basis of a treaty with the Federal Republic of Germany. This proposal was realized in the Basic Treaty and the prerequisites for the membership of both German States in the UN established.

The Basic Treaty regulates the relations between the two German states for the duration of the partition, on the basis of equal rights and non-discrimination, and takes into account the special situation in Germany. This position is mainly determined by the fact that the German nation today is living in two separate states, that a freely agreed peaceful settlement for Germany is still outstanding, and that pending such a settlement, the above-mentioned rights and responsibilities of the Four Powers in respect of Berlin and Germany as a whole continue to apply.

In a statement published in the four capitals on 9 November 1972, the Four Powers declared that the accession to the UN of two German states did not affect the rights and responsibilities of the Four Powers. It was thus made clear that the situation in Germany as such has not been altered by the accession of the two German states to the United Nations. This statement was notified to the Federal Government by the Three Powers, and to the Government of the GDR by the Soviet Union on 9 November 1972.

In addition, the two German states agreed to apply for membership of the United Nations simultaneously.

The Admission of the Federal Republic of Germany to the United Nations

On 18 September 1973, the Federal Republic of Germany was admitted together with the GDR to the United Nations by resolution of the General Assembly.

With the two German states, the UN has for the first time admitted a divided country after the parties concerned had established the prerequisites thereto between themselves.

The admission of the two German states met with international approval. Seventy-five Members, an unusually large number, introduced the draft resolution. The simultaneous and uniform admission in a single resolution and the numerous welcoming speeches conveyed the impression that the community of states was fully aware that this was a case of the admission of two states with a special mutual relationship in which one single nation continued to exist.

The modalities helped to reveal the background of the admission of the two German states. The Security Council and the General Assembly dealt with the applications of the two German states in each case in a single decision which was accepted by acclamation by both bodies. The Federal Chancellor and the Federal Minister for Foreign Affairs made it clear in their speeches that accession of the two German states to the UN did not mean that they tolerated the partition of Germany but that they would continue their efforts to bring about a state of peace in which the German people would regain their unity in free self-determination.

The simultaneous membership of the two German states in the United Nations as brought about under the foregoing circumstances does not prejudice the special situation in Germany. The UN Charter does not have any legal effects by which the partition of Germany is stipulated. A reunification brought about by peaceful means is compatible with the Charter, which confirms the right of self-determination of nations as one of the main principles of international relations. A policy aimed at bringing about a state of peace in Europe in which the German people regain their unity in free self-determination is thus compatible with the United Nations Charter.

The disagreement over the German question cannot, however, be settled in the United Nations as long as it has not been cleared up in Germany itself. But the Federal Republic has, with its admission to the United Nations, gained another international forum before which it can advocate its policy aimed at strengthening the right of self-determination and its peaceful implementation throughout the world.

The Federal Government has been able to represent the interests of Berlin (West) in the United Nations in the form that has long been usual for multilateral treaties.

In conjunction with the application for admission, the Federal Minister for Foreign Affairs made it plain in a letter to the Secretary-General of the United Nations on 13 June 1973 that the Federal Republic of Germany would also take on the rights and obligations contained in the United Nations Charter with regard to Berlin (West) and represent the city's interests in the United Nations, in so far as questions of security and status are not affected. This letter was circulated as an official document of the United Nations. The Federal Chancellor and the Foreign Minister, addressing the General Assembly, re-affirmed that Berlin would be involved in the work of the Federal Republic of Germany in the United Nations.

2. OUTLINES OF COOPERATION AND UNITED NATIONS POLICY

With its accession to the United Nations the Federal Republic of Germany took a step of historic importance: "We are compelled finally to abandon the introversion of our former foreign policy and see ourselves as a part of the universal whole and our own problems in relation to the world as it really is" (the Federal Minister for Foreign Affairs to the German Bundestag on 3 October 1973).

At the time of its admission to the UN, the Federal Republic of Germany found an organization which in the three decades of its existence had undergone a fundamental transformation. The UN had developed from being a limited association of the victorious powers of the Second World War to an almost universal organization and a centre of international co-operation. But it is in that very organization that the tensions and conflicts which determine the world today are discernible.

It is against this background that one must see the co-operation of the Federal Republic of Germany within the UN. It is not aiming at short-term successes. On the contrary, its aim is on a long-term basis to enhance the reputation of the Federal Republic of Germany by solid and constructive co-operation as a reliable partner capable of making an important contribution to the work of the United Nations.

The guiding precepts for the participation of the Federal Republic of Germany in the UN are the purposes and principles of the UN Charter, which were in any case always the basis of its own foreign policy, viz. the safeguarding of peace and international co-operation.

In his speech to the thirtieth General Assembly on 24 September 1975, the Federal Foreign Minister Genscher set forth the demands which, in view of international interdepence, today confront all countries:

"We must proceed from economic egotism to a world-wide reliable regime of co-operation among equals; we must proceed from the proclamation of human rights to their world-wide application and to the implementation of the right of self-determination wherever that right is still being denied; we must proceed from the management of crises to a just and thereby lasting peace."

The Federal Republic of Germany sees its task in the United Nations as the translation of these basic demands for constructive international co-operation into practical policy and advocates a constructive discussion on the demands of the Third World in the economic sector. It endorses a reform of the world economic system aiming at a just balance of interests between industrial states and developing countries. Other focal points of its co-operation are disarmament and arms control, the implementation of the right of self-determination and human rights throughout the world, the struggle to end racial discrimation, and the further development of international law. The Federal Republic of Germany also participates in the peace-keeping operations of the United Nations.

3. MEMBERSHIP IN THE SECURITY COUNCIL AND OTHER IMPORTANT UN ORGANS

During the few years since becoming a Member of the United Nations, the Federal Republic of Germany has been admitted to important UN organs and bodies with a limited number of members, including

- the ECOSOC, the central controlling organ of the UN in the economic and social sector;
- the Commission of Human Rights;
- the Commission on the Status of Women;
- the Geneva Conference on Disarmament (CCD);
- the UN Commission on International Trade Law (UNCITRAL).

A German judge, Professor Mosler, has been a member of the International Court of Justice in The Hague since 1976.

Membership of the Security Council is of particular significance. In 1976, the thirty-First General Assembly elected the Federal Republic of Germany to the Security Council as a non-permanent Member for the two-year period 1977/78. Its membership of the Security Council emphasizes the position the Federal Republic of Germany enjoys in Europe, in East-West relations, and as regards the Third World, as well as the good reputation it has acquired in international and bilateral co-operation. It demonstrates the freedom of action in foreign policy regained through its Eastern policy and intra-German relations. The participation of the Federal Republic in the principal UN organ responsible for the preservation of world peace and international security allows it a greater say in world politics, but it also imposes a greater responsibility. The election of the Federal Republic to the Security Council is also an expression of confidence in the credibility and continuity of its foreign policy. It will continue to pursue this policy, which is geared to constructive co-operation wherever it sees common positions and its partners are willing to do the same within the framework of international multilateral co-operation.

The Federal Minister for Foreign Affairs has outlined the idea of the Federal Government in the Security Council as follows: "We shall base our co-operation in the Security Council on the principles of our foreign policy. We wish to work for the safeguarding of peace in the world and will do our best to ensure that throughout the world the use of force will be rejected as a means of implementing political aims. The right of self-determination of nations shall be the guiding principle for the course taken by the Federal Government. We will strive to ensure respect for human rights all over the world."

4. CO-OPERATION BETWEEN THE MEMBERS OF THE EUROPEAN COMMUNITY

The Federal Republic of Germany also regards itself as a European state in the United Nations. By its co-operation it also wants to strengthen Europe's presence in the United Nations. The Federal Government therefore attaches importance to pursuing its UN policy in close co-ordination with its EC partners.

The framework for this are the meetings within the European Community and the consultations between the representatives of the participants in the European Political Co-operation (EPC) at the UN in New York.

Many joint statements and in many instances an agreed voting policy on the part of the Nine in the General Assembly are impressive proof of the readiness of all concerned to co-operate. The Federal Government will continue its endeavours to intensify European co-operation and will seek close co-operation with other Western allies.

5. MAIN ASPECTS OF CO-OPERATION

The Federal Republic of Germany plays an active and responsible part in all the political, economic, legal, social and humanitarian activities of the principal organs, committees and other bodies of the UN

Participation of the Federal Republic of Germany in UN Peace-Keeping Operations

Participation in UN peace-keeping operations is in line with the principles of the foreign policy of the Federal Republic of Germany, which aims at safeguarding peace. Thus, even before its accession to the UN, it voluntarily supported the UN peace-keeping force for Cyprus and also contributed to UNEF II with voluntary transport services in excess of its obligatory contribution as a Member of the UN. Up to the end of 1976, the Federal Republic took part in UN peace-keeping operations with the following contributions:

— UNFICYP (United Nations Peace-keeping Force for Cyprus) from 1964 to the amount of 15,500,000 dollars; since 1967 the annual voluntary contribution has been one million dollars;

— UNEF II and UNDOF (UN Peace-keeping Force for the Middle East) since the end of 1973 with 20,093,000 US dollars and voluntary transport services of the Federal Armed Forces (transport of about 1,000 soldiers from Ghana and Senegal to Cairo). Of the annual total costs, the Federal Republic provides the amount which is based on its contribution rate for the regular UN budget.

Disarmament

Since its admission to the UN the Federal Republic of Germany has been able to participate actively in international efforts aiming at general and complete disarmament with effective international controls. It devotes these efforts to promoting its policy of safeguarding peace and detente.

In his speech to the thirty-first General Assembly in the autumn of 1976, the Federal Foreign Minister, Hans Dietrich Genscher, urgently called attention to the necessity of disarmament:

"Peace itself and efforts to safeguard it by means of more stable structures are jeopardized by unrelenting efforts in nearly all parts of the world to build up arms strengths. Exports of conventional weapons in particular have increased rapidly. The monstrous waste of scarce resources in the industrial countries as in the developing countries works to the detriment of the people."

"We must not give up hope because of the disappointing results in the field of arms control and disarmament so far. In the process of detente efforts must be redoubled to halt the arms race and, both world-wide and regionally, to translate into reality effective measures of arms control and arms limitation. Balanced and controlled disarmament remains one of the most urgent tasks."

The Federal Government continues to participate in the efforts of the General Assembly to achieve arms controls and disarmament. In this connexion it is anxious to explain its policy of peace and detente in the field of disarmament also before the international forum. The German delegate among other things declared the following in the disarmament debate of the First Committee on 24 October 1974:

"It therefore cannot be denied that there is a danger that the disarmament debate will be regarded by the public at large as a routine matter and that a feeling of hopelessness will ensue. We should do all in our power to resist any such tendency. Complex though the subject may be, it is after all not primarily a question of military and technological problems to which the experts have to give their closest attention, but of political decisions to ensure peace. It is necessary to prevent or eliminate the dangerous instabilities which an armaments race can engender, to initiate controlled disarmament measures and, in addition, to try and concentrate the limited resources of the states on the most urgent tasks of humanity and civilization, the elimination of hunger and want."

The Federal Republic of Germany has been a member of the Geneva Conference on Disarmament (CCD) since 1 January 1975. It is represented in all the CCD's groups of experts.

The Federal Government advocates in the CCD primarily the prohibition of chemical weapons and the discontinuation of all nuclear weapon tests under effective international control. It is thus in agreement with the priority which the General Assembly gives to these questions.

In the International Atomic Energy Agency (IAEA) the Federal Government promotes the peaceful use of nuclear energy in the economic and scientific fields. At the same time it is striving for adequate and efficient control measures in order to prevent the proliferation of nuclear weapons.

The Federal Government will continue to pursue its policy of efficient and controlled steps towards general and complete disarmament in close agreement with friendly and allied states.

Economic Questions and Development Aid

One of the Federal Republic of Germany's main areas of activity in the United Nations is international economic co-operation and multilateral development aid.

Long before its admission to the UN, the Federal Republic of Germany was co-operating in these very fields with the UN Spezialized Agencies and subsidiary organs, and making substantial contributions to multilateral development aid.

The contributions and voluntary services for the UN, including its subsidiary organs, special programmes, and relief agencies, amounted in 1975 to DM 183.6 million (1974: DM 149.2 million). Especially in the case of the UNDP (United Nations Development Programme) the Federal Republic of Germany is one of the leading contributors with the sum of DM 79 million in 1975 (1974: DM 62 million).

Moreover, it was possible to increase the funds for UN special projects (Funds-in-Trust) financed by the Federal Republic of Germany from DM 8.6 million (1974) to DM 15.3 million, thus almost doubling them.

The Federal Republic of Germany has also participated actively in shaping the policy of the various multilateral institutions. In so doing, it has advocated the effective integration of all measures of development policy and an overall plan.

It has, in particular, advocated that, in cases of multilateral development aid, the least developed countries and those most seriously affected by the oil price increase should be given greater consideration.

The Federal Republic of Germany has pledged a contribution of 52 million US dollars for the International Fund for Agricultural Development (IFAD). It hopes that with the establishment of this fund, additional means will be mobilized to increase agricultural production in the developing countries.

Approximately 36 per cent of its food aid, which reached a total volume of DM 323 million in 1975, was contributed via UN Specialized Agencies, chiefly to the particularly poor countries.

So as to make due allowance for the difficult position of many developing countries, the Federal Republic of Germany substantially increased its contributions in 1975 in the monetary sector and to multilateral financing institutions. Within the framework of the fourth IDA replenishment in 1975, the 2nd annual instalment amounting to DM 432 million was paid in cash.

In addition to having interests in the Asian Development Bank and the African Development Fund, the Federal Republic of Germany also joined the Inter-American Development Bank in 1976 as a non-regional member.

By virtue of an agreement with the IMF to refinance the credit pledge from the oil facility in 1975, the Federal Bank made available the sum of 600 million Special Drawing Rights (approx. DM 1,800 million). It also made a contribution of DM 21 million to the interest subsidy account for the oil facility set up on behalf of the poorer developing countries.

Following its admission to the UN, the Federal Republic of Germany has also been elected to several bodies with a limited number of members, for instance, to mention but one, the Economic and Social Council (ECOSOC) which is the central UN steering organ for the economic and social sphere. It also takes an active part in the negotiations improving its organizational structure.

The Federal Republic of Germany will also make a constructive contribution to the North-South Dialogue, that is, to the discussion about the re-organization of the economic relations between the industrial and the developing countries, in order to bridge the affluence gap between North and South and ensure the developing countries a disproportionately larger share in international economic expansion.

Human Rights

The Federal Government regards the promotion of human rights as one of the main areas of its work in the UN. It is actively striving to make human rights a reality not only in Germany but also throughout the world.

In so doing, the rights of the individual are every bit as important as the rights of groups. In its efforts in this connexion the Federal Government refers to the United Nations Charter, the Universal Declaration of Human Rights, the United Nations human rights covenants which came into force in 1976, and the International Convention for the Elimination of All Forms of Racial Discrimination. At the same time, the Federal Government does not underestimate the problems of many countries in the Third World to whom the rights of the community, the struggle against underdevelopment, hunger and unemployment, seem more important than the human rights of the individual. After all, the Federal Government has shown in these very spheres by its financial and technical development aid that it wishes to improve the living conditions of the people in the Third World. It is convinced that the guarantee and protection of human rights must go hand in hand with economic and social development.

Since the accession of the Federal Republic of Germany to the United Nations in September 1973, the Federal Government has given its closest co-operation whenever human rights questions have been dealt with in the plenary session of the General Assembly, in the Third (Social) Main Committee as also in ECOSOC. Because of its vigorous support for the protection and promotion of human rights, the Federal Republic of Germany was elected to the UN Commission of Human Rights in which it has been able since January 1975 — for an initial period of three years — to put forward its opinion on subjects concerning human rights.

Experience in the United Nations so far, however, has also shown that progress in the field of human rights, and in particular those of the individual, can only be achieved gradually and on a long-term basis. Many states reject effective measures to implement human rights at international level and in so doing quote the principles of sovereignty and non-intervention. Moreover, the human rights covenants (on civil and political, as well as economic, social and cultural rights), which the Federal Republic of Germany ratified as early as September 1973, are limited in their effect because they contain numerous reservations.

In spite of all difficulties, the Federal Government steadfastly advocates that the United Nations should not only champion the codification of human rights but also their implementation. It is in this light that the demand put forward by the Federal Minister for Foreign Affairs in the autumn of 1976 at the thirty-first UN General Assembly for the establishment of an international Court of Human Rights similar to the European Convention on Human Rights, is to be understood. It should lend new impulses to the discussion and in the long run ensure the protection of individual human rights throughout the world.

Decolonization and Southern Africa

The Federal Republic followed the process of decolonization, which had, in the main, already been completed before its access to the UN, with great sympathy; it has always claimed the right of self-determination for all nations all over the world. The Federal Republic established relations without delay with the African states that had become independent and included them in the field of economic co-operation.

The Federal Government supports all measures of the UN promoting the necessary changes in southern Africa without the use of force. In its view the only thing that can prevent the otherwise inevitable catastrophe of a racial war is a renunciation of the use of force. In the General Assembly the Federal Government has constantly advocated that in the reorganization in southern Africa the right of self-determination, human rights and the principle of non-intervention should be observed.

With regard to Southern Rhodesia, it accepted and strictly applied the boycott resolutions of the Security Council even before its accession to the UN. Together with its European partners, the Federal Government supports the right of self-determination and independence of the Rhodesian people as also a speedy and peaceful transfer of government power to the majority of the population.

As regards Namibia, the Federal Republic advocates that the domination by South Africa should be put an end to as soon as possible and that all political forces should participate in preparing its independence under the aegis of the UN.

In southern Africa it is a question of whether blacks and whites will find a form of equal co-existence which will also continue to endure in the future. The rule of the majority must be realized but the just interests of minorities must be protected as well. In the view of the Federal Government the policy of the United Nations should aim at safeguarding structures of peace and co-operation in that part of the African continent too.

The Federal Republic rejects the policy of apartheid practised by the South African Government. It endorsed the condemnation of the apartheid policy by the United Nations at a time when it was itself still a yet member of that organization. Since 1963 it has adhered strictly to the arms embargo imposed on South Africa by the United Nations.

Together with its western allies, the Federal Government has repeatedly and emphatically asked the South African Government to abandon its policy of racial segregation, not to shut its eyes to inevitable an evolution, and to create a new society in which both black and white Africans have equal rights.

Legal Questions

In the work of the United Nations in the field of international law, the Federal Government sees an important contribution towards consolidating international order. The peaceful co-existence of nations necessitates that the states submit to legal obligations, principles and rules of conduct. The increasing complexity of international relations requires that these rules be constantly developed and expanded. The Federal Republic of Germany therefore attaches particular importance to the work of the United Nations in the sphere of international law and has actively participated in it since its accession to the UN.

At the thirty-first General Assembly, Foreign Minister Genscher proposed a convention against the taking of hostages. The General Assembly approved the German proposal unanimously on 15 December 1976.

It set up a committee to draft a convention. Thus the initiative of the Federal Republic has produced a first step by the family of nations in the fight against a particularly cruel form of the use of force.

In its co-operation in the UN bodies that deal with legal questions, it can draw on its great, internationally acknowledged legal tradition and provide important impulses.

In the opinion of the Federal Republic, the regulating power of international law must play a central part in international relations. This also determines the relationship of the Federal Republic to the International Court of Justice: the Federal Republic first submitted to its jurisdiction as far back as 1955 and has appealed to it twice, in each case with success: in 1969 in the dispute with the Netherlands and Denmark over the continental shelf and, in 1974, in the fisheries dispute with Iceland.

On 17 November 1975, the Heidelberg expert on international law, Professor Hermann Mosler, was elected as a judge of the International Court of Justice. This election, by which a German joined for the first time since the League of Nations the highest international organ of jurisdiction, may be regarded not only as a great distinction for the person concerned but also as an indication of the importance of the co-operation of the Federal Republic in the efforts of the UN for the further development and consolidation of international law.

The Federal Republic
and the UN Conference on the Law of the Sea

The purpose of the Third Conference on the Law of the Sea is to adjust the legal position as regards the exploitation of the seas by a comprehensive convention on the law of the sea. In the case of the rights of exploitation as applied to the seas and the seabed, far-reaching economic interests are involved. We, and generations after us, will be affected by the results of this Conference.

In 1969 the twenty-fourth General Assembly asked nations to refrain from exploiting the resources of the seabed outside the limits of international jurisdiction, until an international seabed regime had entered into force (Moratorium Resolution 2574 D XXIV). In 1970, the 25th General Assembly declared the seabed and its resources the "common heritage of mankind". For the utilization thereof an international regime was to be created which would take into account the interests of all mankind and in particular those of the developing countries.

The 25th General Assembly convened the Third UN Conference on the Law of the Sea for 1973. Since then, five sessions of the Conference have been held. The sixth session is due to begin in 1977 in New York. The following are central problems of the Conference:

— Establishment of an international seabed regime beyond the limits of national jurisdiction, for the utilization of the "common heritage of mankind",

— Establishment of the outmost limits of coastal waters (12 nautical miles) and solution of the problems contingent thereon,

— Formation of economic zones beyond the coastal waters,

— Establishment of a new outer limit of the continental shelf,

— Protection of the marine environment,

— Regulation of marine research and of the transfer of marine technology,

— A system of compulsory settlement of disputes.

In this context, there are fundamental differences of interests to be overcome especially between industrial and developing countries, consumers and producers, coastal and land-locked countries, countries with an extensive seaboard and geographically handicapped countries. The Convention is intended to prevent individual countries from taking unilateral measures by virtue of their geographical position or their military or political strength.

For the Federal Republic of Germany there are manifold, vital interests at stake. Fishing and shipping have at all times been of eminent importance to the German economy. It will also be dependent on future marine mining because the deposits of the most important industrial raw materials in its territory are negligible. It considers the Conference on the Law of the Sea to be of paramount importance for the peaceful co-existence of states. In view of the threat of anarchy and conflicts in the seas of the world, the Federal Government considers it necessary and encouraging that the community of states is endeavouring to settle anew the rights and obligations with regard to the seas by way of a harmonization of interests.

The Federal Govnernment co-operates actively and constructively in all spheres of the Conference. The result of the Conference can be no more than a compromise between the multiple and often conflicting interests of all the states participating in the Conference. The Federal Republic will continue to help bring about the establishment of a well-balanced Convention on the Law of the Sea acceptable to all states.

German Personnel in the United Nations

Even before its admission to the UN in 1973, the Federal Republic of Germany was represented by about 20 employees in the subsidiary organs UNIDO, UNCTAD and ECE by reason of a special membership status.

Its admission to the UN gave it access for example to the UN Secretariat in New York together with its Geneva Office as well as to the non-European regional commissions. Secretary-General Waldheim summoned a German to New York, appointing him head of the budgetary and financial system (controller) with the rank of an assistant Secretary-General.

In accordance with its budgetary contribution of so far 7.1 per cent, the Federal Republic of Germany is entitled to between 116 and 161 of the total 2,600 positions for comparable professions which under the UN Charter should be filled on the broadest possible geographical basis.

As of 1 September 1976, a total of 74 posts within the scope of the regular UN budget were filled by applicants from the Federal Republic of Germany. Of these, 23 are in the UN Secretariat in New York, 8 in the UN Office in Geneva, 20 in UNIDO in Vienna, 9 with UNCTAD in Geneva, 7 with ECE in Geneva, 3 with UNEP in Nairobi, 3 with ECLA in Santiago de Chile, and 1 with UNDRO in Geneva. Compared with its moderate personnel quota of 138 posts, the Federal Republic of Germany last autumn still had a deficit of 64.

The decisions for appointments are made autonomously by the UN Secretariat. German applicants must compete with qualified candidates from numerous other UN Member States. The Federal Foreign Office together with the other Federal Ministries endeavours to find suitable applicants for service in the UN. In so doing, it is assisted by the Office for Leading Employees for International Organizations under the Central Employment Agency (Feuerbachstraße 44, Frankfurt/Main). This Agency informs and advises those interested, collects the personal records of suitable applicants, registers advertised situations and vacancies, and passes them on to interested persons and institutions.

Candidates for posts in the United Nations must as a rule have a university degree, excellent linguistic knowledge and, depending on the vacancy in question, relevant professional experience.

Financial Contributions,
Co-operation in the Budgetary and Administrative Sphere

The regular budget of the United Nations is covered by the contributions of the Member States. The size of a country's contribution depends mainly on its gross national product and income per head of the population. In 1976, the Federal Republic of Germany, with a rate of 7.1 per cent, paid a contribution of approximately

DM 58.3 million (22.7 million US dollars). The contribution of the Federal Republic of Germany for the years 1977—1979 is expected to be fixed at 7.74 per cent. Among the UN Member States the Federal Republic of Germany comes fourth after the USA (25 per cent), the USSR (including the Ukrainian and Byelorussian SSR 13.23 per cent) and Japan (8.66 per cent). The large contributions which amounted to roughly DM 897 million in 1975 for its overall UN activity (for detailed allocation v. Part V, Section 1) have strengthened the position of the Federal Republic of Germany in the United Nations.

Irrespective of the size of its budget contribution, each Member of the United Nations has one vote. The distribution of personnel posts in the narrower UN sphere is, however, calculated mainly according to the size of the contribution (cf. Section on "German Personnel in the United Nations").

The Federal Government co-operates intensively in all the bodies within the scope of the UN dealing with financial questions, and finds due recognition in this connexion. Thus, for instance, at the 30th General Assembly in autumn 1975, a representative of the Federal Republic of Germany was co-opted on to the Advisory Committee for Administrative and Budgetary Questions. This committee has extensive competence for the preliminary examination of budgetary questions, fundamental personnel matters and administrative questions of the United Nations, and in part, too, for the sphere of the United Nations Specialized Agencies. The final decisions for the UN budget, which amounts to 746 million US dollars, rest with the UN General Assembly.

Approximately 80 per cent of the regular budget of the United Nations covers personnel costs. Independent of this, various relief programmes such as the UN Development Programme (UNDP), the Children's Fund (UNICEF), the High Commissioner for Refugees (UNHCR) and the Relief and Works Agency for the Palestine Refugees in the Middle East (UNRWA) each have their own particular budgets.

Part III
Subsidiary Organs and Relief Agencies
Specialized Agencies
Intergovernmental Organizations

1. The Subsidiary Organs and Relief Agencies of the United Nations

A. United Nations Development Programme UNDP

A. Establishment: As a result of A/Res. 2029 (XX) of November 22, 1965, as a subsidiary organ under the supervision of the UN Economic and Social Council (ECOSOC) and of the UN General Assembly. Headquarters: 866 UN Plaza, New York, N. Y. 10017. Arose out of the combination of the 1949 Expanded Programme of Technical Assistance (EPTA) and the Special Fund.

Organs:

a. Governing Council:

Function: Supervision. Meets twice a year. 48 Member States (including 27 developing countries) are represented. Normally, Members are elected for a period of 3 years, at present by ECOSOC acting for the UN General Assembly. Re-election possible. The geographical distribution of the seats is as follows:

Africa group: 11

Asia and Yugoslavia: 9

Latin America: 7

Western industrial countries: 17

Eastern Europe: 4

b. UNDP Administration:

The UNDP is headed by the Administrator who bears overall responsibility for all UNDP programmes:

Bradford Morse, USA (since 1 January 1976).

Deputy Administrator:

I. G. Patel, India.

Inter-Agency Consultative Board (IACB)

Members:

Administrator, UN Secretary-General, Heads of Specialized Agencies and subsidiary organs.

Function:

Co-ordination.

Functions:

Today, UNDP as one of the most important UN subsidiary organs is largely self-governing and, as a central organization, in charge of about two thirds of all technical co-operation of UN organs and Specialized Agencies.

At present, UNDP carries on activities in 147 countries and territories with a view to:

Assisting the developing countries in their economic and social development within the framework of several-year national programmes. UNDP mainly provides services of international experts, equipment, training facilities and scholarships;

Implementation of UNDP projects mainly through UN subsidiary organs and Specialized Agencies;

On behalf of the General Assembly, UNDP administers several special funds and the UN Volunteer Programme (cf. pp. 48 f. and 50).

B. Participation of the Federal Republic of Germany

The Federal Republic of Germany was a Founder Member of the UNDP.

a. *Contributions of the Federal Republic of Germany in mill. US dollars:*

1969	1970	1971	1972	1973	1974	1975
10.2	11.2	13.7	15.5	21.3	24.3	29.3

Total budget of UNDP in mill. US dollars:

1971	1972	1973	1974	1975
343	358	356	383	457

Main contributors in 1975 — in mill. US dollars:

		%
United States	77.8	19.1
Sweden	51.7	12.7
Denmark	39.3	9.7
Netherlands	38.6	9.5
Federal Republic of Germany	29.3	7.2
United Kingdom	24.9	6.1
others	144.8	35.6

b. *German personnel:*

Absolute	Percentage	Germans in leading positions	Total personnel UNDP	German financial contribution %
28	3.7	5	749	7.2

c. *Main areas of activity of the Federal Republic of Germany:*

The Federal Republic of Germany firmly upholds the principle of self-determination in a country's development, which characterizes the international co-operation within the framework of UNDP. It therefore encourages those tendencies which will strengthen the central role of UNDP in multilateral technical co-operation within the framework of UN development organizations. By substantially increasing its voluntary contributions, it has considerably helped to further UNDP aims. The re-allocation of available funds as advocated by the Federal Republic will secure relatively more assistance for the least developed countries. It supports UNDP in encouraging wider co-operation among developing countries.

d. *Competency in the Federal Republic of Germany:*

Federal Ministry for Economic Co-operation; Federal Foreign Office. Permanent Mission of the Federal Republic of Germany to the United Nations, 600, 3rd Ave. New York, N. Y. 10016, USA

47

Appendix 1

UNDP also comprises the United Nations Fund for Population Activities (UNFPA).

A. Establishment: On the strength of A/Res. 2211 (XXI) of 17 December 1966, established in 1967 as a Trust Fund of the UN Secretary-General, placed under the charge of the UNDP Administrator in 1969. Pursuant to A/Res. 3019 (XXVII) of 18 December 1972, UNFPA today is a subsidiary organ of the UN, holds a semi-autonomous position under UNDP, and is under the general political control of ECOSOC and the UN General Assembly. Headquarters: 485 Lexington Ave. New York, N. Y. 10017.

Organs:

a. Governing Council of UNDP; composition see under UNDP.

   Function: Supervision.

b. Executive Director:

   The Executive Director conducts the activities of UNFPA as a semi-autonomous body of UNDP.

   Rafael M. Salas, Philippines (since May 1971).

Functions:

Making nations aware of the interdependence of population growth and economic and social development. Whilst respecting the sovereignty of states, UNFPA, if so requested, helps solve population problems and establish family planning institutions in developing countries. Co-ordination of all UN measures in this field. Since the 1974 World Population Conference, requests to UNFPA have increased dramatically.

B. Participation of the Federal Republic of Germany

a. *Contributions of the Federal Republic of Germany in mill. US dollars:*

Total UNFPA revenue in mill. US dollars (voluntary contributions in parentheses):

1973	1974	1975
42.5	52.0	65.1
(42.57)	(50.0)	(63.1)

Contributions of the Federal Republic of Germany in mill. US dollars: (percentage of total contributions in parentheses):

1973	1974	1975
4.3	5.7	7.5
(10.1 %)	(10.6 %)	(11.9 %)

Main contributors 1975 in mill. US dollars:

USA	20.0
Federal Republic of Germany	7.5
Netherlands	7.1
Japan	7.0
Sweden	5.7

b. *German personnel:*

Absolute	Percentage	Germans in leading positions	Total UNFPA personnel	German financial contribution %
3	4 %	3	77	7.5

c. *Main areas of activity of the Federal Republic of Germany:*

As one of the main contributors, the Federal Republic plays an active part in the decision-making process of UNFPA, particularly in the Governing Council. Thanks to its efforts, criteria for the allocation of funds were elaborated, with activities concentrating on family planning.

d. *Competency in the Federal Republic of Germany:*

Federal Ministry for Economic Co-operation; Federal Foreign Office; Permanent Mission of the Federal Republic of Germany to the United Nations, 600, 3rd Ave., New York, N. Y. 10016, USA.

Appendix 2

The programme of United Nations Volunteers (UNV) was set up under the responsibility of UNDP.

A. Established pursuant to Res. 2659 (XXV) of 7 December 1970 on the basis of ECOSOC proposals (4/4790), entering into force on 1 January 1971.
Headquarters: Palais des Nations, Geneva.

Organs:

John Gordon, Canada, has been co-ordinator of UNV since 1 January 1971.

Functions:

Preparation and organization of recruitment and assignments of volunteers from developed and developing countries under UN projects with particular reference to the least developed countries. On 30 April 1975, 242 volunteers from 48 nations were engaged in activities in 41 countries, 48 % of them in least developed countries. 38 % of the volunteers came from developing countries. In addition, UNV helps in the development of youth services in the Third World.

B. Participation of the Federal Republic of Germany

a. *Contributions of the Federal Republic of Germany:*

UNV budget (part of the UNDP budget and Special Fund):
1976: US dollars 1.066,900

Additional voluntary contributions by the Federal Republic to the UNV Special Fund in excess of its UNDP contribution (in US dollars):

1972/73	1974	1975
62,465	74,627	205,128

Main contributors to UNV Special Fund (accumulated amounts up to 1975):

USA	400,000
Federal Republic of Germany	342,220
Netherlands	150,000
Switzerland	66,391
Iran	30,000

b. *German personnel:*

One of the 12 members of the UNV Administration is a German.

B. United Nations Industrial Development Organization UNIDO

A. Establishment: By Resolution A/Res. 2152 (XXI) of 17 November 1966, as a subsidiary organ*) of the United Nations with headquarters at Felderhaus, Rathausplatz 2, Vienna.

Organs:

a. Industrial Development Board:

Meets annually. 45 Members are elected by the UN General Assembly for a term of 3 years, 15 being elected each year. To ensure an equitable geographical distribution the seats are arranged in the following 4 groups:

1. Africa, Asia and Yugoslavia: 78 countries (18 seats)

2. Western industrial countries: 30 countries (15 seats)

3. Latin America: 25 countries (7 seats)

4. Eastern Europe: 10 countries (5 seats).

b. Permanent Committee:

Meets every six months; main function: programme consultations.

c. Secretariat:

This is headed by an Executive Director appointed by the Secretary-General and confirmed by the General Assembly.

Abd-er Rahman Khane, Algeria (since 1 January 1975).

Functions:

Promotion of industrial development in Third World countries. Co-ordination of all activities of the United Nations system in the field of industrial development.

146 Member States (1972)

---

*) By resolution of the 1975 General Assembly of UNIDO in Lima, it is to be converted into a Specialized Agency. Negotiations on this are in progress.

B. Participation of the Federal Republic of Germany

The Federal Republic of Germany is a Founder Member of the UNIDO.

a. *Contributions of the Federal Republic of Germany — in US dollars:*

1970	1971	1972	1973	1974
656,536	708,466	837,148	9,22,467	718,528

(since 1975 part of regular UN contribution)

UNIDO budget — in US dollars (part of UN budget):

1969	1970	1972	1973	1974-75
9,693,200	10,250,000	14,419,000	14,634,700	36,792,000

Main contributors — in US dollars:

	1969	1970
Federal Republic of Germany	—	656,536
Italy	—	600,000
Soviet Union	555,556	555,556
Egypt	109,246	—
Yugoslavia	75,000	100,000

b. *German share of personnel:*

Absolute	Percentage	Germans in leading positions	Total personnel	German financial contribution %
9	5.7	4	334	6

c. *Main areas of activity of the Federal Republic of Germany:*

The Federal Republic of Germany particularly supports the efforts of the UNIDO in building up small- and medium-scale industries in developing countries, in industrializing the least developed countries and in co-operation with the World Bank. Through delegating qualified personnel to the Central Administration and to UNIDO projects in the developing countries and through voluntary financial contributions the Federal Republic of Germany has helped to increase the efficiency of the Organization.

d. *Competency in the Federal Republic of Germany:*

Federal Ministry for Economic Co-operation; Federal Foreign Office.
Diplomatic representation: Mission of the Federal Republic of Germany to the International Organizations at Metternichgasse 3, A-1030 Vienna.

C. United Nations Relief and Works Agency for Palestine Refugees in the Middle East UNRWA

A. Established by Resolution A/Res. 302 (IV) of 8 December 1949. One year later the Agency's mandate was extended. Headquarters: Beirut, Lebanon (temporarily transferred to Vienna because of the situation in Lebanon), UNRWA. Headquarters, Museitbeh Quarter. Liaison offices in Bagdad, Amman, Geneva and New York.

Organs:

a. *Advisory Commission:*

4 Members were appointed by the General Assembly: France, United Kingdom, Turkey and the United States.

5 other Members were appointed with the authorization of the General Assembly: Belgium, Egypt, Jordan, Lebanon, Syria.

b. *Commissioner-General:*

Sir John Rennie, United Kingdom (since 1972).

Functions:

Relief for the Palestine refugees who became homeless in the process of the establishment of the State of Israel and in the two Middle East wars to create a tolerable economic existence in the neighbouring countries.

Consultations with the Middle East Governments concerning measures to be taken by them preparatory to the time when UNRWA assistance is no longer available.

UNRWA's operations are financed by voluntary contributions from about 100 countries (as well as the European Community).

53

B. Participation of the Federal Republic of Germany

The Federal Republic of Germany contributed since 1952 on a voluntary basis.

a. *Contributions of the Federal Republic of Germany — in mill. US dollars:*

1969	1970	1971	1972	1973	1974	1975	1976
3.1	3.2	3.3	3.5	5.0	3.0	3.7	3.5

The programme budget of UNRWA (made up of voluntary contributions):

1969	1970	1971	1972	1973	1974	1975	1976
42.5	45.1	48.5	53.0	63.0	88.0	124.0	128.0

Main contributors — in mill. US dollars:

	1969	1971	1975
United States	22.2	22.9	42.0
Saudi Arabia	—	—	11.2
United Kingdom	4.5	4.5	5.3
Japan	—	—	5.0
Sweden	2.2	2.4	4.9
Federal Republic of Germany	3.1	3.3	3.7

b. *Main areas of activity of the Federal Republic of Germany:*

Extensive assistance immediately following the Middle East wars and the civil war in Jordan in 1970 by making available evacuation hospitals and clearing stations, personnel, food and medicines. Funds for the development and running of a trade school in Amman, for hygiene etc. In April 1971, schools built with donations from the Federal Government at Baddawi and Nahrel Bared near Tripoli (Lebanon) were opened. Financial participation in UNRWA's vocational school programme. Scholarships for refugees to study in Germany. Donations from private firms for vocational training in the Federal Republic of Germany.

c. *Competency in the Federal Republic of Germany:*

Federal Foreign Office.

D. United Nations Conference on Trade and Development UNCTAD

A. Established as a permanent organ of the United Nations by Resolution A/Res. 1995 (XIX) of 30 December 1964. Headquarters: Geneva.

Organs:

a. Conference on Trade and Development:

Met so far every four years. The fourth Conference was held from 5 May to 31 May 1976 in Nairobi. The Conference on Trade and Development is directly responsible to the United Nations General Assembly. Its Secretary-General is appointed by the Secretary-General of the United Nations with the approval of the General Assembly. The Conference's expenses form part of the United Nations budget.

b. Trade and Development Board:

Since 1972 the Members total 68 (earlier 55), elected by the 1972 Conference with the approval of the General Assembly. The fourth Conference decided that, subject to approval by the General Assembly, any UNCTAD Member may become a Member of the Board.

The countries have been divided into regional groups:

A. African and Asian countries and Yugoslavia

B. Developed countries with market economies

C. Latin America

D. Socialist countries

The groups A and C together form the "Group of 77" (developing countries).

The Trade and Development Boards has established 6 main Committees:

1. Committee on Commodities

2. Committee on Manufactures and Semi-manufactures

3. Committee on Invisibles and Financing relating to Trade

4. Committee on Shipping

5. Committee on Transfer of Technology

6. Special Committee on Preferences

The fourth Conference advocated the establishment of another main Committee on Economic Co-operation among developing countries.

In addition, there are a number of groups of Government representatives and experts.

Functions:

Promotion of international trade; raising of the standard of living in all countries, particularly in the developing countries. Main areas: commodities, manufactures, financing of development aid.

153 Member States (1976; cf. p. 229)

Secretary-General:

Gamani Corea, Sri Lanka (since 1 April 1974).

B. Participation of the Federal Republic of Germany

The Federal Republic of Germany has been a Member of the UNCTAD since 1964.

a. *Contributions of the Federal Republic of Germany — in US dollars:*

1969	1970	1971	1972	1973
617,504	557,169	621,787	701,964	662,048

UNCTAD budget — in US dollars:

1969	1971	1973
8,326,200	10,330,000	19,505,000

b. *German personnel:*

9 Germans

c. *Main areas of activity of the Federal Republic of Germany:*

Ever since the establishment of UNCTAD intensive co-operation in all Committees. As the world's second biggest trading country, the Federal Republic of Germany has made a very large financial contribution, this amounting in each of the years 1970 to 1973 to 7.01 % of the total contributions of all UNCTAD Member States.

d. *Competency in the Federal Republic of Germany:*

Federal Ministry of Economics; Federal Foreign Office.

Permanent Mission of the Federal Republic of Germany to the International Organizations, 28 D, Chemin du Petit-Saconnex, CH-1211 Geneva 19

E. Economic Commission for Europe
ECE

A. Established as a regional economic commission of the UN Economic and Social Council (ECOSOC) pursuant to E/Res. 36 (IV) of 28 March 1947. Headquarters: Palais des Nations, Geneva, Switzerland.

Organs:

a. Commission:

The Commission is composed of the European Members of the United Nations and the United States, Canada and Switzerland (total: 34 Members):

Albania, Austria, Belgium, Bulgaria, Byelorussian S.S.R., Canada, Cyprus, Czechoslovakia, Denmark, Finland, France, Federal Republic of Germany, German Democratic Republic, Greece, Hungary, Iceland, Ireland, Italy, Luxembourg, Malta, Netherlands, Norway, Poland, Portugal, Romania, Spain, Sweden, Turkey, Ukrainian S.S.R., U.S.S.R., United Kingdom, United States, Yugoslavia, Switzerland.

The Commission holds one public session each year.

b. Twelve committees

c. Secretariat:

Headed by the Executive Secretary,
Janez Stanovnik, Yugoslavia (since 1968).

Functions:

Promoting the economic reconstruction of Europe after the war; raising the level of economic activity in Europe. Important fields of operation: trade, energy, transport, technology, human environment.

The ECE is the only body in which all Western and Eastern states are represented. It provides systematic and specialized economic and statistical information and analyses. The CSCE Final Act underlines its role in the multilateral implementation of CSCE provisions concerning co-operation in the fields of economy, science and technology as well as the environment.

B. Participation of the Federal Republic of Germany

The Federal Republic of Germany became a Member of the ECE on 21 February 1956, after the terms of reference had been extended by ECOSOC on 15 December 1955.

a. *Contributions of the Federal Republic of Germany — in US dollars:*

1969	1970	1971	1972	1973	1974
379,599	443,284	453,056	487,968	648,412	397,845

It should be noted that the 1973 figure includes outstanding payments from 1971 and 1972; the 1974 contributions are outstanding contributions for the 1973 period up to the date of accession of the Federal Republic of Germany to the UN Charter; subsequently, contributions to the ECE were part of the regular membership contributions paid to the UN.

b. *Main areas of activity of the Federal Republic of Germany:*

Co-operation in all committees and working groups; working out multilateral arrangements concerning aspects of European transport; statistics concerning accidents throughout Europe; standardized traffic signs and traffic regulations; facilitating customs procedures in passenger and goods traffic; questions concerning the mechanization of agricultural businesses; questions concerning the standardization of agricultural products; problems concerning mass-produced buildings, the opening up of building land etc.; questions concerning environmental pollution, the manpower market and the utilization of energy (coal, electricity and gas); container traffic; problems of trade and of industrial co-operation in the ECE countries.

c. *Competency in the Federal Republic of Germany:*

Federal Ministry of Economics, in special cases the Federal Ministry of Transport, the Federal Ministry of Agriculture, other departments; Federal Foreign Office.

F. United Nations Children's Fund UNICEF

A. Established by Resolution A/Res. 802 (VIII) of 6 October 1953 as a permanent body of the United Nations to provide assistance to children throughout the world. Headquarters: 4-1234 T. Plaza, New York, N. Y. 10017.

Organs:

a. Executive Board:

Consists of 30 Members elected for 3-year terms. Ten retire each year with a further ten elected. Annual meetings in the spring in NewYork.

b. Committees:

Programme Committee, Administration and Finance Committee.

c. Secretariat:

Headed by an Executive Director:
Henry R. Labouisse, United States (since June 1965).

Functions:

Assistance to needy children and young people, above all in developing countries. UNICEF assists the Governments of Third World countries particularly in the case of programmes for assisting mother and child, health and welfare services, food and education. A permanent function of UNICEF is also to provide assistance in the case of disasters.

B. Participation of the Federal Republic of Germany

The Federal Republic of Germany has again been a Member of the Executive Board of UNICEF since 1972.

a. *Contributions of the Federal Republic of Germany to the regular budget – in mill. US dollars:*

1969	1970	1971	1972	1973	1974	1975	1976
1.8	2.6	2.1	2.4	3.4	3.4	3.1	3.1

UNICEF's total budget – in US dollars:

1971	1972	1974	1975	1976
about 72 mill.	about 90 mill.	about 99 mill.	about 138 mill.	about 150 mill.

Besides the Federal Republic of Germany the main contributors are: United States, Sweden, United Kingdom, Norway, Netherlands.

b. *German personnel:*

Absolute	Percentage	Germans in leading positions	Total UNICEF personnel	German financial contribution %
15	5.7	6	261	6.4

c. *Main areas of activity of the Federal Republic of Germany:*

The Federal Republic of Germany, which received considerable assistance from UNICEF immediately after the Second World War, supports this organization very actively. Apart from contributions to the regular budget it has also placed special funds at UNICEF's disposal to assist trust projects and provide relief following disasters.

d. The German Committee for UNICEF (Steinfeldergasse 9, 5000 Cologne 1) plays a large part in making the Organization's objectives and tasks known in the Federal Republic of Germany. It organizes campaigns for donations and the sale of greetings-cards for the benefit of UNICEF.

e. *Competency in the Federal Republic of Germany:*

Federal Foreign Office.

G. United Nations High Commissioner for Refugees UNHCR

A. By Resolution 319 (IV) of the United Nations, the Office of the United Nations High Commissioner for Refugees was established on 3 December 1949, initially for a 3-year term. Since 1953 the mandate has been extended for, in each case, five years. The current term will end in December 1978. Headquarters: Palais des Nations, Geneva.

Organs:

a. High Commissioner for Refugees:

   Elected for a 5-year term by the UN General Assembly and the Secretary-General. He is responsible to the ECOSOC and the UN General Assembly.

   Prince Sadruddin Aga Khan, Iran (since 1 January 1966).

b. Executive Committee:

   Meets at least once a year in Geneva. It consists of 31 representatives of the Governments of the States which have devoted special attention to the solution of the refugee problem.

   The Office of the High Commissioner for Refugees has at its disposal more than 30 branches in the principal countries providing and receiving assistance for refugees, as well as offices of correspondents and special representatives.

Functions:

Assistance to refugees who have been persecuted and expelled on account of their race, religion or political conviction. The efforts are directed towards a final solution as a result of voluntary repatriation or permanent assimilation of the refugees in their new environment. This includes in particular legal protection.

B. Participation of the Federal Republic of Germany

Ever since the Office of the High Commissioner for Refugees was established the Federal Republic of Germany has supported it with very considerable contributions.

a. *Contributions of the Federal Republic of Germany — in US dollars:*

1969	1971	1972	1974	1975	1976
325,000	530,000	629,510	780,537	784,314	775,194

Budget of the High Commissioner for Refugees — in US dollars:

1971	1972	1974	1975	1976
7,052,000	7,968,900	11,808,000	14,117,000	14,851,000

Main contributors — in US dollars:

	1969	1970	1974	1975
United States	900,000	1,000,000	1,100,000	1,056,000
Sweden	755,000	955,000	803,690	800,000
Denmark	399,978	859,817	—	—
Federal Republic of Germany	325,000	409,836	780,537	784,314
France	385,930	389,842	521,250	588,706
Canada	370,370	386,473	567,010	588,235
Norway	333,720	367,088	578,231	693,878
United Kingdom	359,971	359,971	500,000	541,176
Netherlands	—	—	576,923	832,917

b. *German personnel:*

Absolute	Percentage	Germans in leading positions	Total UNHCR personnel	German financial contribution %
4	3.2	1	124	5.5

c. *Additional voluntary services of the Federal Republic of Germany:*

Assistance to refugees from and in Vietnam and Cyprus. Assistance to resettle refugees in Guinea-Bissau, reception in the Federal Republic of Germany of about 1,800 refugees from Chile.

In terms of total contributions to UNHCR, the Federal Republic of Germany occupied 7th position in 1975.

d. *Competency in the Federal Republic of Germany:*

Federal Foreign Office.

e. *Office of the UNHCR in the Federal Republic of Germany:*

Rheinallee 18, 5300 Bonn-Bad Godesberg.

H. United Nations Institute for Training and Research UNITAR

A. Established as an autonomous institution within the framework of the United Nations by Resolution 1934 (XVIII) of 11 December 1963. Headquarters: 801 United Nations Plaza, New York.

Organs:

a. Board of Trustees:

Consists of 4 permanent and — at present — 21 elected Members; meets annually. The Members are appointed for 3-year terms by the UN Secretary-General.

b. Executive Director:

Appointed by the UN Secretary-General:

Davidson Nicol, Sierra Leone (since August 1972).

Functions:

Since the Institute became operational in 1966 numerous training programmes have been carried out for the United Nations (courses, seminars, symposia etc.). — At the suggestion of organs of the United Nations or of Members, the Studies Department investigates international problems, e. g., technology transfer, development management, further development of international law, peace research, and improvement of the system of the United Nations. The Project on the Future, established in 1975, deals with important problems in connection with commodities, questions of population, economic growth and protection of the environment.

B. Participation of the Federal Republic of Germany

The Federal Republic of Germany has been a Member of the UNITAR Board of Trustees since 1963.

a. *Contributions of the Federal Republic of Germany — in US dollars:*

1969	1971	1973	1974	1975
75,000	120,127	205,900	239,423	240,000

UNITAR budget — in US dollars: in 1975: about 2.3 mill.

Main contributors — in US dollars:

	1969	1970	1973	1974
United States	400,000	400,000	400,000	400,000
Federal Republic of Germany	75,000	75,000	205,900	239,423
Sweden	—	—	3,104	68,729
Belgium	50,140	50,275	60,452	64,450
Canada	55,556	57,971	60,000	61,856
Japan	2,000	80,000	40,000	50,000

b. *German personnel:*

Absolute	Percentage	Germans in leading positions	Total UNITAR personnel	German financial contribution %
1	1.4	—	66	1.5

c. *Main areas of activity of the Federal Republic of Germany:*

Within the framework of the Officer Attachment Scheme six German officials were active at the UNITAR for between two and 18 months. Participation in the so-called Peace Research Project.

d. *Competency in the Federal Republic of Germany:*

Federal Ministry for Economic Co-operation; Federal Foreign Office.

2. The Specialized Agencies of the United Nations

A. International Bank for Reconstruction and Development IBRD

A. Established at the monetary and financial conference of the United Nations at Bretton Woods, held from 1 to 22 July 1944; the Articles of Agreement were signed and entered into force on 27 December 1945; Specialized Agency of the United Nations pursuant to A/Res. 124 (II) of 15 November 1947. Headquarters: 1818 H Street N. W., Washington 25 D. C.

Organs:

a. Board of Governors; meets annually. Each Member delegates one representative.

b. 20 Executive Directors, of which 5 are permanent Directors appointed by the largest subscribers to the capital stock (the United States, the United Kingdom, the Federal Republic of Germany, France and Japan), and fifteen elected every two years by the Governors of the remaining members.

c. President, who is elected by the Executive Directors and is their chairman.

At the same time they constitute the administrative organs of the organizations belonging to the World Bank group — the International Development Association (IDA) and the International Finance Corporation (IFC) — among which close co-operation is maintained.

Functions:

The World Bank is an international financial institution granting long-term loans for the reconstruction and economic development of its Members. Membership is restricted to Governments which are members of the International Monetary Fund.

According to its Articles, the following are the Bank's most important functions:

a. Assisting in the reconstruction and development of the member countries by granting loans for productive projects which will lead in the long run to a balanced extension of foreign trade, the opening of production resources, higher productivity, higher standards of living, and better working conditions.

Promoting international private investment activity by undertaking guarantees or participating in loans and other investments on the part of private enterprises.

127 Members (1976; cf. p. 229)

President:

Robert S. McNamara, United States (1 April 1968 to 31 March 1978).

B. Participation of the Federal Republic of Germany

The Federal Republic of Germany acceded to the World Bank on 14 August 1952.

a. *Contributions of the Federal Republic of Germany — in US dollars:*

1969	1971	1972	1973
3,450,000	6,222,250	6,200,673	7,024,00

Subscribed capital — in US dollar 25,581.3 mill.

Largest subscribers to the capital stock:	(capital shares) in %	(voting right shares) in %
United States	25.3	22.6
United Kingdom	10.2	9.1
Federal Republic of Germany	5.3	4.8
France	5.0	4.5
Japan	4.0	3.6
Canada	3.7	3.4
India	3.5	3.2

Income of the World Bank — in mill. US dollars:

	1972	1973	1974	1975
gross	646.0	758.0	929.3	1,157.0
net	182.6	185.6	215.8	275.0

b. *German personnel:*

Absolute	Percentage	Germans in leading positions	Total World Bank personnel
117	5.4	11	2,160

c. *Main areas of activity of the Federal Republic of Germany:*

The Federal Republic of Germany is one of the World Bank's largest sub-scribers of capital stock. Through her financial payments she makes a vital contribution towards the implementation of all important loan programmes of the Bank with annual commitments totalling at present more than 5 bill. US dollars. The German capital market plays a significant role in the Bank's refinancing with an average 24 % of the capital raised by the Bank. This close co-operation is also demonstrated by the agreement of 6 December 1974, concluded between the Federal Republic of Germany and the Bank on the joint financing of programmes and projects of development aid.

Points of main effort of this joint financing are projects for the improvement of infrastructure and agriculture.

The Federal Republic of Germany is a member of the consortia concerned with relief for India and Pakistan and of the advisory groups for Colombia, Korea, Malaysia, Morocco, Nigeria, Peru, Sri Lanka, Sudan, Thailand and Tunisia.

d. *Competency in the Federal Republic of Germany:*

Federal Ministry for Economic Co-operation; Federal Foreign Office.

B. International Monetary Fund
IMF

A. Established on 27 December 1945, as a result of the signing of the resolutions of the Bretton Woods Conference (1944). Constitution as a Specialized Agency of the United Nations as a result of the agreement of 15 April 1948. Headquarters: Washington, D. C.

Organs:

a. Board of Governors:

Supreme organ in which every Member is represented.

b. Executive Directors:

Administrative organ with 20 directors, 5 of whom are appointed by member states with the largest quotas. The other 15 are elected by the Governors of the remaining member states every 2 years.

c. IMF Interim Committee:

Consultative organ of the IMF Board of Governors for the supervision and further development of the international monetary system. Membership as with the Executive Directors. Set up in 1974 to replace the Committee of Twenty.

Functions:

Promotion of international monetary co-operation; facilitation of the growth of international trade; promotion of exchange stability; granting of credits to Members in dealing with temporary balance of payments difficulties.

128 member states (1976, cf. p. 229)

Managing Director:

Prof. Dr. Hendrikus Johannes Witteveen, Netherlands (since 1 September 1973).

B. Participation of the Federal Republic of Germany

The Federal Republic of Germany acceded to the IMF on 14 August 1952.

a. *Participation of the Federal Republic of Germany in the quota investments (in mill. US dollars) and Special Drawing Rights (SDR):*

1952	1959	1966	1972	1977
330	787.5	1,200	1,600	2,100 mill. SDR
			(of which 25.0 % paid in gold)	5.53 %

Amount of the total quotas:

1972	1977
29.169 bill. SDR	39 bill. SDR

b. *Assignment of Special Drawing Rights (in billions)*

1970	1971	1972
3.4	2.9	2.9

c. *Personnel of the Federal Republic of Germany:*

Absolute	Percentage	Germans in leading positions	Total IMF personnel Senior officials	German financial contribution %
30	4	12	766	5.53

d. *Main areas of activity of the Federal Republic of Germany:*

The DM is among the currencies for which there has so far been the largest demand in drawings by IMF Members. The Federal Republic has stated its readiness to furnish credit lines (DM 4 billion) in certain circumstances under the General Agreement on Credits among the ten most important industrial countries, if it should be necessary, in meeting their credit requirements, to provide additional amounts in order to forestall an impairment of the international monetary system. The Federal Republic advocates the strengthening of the competencies and responsibilities of the IMF within the scope of the new IMF Agreement that will enter into force in 1977.

e. *Official offices of the IMF in the Federal Republic of Germany:*

None.

f. *Competency in the Federal Republic of Germany:*

Federal Ministry of Finance; Federal Foreign Office.

C. International Finance Corporation IFC

A. The IFC was established as a Specialized Agency of the United Nations and a subsidiary of the World Bank pursuant to A/Res. 1116 (XII) of 20 February 1957. Headquarters: 1818 Street N. W., Washington, D. C.

Branches in New York, London, Paris, Tokyo, Nairobi.

Organs:

The administrative organs correspond to those of the World Bank. The IFC has, however, its own operating staff.

Functions:

In accordance with the Statutes, the function of the IFC is to further economic development by investing in productive private enterprises in its member countries, particularly in those that are less developed. For this purpose the IFC

a. assists, in association with private investors, in the financing (without Government guarantee) of enterprises which contribute towards the development where sufficient private capital is not available on reasonable terms;

b. creates opportunities for investment by bringing together private capital, both foreign and domestic, and experienced management.

The IFC fulfils this function mainly through direct investments in productive private enterprises. In particular, it assists partnership concerns which provide an opportunity to link up domestic enterprises and a knowledge of the domestic market and other local circumstances with the technical and economic experience acquired in the developed countries.

105 members states (1976, cf. p. 229)

President: (as also of the World Bank)

Robert S. McNamara, United States (since 1 April 1968).

B. Participation of the Federal Republic of Germany

The Federal Republic of Germany is a Founder Member of the IFC.

a. *Contributions of the Federal Republic of Germany:*

With a capital investment amounting to $ 3.66 million (non-recurring payment), it contributes the fifth largest amount among all member states. Subscribed capital of the IFC: $ 100 million.

Gross commitments IFC (altogether) — in mill. US dollars:

1969	1970	1971	1972	1973	1974	1975
92.865	111.848	101.297	115.946	146.4	203.4	211.7

Largest subscribers of capital

	in % (capital shares)	in % (voting right shares)
United States	32.8	26.8
United Kingdom	13.4	11.1
France	5.4	4.6
India	4.1	3.5
China (Taiwan)	3.9	3.3
Federal Republic of Germany	3.4	3.0
Canada	3.4	2.9

b. *Main areas of activity of the Federal Republic of Germany:*

As one of the chief subscribers of capital and contributors, the Federal Republic of Germany makes a vital contribution towards achieving the aims of the Corporation. Commitments have mainly been concentrated on the iron and steel, cement, textile and paper industries.

c. *Competency in the Federal Republic of Germany:*

Federal Ministry for Economic Co-operation; Federal Foreign Office.

D. International Development Association IDA

A. The establishment of the IDA as a Specialized Agency of the United Nations was based on A/Res. 1420 (XIV) of 5 December 1959. The agreement was signed on 26 January 1960 and headquarters were set up in September 1960 at 1818 H Street N. W., Washington 25, D. C. The IDA is an affiliate of the World Bank, its administrative organs being identical with those of the World Bank.

Organs:

The administrative organs correspond to those of the World Bank.

Functions:

Promoting the economy in the developing countries; providing finance on easier and more flexible terms than those of conventional loans. Interest-free development credits are repayable over a 50-year period, only administrative fees being charged. It promotes projects which can be financed neither out of private capital nor solely through World Bank loans. On principle only those member countries receive loans whose per-capita income is under 375 US dollars p. a.

116 member states 1976 (membership is open to any member of the World Bank, cf. p. 229)

Group I

consists of 18 economically advanced countries which have to pay their entire subscription in gold or in freely convertible currency. Financing is effected out of budgetary funds.

Members of Group I:

Australia, Austria, Belgium, Canada, Denmark, Finland, France, Federal Republic of Germany, Italy, Japan, Kuwait, Luxembourg, Netherlands, Norway, South Africa, Sweden, United Kingdom, United States.

Group II

consists of all other countries. They have to pay only one-tenth of their subscriptions in convertible currency and the remaining portions in their own currency.

President:

According to the Statutes, the President of the World Bank is always simultaneously the President of the IDA.

B. Participation of the Federal Republic of Germany

The Federal Republic of Germany is a Founder Member of the IDA.

a. *Contributions of the Federal Republic of Germany — in US dollars:*

— original subscription and participation in first 3 replenishment rounds: 574,879,000 US dollars.

— IVth replenishment (financial years 1975—77): 527,392,000 US dollars.

Disposable funds of the IDA — in mill. US dollars:

from:	Ist repl.	IInd repl.	IIIrd repl.	IVth repl.
	753.4	1,200.0	2,409.0	4,501.3

Largest donors of capital

	in %	in %
	(capital shares)	(voting right shares)
United States	37.8	24.0
United Kingdom	11.7	8.2
Federal Republic of Germany	10.1	6.7
Japan	7.4	5.2
France	6.3	4.3
Canada	6.1	4.0

b. *German personnel: see World Bank.*

c. *Main areas of activity of the Federal Republic of Germany:*

As one of the IDA's chief contributors, the Federal Republic of Germany, together with other granters of loans, contributes financially to an ever increasing number of socially oriented projects, in particular for rural development. Main borrowers from the IDA are India, Pakistan, and Bangladesh with 56 % of all credits granted so far, followed, with a large gap, by Ethiopia, Egypt and Tanzania.

d. *Competency in the Federal Republic of Germany:*

Federal Ministry for Economic Co-operation; Federal Foreign Office.

E. United Nations Educational, Scientific and Cultural Organization UNESCO

A. Established as a Specialized Agency of the United Nations pursuant to A/Res. 50 (I) of 14 December 1946. Headquarters: 7-9, Place de Fontenay, F-75700 Paris 7e.

Organs:

a. General Conference (held biennially):

19th conference in 1976 in Paris.

b. Executive Board:

Up to the 17th General Conference 34 members and since then 40; each is elected for a four-year term — immediate re-election not allowed — by the General Conference.

Group I (Western Europe, United States, Canada) 10 seats:
Australia, Austria, Belgium, France, Federal Republic of Germany, Italy, Norway, Spain, United Kingdom, United States.

Group II (Eastern Europe, Soviet Union, Byelorussian S.S.R.) 4 seats:
GDR, Bulgaria, Soviet Union, Yugoslavia.

Group III (Latin America) 7 seats:
Argentina, Brazil, Chile, Colombia, Cuba, Jamaica, Uruguay.

Group IV (Asia) 6 seats:
China, India, Iran, Japan, Nepal, Philippines.

Group V (Africa) 13 seats:
Benin, Egypt, Gabon, Ghana, Kenya, Mauritania, Saudi Arabia, Syria, Togo, Tunisia, Uganda, Upper Volta, Zaire.

c. Secretariat

Functions:

Promotion of international co-operation in the fields of education, science, communication and documentation without distinction as to race, sex, language or religion; access of all people to education and culture on the basis of equal rights; general education of the masses; assurance of universal respect for human rights; raising of the level of education.

Points of main effort in present programmes: Aid to the Third World.

137 member states (1976, cf. p. 229)

Director-General:

Amadou Mahtar M'Bow, Senegal (since 1 November 1974).

B. Participation of the Federal Republic of Germany

The Federal Republic of Germany acceded to UNESCO on 21 June 1952.

a. *Contributions of the Federal Republic of Germany — in US dollars:*

1969	1970	1971	1973	1975
2,335,384	2,335,384	2,569,708	3,465,648	5,483,456

Total budget of UNESCO — in US dollars (for two years):

1969–70	1971–72	1973–74	1975–76
71,550,000	81,300,000	119,954,000	169,992,000

Main contributors:	1969/70	1971/72	1973/74	1975/76
United States	21,271,815	24,227,400	31,598,104	38,945,000
	29.73 %	29.80 %	29.41 %	25.00 %
Soviet Union	9,838,125	10,902,330	14,214,312	23,398,156
	13.75 %	13.41 %	13.23 %	15.02 %
Japan				11,044,802
				7.09 %
Federal Republic	4,722,300	5,227,590	6,008,096	10,966,912
of Germany	6.60 %	6.43 %	6.34 %	7.04 %

With this, the Federal Republic of Germany takes fourth place among the contributors.

b. *German personnel:*

Absolute	Percentage	Germans in leading positions	Total UNESCO personnel	German financial contribution %
35	4.5	3	773	7.0

c. *Main areas of activity of the Federal Republic of Germany:*

Education and training, including educational assistance in all its aspects, particularly with respect to adult education and further education; educational reforms; environmental questions and ecology; maritime research and hydrology; technical progress and its application in communication systems; preservation of cultural heritage.

d. *Official offices of UNESCO in the Federal Republic of Germany:*

German Commission for UNESCO, Cäcilienstraße 42–44, 5000 Cologne.

e. *Competency in the Federal Republic of Germany:*

Federal Foreign Office; liaison address:
Permanent Mission of the Federal Republic of Germany to UNESCO, 13–15, Avenue Franklin D. Roosevelt, F-75008 Paris 8ᵉ.

F. World Intellectual Property Organization WIPO

A. The World Intellectual Property Organization was established on 14 July 1967 as the successor to the United International Bureau for the Protection of Intellectual Property (BIRPI) in Stockholm. By Resolution of the 29th General Assembly of the United Nations of 17 December 1974, it was converted into a Specialized Agency pursuant to article 57 of the UN Charter.

Headquarters: 32, Chemin des Colombettes, Geneva

Organs:

a. General Assembly:

The General Assembly consists of the signatories to the Stockholm Convention of 14 July 1967 who are at the same time members of at least one of the following Unions:

1. Paris Union, i. e. the International Union for the Protection of Industrial Property established by the Paris Convention of 20 March 1883,

2. The Bern Union, i. e. the Union for the Protection of Literary and Artistic Works established by the Bern Convention of 9 September 1886.

The General Assembly is held every 3 years at the organization's headquarters. Extraordinary General Assemblies may be convened by the Director General. The last General Assembly was held from 27 September to 5 October 1976.

b. Conference:

The Conference is formed by the signatories to the Stockholm Convention of 14 July 1967, irrespective of whether they are members of one of the unions or not. The members of the Conference meet at the same time and at the same place as the General Assembly .

Extraordinary meetings may be held at the request of the majority of the members states.

c. Co-ordinating Committee:

The Co-ordinating Committee consists of the signatories to the Stockholm Convention, the members of the Executive Committee of the Paris Union, of the Executive Committee of the Bern Union, or both Committees.

d. International Bureau:

The International Bureau is the Secretariat of the organization and is headed by the Director-General assisted by two or more Deputy Directors-General.

Functions:

WIPO is the world-wide international organization for the protection of intellectual property, i. e. industrial property and copyright, literary and artistic works, and promotes measures for the harmonization of national law in this field.

Member states (1976; cf. page 229)

WIPO	Paris Union	Bern Union
60	81	64

Director General: Dr. Arpad Bogsch, United States (since 1 December 1973).

Deputy Directors General:

Dr. Klaus Pfanner, Federal Republic of Germany, Felix Alexandrowitsch Swiridow, Soviet Union, Ketty-Lina Linguier-Laubhouet, Ivory Coast.

B. Participation of the Federal Republic of Germany

Participation for the most part in the following six international conventions and agreements:

- Paris Union for the Protection of Industrial Property of 20 March 1883
- Bern Union for the Protection of Literary and Artistic Works of 9 September 1886
- Nice Convention for the Classification of Goods and Services for the Registration of Trade Marks of 15 June 1957
- PCT = International Co-operation in the Field of Patents of 19 June 1970
- IPC = Strasbourg Convention on International Patent Classification of 24 March 1971
- ICIREPAT = International Patent Documentation.

a. *Contributions of the Federal Republic of Germany in DM*

1966	1972	1973	1974	1975	1976
75,000	326,000	342,200	469,600	547,500	638,700

b. *German personnel:*

Absolute	Percentage (only admin. grades)	Germans in leading positions	Total WIPO personnel in admin. grades	German financial contributions in %
5	3.6	2	56	7.67

c. *Main areas of activity of the Federal Republic of Germany:*

Protection of industrial property rights in particular

d. *Competency in the Federal Republic of Germany:*

Federal Ministry of Justice; Federal Foreign Office; Permanent Mission of the Federal Republic of Germany to the International Organizations, 28 D, Chemin du Petit-Saconnex, CH-1211 Geneva 19.

G. Food and Agriculture Organization
FAO

A. Established as the first Specialized Agency of the United Nations pursuant to A/Res. 50 (I) of 14 December 1946. Headquarters: Via delle Terme di Caracalla, Rome.

Organs:

a. General Conference (meets biennially). 18th conference 8—27 November 1975, in Rome.

b. Council: its 42 members, elected by the General Conference, serve for a term of three years, with eleven retiring on each of two successive years and twelve in the third year.

   Members of the Council (1976):

   Argentina, Brazil, Bulgaria, Burundi, Canada, China, Colombia, Congo, Ecuador, Egypt, Finland, France, Gabon, Gambia, Federal Republic of Germany, Guinea, India, Indonesia, Italy, Japan, Jordan, Libya, Malawi, Mauritius, Mexico, Netherlands, New Zealand, Niger, Pakistan, Panama, Peru, Philippines, Spain, Sri Lanka, Sudan, Thailand, Trinidad, Tobago, Tunisia, United Kingdom, United States, Yugoslavia.

c. Secretariat and 5 regional offices

d. Committees:
   1. Programme Committee
   2. Finance Committee
   3. Committee on Constitutional and Legal Matters
   4. Committee on Commodity Problems
   5. Committee on Fisheries
   6. Committee on Forestry
   7. Committee on Agriculture
   8. Committee on World Food Security

Functions:

Raising the levels of nutrition and standards of living throughout the world, improving in particular agricultural production and distribution of food, creation of better living conditions for rural population including the people employed in food, fishing and forestry industries, promoting the expansion of the world economy.

136 member states (1976, cf. page 229)

Director-General:

Edouard Saouma, Lebanon (since 1 January 1976).

B. Participation of the Federal Republic of Germany

The Federal Republic of Germany acceded to the FAO on 10 November 1950.

a. *Contributions of the Federal Republic of Germany — in US dollars:*

1969	1972	1973	1974	1975	1976	1977
2,607,642	3,379,032	3,379,039	4,828,175	4,828,175	7,375,736	7,375,736

Total budget of FAO — in US dollars: (in each case for two years)

1970/71	1972/73	1974/75	1976/77
71,325,000	85,998,000	106,700,000	167,000,000

Main contributors — in US dollars:

	1970/71	1974/75	1976/77
United States	2 x 11,722,629	2 x 13,547,500	2 x 20,797,500
Federal Republic of Germany	2 x 2,817,108	2 x 4,828,175	2 x 7,375,736
United Kingdom	2 x 2,660,602	2 x 4,860,185	2 x 7,432,849
France	2 x 2,412,006	2 x 3,985,245	2 x 6,094,773

b. *German personnel (admin. grades):*

Absolute	Percentage	Germans in leading positions	German financial contribution %
55	6.68	24	9.05

c. *Main areas of activity of the Federal Republic of Germany:*

As an FAO Member, the Federal Republic of Germany participates in all activities of working groups and other bodies and strives to strengthen the role of the FAO and improve its effectiveness. The World Food Conference convened by the United Nations in 1974 has called the fight against hunger all over the world one of the most urgent priorities. The Federal Republic of Germany has accorded priority to this problem, in its bilateral and multilateral co-operation with developing countries. The FAO work programme has been extended in particular with relation to production-oriented measures. Moreover, the Federal Republic of Germany gives support to the "Deutsche Welthungerhilfe", the national committee of FAO in its Freedom from Hunger/ Action for Development Campaign.

In the view of the Government of the Federal Republic, FAO activities should be concentrated on the following priorities:

1. Efforts to increase agricultural production and efficiency and improve the food situation in the developing countries.

2. For the rural areas, mobilization of manpower and improvement of living conditions.

3. Preservation of natural resources, as well as control of disease and vermin.

4. World food security through international co-ordination of national storage policies, formation of stocks in developing countries as well as the establishment of an effective worldwide information and early-warning system for the avoidance of supply shortages.

d. *Competency in the Federal Republic of Germany:*

Federal Ministry of Food, Agriculture and Forestry; Federal Foreign Office.

H. World Health Organization
WHO

A. The WHO was established as a Specialized Agency of the United Nations pursuant to A/Res. 124 (III) of 15 November 1947. Headquarters: Avenue Appia, Geneva.

Organs:

a. World Health Assembly, held annually in Geneva.
152 member states (1976; cf. page 229)

b. Executive Board:

31 members, elected by the World Health Assembly for 3-year terms.

c. Six regional offices of the WHO:

1. Europe including Algeria, Morocco and Turkey
Headquarters: 8 Scherfigsvej, Copenhagen.

2. North, Central and South America
Headquarters: Washington.

3. Eastern Mediterranean including Afghanistan, Iran, Pakistan and Sudan
Headquarters: Alexandria.

4. South-East Asia including Mongolia
Headquarters: New Delhi.

5. Western Pacific including China
Headquarters: Manila.

6. Africa
Headquarters: Brazzaville.

Bodies of experts advise the WHO on the planning and execution of programmes and measures.

d. Secretariat

Director-General:

Dr. Halfdan Mahler, Denmark (since 21 July 1973).

The President of the World Health Assembly is also elected by the Assembly.

Functions:

Exchange of experiences and further training by means of international conferences, seminars, working-groups, courses and studies;

Assistance, when wished by a member state, in improving that country's hygienic and sanitary conditions;

Assistance in eradicating plagues and epidemic diseases;

Promoting research in all fields of health and hygiene;

Assisting and improving the training of members of the health services and professions;

Assistance with problems of the protection of the human environment;

Establishing international norms for biological and pharmaceutical products;

A subsidiary organ of the WHO is the International Agency for Research into Cancer (IARC). Headquarters: Lyons. In this Agency the Federal Republic of Germany is also an active member.

B. Participation of the Federal Republic of Germany

The Federal Republic of Germany acceded to the WHO on 29 May 1951.

a. *Contributions of the Federal Republic of Germany — in mill. US dollars:*
   not including additional payments for IARC

1969	1971	1973	1974	1975	1976
3.96	4.769	5.654	6.558	7.958	8.575
6.30 %	6.30 %	6.13 %	6.12 %	6.90 %	6.90 %

Total budget of WHO — in mill. US dollars:

1971	1972	1973	1974	1975	1976
76.101	84.489	92.782	100.113	129.665	153.307

Main contributors — in mill. US dollars:

	1971	1972	1973	1974	1975	1976
United States	23.7	26.3	28.8	31.7	30.1	32.4
Soviet Union	11.2	12.2	13.3	13.6	14.9	16.1
Federal Republic of Germany	4.8	5.1	5.7	6.5	7.9	8.5
Japan	2.5	4.0	4.5	5.2	8.0	8.6
France	4.1	4.6	5.0	5.8	6.6	7.1
United Kingdom	4.5	4.5	4.9	5.6	6.1	6.5

b. *German personnel:*

Absolute	Percentage	Germans in leading positions	Total WHO personnel	German financial contribution %
49	2.5	37	1,950	6.12

c. *Main areas of activity of the Federal Republic of Germany:*

Investigating and combatting cancer, cardio-vascular diseases, small pox, rabies, cholera, malaria, onchocereosis, programmes and measures in all fields of psychiatric care, clinical pharmacology, dental surgery and protection of the human environment.

The Federal Republic of Germany receives an increasing number of WHO fellowship holders.

d. *Competency in the Federal Republic of Germany:*

Federal Ministry of Youth, Family Affairs and Health; Federal Foreign Office. Permanent Mission of the Federal Republic of Germany to the International Organizations; 94, rue de Lausanne, Geneva, Switzerland.

I. International Labour Organization ILO

A. Established in 1919 as an International Labour Office under the League of Nations. After the Second World War it was constituted on 14 December 1946 as a Specialized Agency of the United Nations pursuant to A/Res. 50 (I). Headquarters: CH-1211 Geneva 22.

Organs:

a. International Labour Conference (meets annually):

60th session June 1976 in Geneva
(convening of extraordinary conferences, e. g. World Employment Conference in June 1976, Geneva).

b. Governing Body:

56 members, including 28 government representatives, 14 employers' representatives and 14 workers' representatives. The Federal Republic of Germany's representative is included among the ten delegates of the leading industrial nations, with special prerogatives, e. g., permanent membership of the Governing Body.

Permanent members of the Governing Body:

Canada, China, France, Federal Republic of Germany, India, Italy, Japan, Soviet Union, United Kingdom, United States.

For the 1975—76 period, the Federal Republic's government representative was elected Chairman of the Governing Body.

c. International Labour Office.

d. Regional conferences, industrial committees, other committees and groups of experts.

Functions:

Initiation of decent working and living conditions through the adoption of international Labour Conventions and Recommendations. Basic principle: the right of all people to economic security and cultural development with the same opportunities and with the preservation of man's freedom and dignity without distinction of race, origin and sex.

132 member states (1976, cf. p. 229)

Director-General: Francis Blanchard, France (since 26 February 1974).

B. Participation of the Federal Republic of Germany

The Federal Republic of Germany acceded to the ILO on 12 June 1951.

a. *Contributions of the Federal Republic of Germany — in US dollars:*

1973	1974	1975	1976
1,978,742	2,717,097	2,879,581	5,454,060
5.68 %	6.02 %	6.38 %	6.73 %

Total budget of ILO — in US dollars:
(in each case for two years)

1972/73	1974/75	1976/77
71,503,000	95,069,000	160,616,406

Main contributors — in US dollars:

	1975	1976
United States	25.00 % = 11,283,625	25.00 % = 20,260,250
Soviet Union	13.45 % = 6,061,562	12.27 % = 11,564,551
Federal Republic of Germany	6.38 % = 2,879,581	6.73 % = 5,454,060

b. *German personnel:*

Absolute	Percentage	Germans in leading positions	Total ILO personnel (admin. grades)	German financial contribution %
33	4.5	6	726	5.3

c. *Main areas of activity of the Federal Republic of Germany:*

Collaboration in the working out of minimum standards in such fields as the protection of labour, social security, improvement of working and living conditions, and working environment; support of the ILO's programmes for technical co-operation with the developing countries (finance and personnel).

The programmes relate in particular to the creation of places of work in connection with the ILO's world employment programme, vocational training and advanced training, and the development of social institutions.

d. *Official agencies of the ILO in the Federal Republic of Germany:*

International Labour Office: branch office: Hohenzollernstrasse 21, 5300 Bonn-Bad Godesberg.

e. *Competency in the Federal Republic of Germany:*

Federal Ministry of Labour and Social Affairs; Federal Foreign Office.

Permanent Mission of the Federal Republic of Germany to the International Organizations, 28 D, Chemin du Petit-Saconnex, CH-1211 Geneva 19.

K. International Civil Aviation Organization ICAO

A. Established as a Specialized Agency of the United Nations pursuant to A/Res. 50 (I) of 14 December 1946. Headquarters: International Aviation Building, 1000 Sherbrooke Street West, Montreal, Canada.

Organs:

a. General Assembly (at least every three years):

21st General Assembly in 1974 in Montreal. The convening of extraordinary assemblies is possible.

b. ICAO Council:

At present 30 members*) arranged in three categories each consisting of ten states. Election: for three years.

Category 1 (states of chief importance in air transport):
Australia, Brazil, Canada, France, Federal Republic of Germany, Italy, Japan, Soviet Union, United Kingdom, United States.

Category 2 (states of medium importance in air transport):
Argentina, China, Czechoslovakia, Egypt, India, Lebanon, Mexico, Spain, Pakistan, Sweden.

Category 3 (states which through their election ensure the representation of the most important geographical regions of the world on the Council):
Colombia, Costa Rica, Indonesia, Kenya, Nigeria, Madagascar, Morocco, Senegal, Trinidad and Tobago, Yugoslavia.

c. Air Navigation Commission.

d. Secretary-General:

Yves Lambert, France (since 1 January 1975).

Functions:

Further development of the principles and technology of international civil aviation, ensuring a safe and orderly growth of international aviation, development and operation of aircraft for peaceful purposes; promoting the extension of air routes and the extension and improvement of airports and traffic safety facilities; satisfying demand for safe, well-planned and economically efficient air traffic; improvement of traffic safety in international aviation; promotion of the free development of each branch of international civil aviation.

134 member states (1976, cf. p. 229)

President of the ICAO Council:

Dr. Assad Kotaite, Lebanon (since 1 January 1975).

---

*) According to a decision taken at the 21st General Assembly, the number of Members of the ICAO Council is being increased to 33.

B. Participation of the Federal Republic of Germany

The Federal Republic of Germany acceded to the ICAO on 8 June 1956.

a. *Contributions of the Federal Republic of Germany — in US dollars:*

1969	1972	1973	1974	1975	1976
488,451	468,283	531,002	532,901	820,610	872,588

Net budget of ICAO — in mill. US dollars:

1969	1972	1973	1974	1975	1976
6,587	8,855	10,029	9,778	12,659	13,493

Main contributors (percental of total budget):

	1969	1972	1973	1974	1975	1976
United States	30.87	28.75	28.75	28.75	25.00	25.00
Soviet Union	—	13.48	13.39	13.33	13.24	13.03
United Kingdom	8.32	5.87	5.82	5.80	5.63	5.54
France	6.92	5.54	5.50	5.48	5.65	5.55
Federal Republic of Germany	7.30	5.51	5.47	5.45	6.00	6.20
Japan	—	—	4.96	5.18	5.70	6.27

b. *German personnel:*

Absolute	Percentage	Germans in leading positions	Total personnel ICAO Secretariat	German financial contribution %
5	1.93	1	259	6.2

c. *Main areas of activity of the Federal Republic of Germany:*

Air traffic control; flying operations; airworthiness; meteorological services; air navigation regulations; training of air navigation personnel.

d. *Competency in the Federal Republic of Germany:*

Federal Ministry of Transport; Federal Foreign Office.

L. Intergovernmental Maritime Consultative Organization IMCO

A. Established in 1948 on the strength of a Convention concluded by 35 states, pursuant to A/Res. 204 (III) of 18 November 1948, as a Specialized Agency of the UN. Headquarters: London W 1, 101-104, Piccadilly.

Organs:

a. General Assembly (every two years):

8th session 1975 in London.

b. Council:

18 members elected by the General Assembly for two years. Arranged in three categories: (1976—77)

1. Six states with particularly large merchant fleets:
   Greece, Japan, Norway, Soviet Union, United Kingdom, United States.
2. Six states with a particular interest in providing international shipping services:
   Brazil, Canada, China, France, Federal Republic of Germany, Italy.
3. 6 other states (with account taken of regional representation):
   Algeria, Argentina, India, Indonesia, Nigeria, Poland.

c. Maritime Safety Committee:

16 members. Elected by the General Assembly for four years.

d. Secretariat.

Subsidiary Organs:

e. Marine Environment Protection Committee.

f. Legal Committee.

g. Facilitation Committee.

h. Committee on Technical Cooperation.

Functions:

Consultation on shipping matters within the framework of the UN; exchange of information between Governments; treatment of technical matters of all kinds affecting shipping; safety at sea; protection of the environment at sea; technical assistance in maritime matters for the developing countries.

96 member states (1976, cf. p. 229)

Secretary-General:

C. P. Srivastava, India (since 1 January 1974).

B. Participation of the Federal Republic of Germany

The Federal Republic of Germany acceded to IMCO on 7 January 1959.

a. *Contributions of the Federal Republic of Germany — in US dollars:*

1969	1972	1973	1974	1975
37,547	66,098	66,189	79,610	82,079

Total budget of IMCO:

1969	1972	1973	1974	1975
1,234,924	1,969,900	2,075,156	2,924,000	3,203,563

Main contributors — in US dollars:

	1969	1972	1973	1974	1975
Liberia	202,038	208,702	257,888	355,397	378,684
United Kingdom	116,759	232,471	214,226	292,110	316,904
Japan	104,753	164,653	173,664	227,645	245,171
Norway	103,164	290,702	326,559	478,728	543,292

b. *German personnel:*

Absolute	Percentage	Germans in leading positions	Total IMCO personnel	German financial contribution %
2	1	1	206	2.5

c. *Main areas of activity of the Federal Republic of Germany:*

Participation in all committees and subcommittees; for many years chairmanship of the Maritime Safety Committee.

Co-operation in agreements for the prevention of collisions at sea; standardization of the regulations concerning limits of national areas all over the world; studies for the prevention of oil pollution at sea; contact frequencies between ships and aircraft; meteorological forecasts.

d. *Competency in the Federal Republic of Germany:*

Federal Ministry of Transport; Federal Foreign Office.

M. International Telecommunication Union ITU

A. Established 17 May 1865 as the International Telegraph Union, converted into International Telecommunication Union (Union internationale des télécommunications) in 1932. — International Telecommunication Convention, Madrid 1932 (Convention internationale des télécommunications). — Specialized Agency of the United Nations pursuant to the Agreement concluded between the United Nations and the International Telecommunication Union, Lake Success, August 1947. A/Res. 124 (III) of 15 November 1947.

Contractual basis: International Telecommunication Convention of 25 October 1973 (Malaga-Torremolinos). Headquarters: Place des Nations, CH-1211 Geneva 20.

Organs:

a. Plenipotentiary Conference:

Meets at regular intervals, usually every 5 years. Last conference at Malaga-Torremolinos, Spain, in 1973. Next conference scheduled for Nairobi, probably in 1980.

b. Administrative Conferences:

Meet as required and convened with the consent of the majority of members as world-wide or regional Administrative Conferences.

c. Administrative Council: 36 member states (1973). Its composition is (since 1973 until next Plenipotentiary Conference):

Region 1 (North and South America):
Argentina, Brazil, Canada, Mexico, United States, Venezuela, Trinidad and Tobago

Region 2 (Western Europe):
Federal Republic of Germany, France, Italy, Spain, Sweden, Switzerland, United Kingdom

Region 3 (Eastern Europe and Northern Asia):
Hungary, Poland, Romania, Soviet Union

Region 4 (Africa):
Algeria, Cameroon, Egypt, Ethiopia, Morocco, Nigeria, Senegal, Tanzania, Zaire

Region 5 (Asia and Australasia):
Australia, China, India, Iran, Japan, Lebanon, Malaysia, Saudi Arabia, Thailand

Normally meets every year. Acts as an agent for the Plenipotentiary Conference, controls and co-ordinates TV activities and exercises financial control of the permanent organs.

d. Permanent Organs:

1. General Secretariat
2. International Frequency Registration Board (IFRB)
3. International Radio Consultative Committee (CCIR)
4. International Telegraph and Telephone Consultative Committee (CCITT).

Functions:

Maintaining and extending international co-operation in all fields of communication by telegraph, telephone, cable and radio, including the allocation of frequencies; radio in space; all questions of telecommunications, including co-operation with the United Nations Development Programme (UNDP).

148 member states (1976, cf. p. 229)

Secretary-General:

Mohamed Ezzedine Mili, Tunisia (since 1967).

Deputy Secretary-General:

Richard E. Butler, Australia.

B. Participation of the Federal Republic of Germany

The Federal Republic of Germany acceded to the ITU on 17 April 1952.

a. *Contributions of the Federal Republic of Germany — in Swiss Francs:*

1973	1974	1975	1976	1977
1,352,000	1,563,480	2,178,400	2,240,840	3,225,000
4.16 %	4.12 %	4.81 %	4.80 %	5.90 %

Total budget of the ITU — in mill. Swiss Francs (official currency unit):

1969	1971	1972	1973	1974	1975	1976
21,876	27,571	29,718	36,220	45,444	50,296	50,231

Main contributors:

(The contribution system is based on voluntary classes ranging between the class units $1/2$ and 30.)

	1973	1974	1975	1976	1977
Total units:	480 $1/2$	486 $1/2$	415 $1/2$	416 $1/2$	423 $1/2$
United States	30	30	30	30	30
United Kingdom	30	30	30	30	30
Soviet Union	30	30	30	30	30
France	30	30	30	30	30
Federal Republic of Germany	20	20	20	20	25
Japan	20	20	20	20	20

b. *German personnel:*

Absolute	Percentage	Germans in leading positions	Total ITU personnel	German financial contribution %
8	4.85	1	165	4.81

c. *Main areas of activity of the Federal Republic of Germany:*

Co-operation in the Administrative Council; proposals for the form of the new International Telecommunication Convention; collaboration in the revising and supplementing of executive regulations (executive regulations for the telegraph services; executive regulations for the telephone services; executive regulations for the radio services; supplementary executive regulations for the radio services); collaboration in working out recommendations of the International Consultative Committees; co-operation in the International Frequency Registration Board for the purpose of exploiting the frequency spectrum and avoiding mutual disturbances in the radio services; making experts available for the ITU's development aid projects (1975: 81 experts on 87 assignments); informing ITU fellowship holders about telecommunications in the Federal Republic of Germany.

d. *Competency in the Federal Republic of Germany:*

Federal Ministry of Posts and Telecommunications; Federal Foreign Office.

Permanent Mission of the Federal Republic of Germany to the International Organizations: 28 D, Chemin du Petit-Saconnex, CH-1211 Geneva 19.

N. Universal Postal Union
UPU

A. Established in 1874 as the International Postal Union (since 1878 the "Universal Postal Union"); from 1948: Universal Postal Union constituted as Specialized Agency of the United Nations pursuant to A/Res. 124 (III) of 15 November 1947. Headquarters: Weltpoststrasse 4, CH-3000 Bern 15.

Organs:

a. Universal Post Congress

Meets every 5 years. 17th Congress (together with centenary celebration) met in 1974 in Lausanne, Switzerland. Extraordinary sessions may be held at the request or with the consent of two-thirds of the members. 18th Universal Post Congress will be held in Rio de Janeiro, Brazil, in 1979.

b. Executive Council (Conseil exécutif, CE)

40 member states. 39 out of these are elected by the Universal Post Congress for the intervals between two congresses. Re-election for one more term possible. Distribution into 5 geographical groups on the basis of equitable geographic distribution.

Zone 1 Western Hemisphere (8 seats):

Argentina, Brazil, Canada, Colombia, Cuba, Jamaica, Uruguay, Venezuela.

Zone 2 Eastern Europe and Northern Asia (4 seats):

Czechoslovakia, Romania, Ukrainian S.S.R., Yugoslavia.

Zone 3 Western Europe (6 seats):

Federal Republic of Germany, Iceland, Italy, Netherlands, Spain, United Kingdom.

Zone 4 South-East Europe, Southern Asia, Oceania (10 seats):

Australia, Bangladesh, China, Indonesia, Japan, Lebanon, Malaysia, Pakistan, Sri Lanka, Syria.

Zone 5 Africa (11 seats):

Cameroon, Congo, Guinea, Kenya, Liberia, Libya, Mali, Mauritius, Morocco, Niger, Sudan.

As a rule, the chairmanship of the Executive Council lies with the host country of the last Congress, i. e. at present Switzerland, which because of this chairmanship also is a member of the Executive Council.

c. Consultative Committee for Postal Studies (Conseil Consultatif des Études Postales — CCEP):

30 member states.

d. International Bureau.

Functions:

Securing and improvement of the postal services in international collaboration; technical assistance within the scope of UN programmes, but also directly.

Member states and territories of the UPU constitute a single postal territory for the reciprocal exchange of mail. Freedom of transit is guaranteed throughout the Union territory. Apart from the obligatory international mail service, members can decide themselves about other services (registered mail, parcels, money orders, postal cheques), under the appropriate agreements of the UPU.

154 member states (1976, cf. p. 229)

Director-General of the International Office of the UPU:

Mohammed I. Sobhi, Egypt (since 1 January 1975).

B. Participation of the Federal Republic of Germany

The Federal Republic of Germany acceded again to the Universal Postal Union in 1955 (the German Reich was one of the 22 Founder Members of the International Postal Union).

a. *Contributions of the Federal Republic of Germany — in Swiss Francs*:*
   (including voluntary payments for the Fonds spécial)

1972	1973	1974	1975	1976 (estimate)
253,691	274,490	299,785	321,500	650,000

Total budget of UPU — in Swiss Francs (gross):

1972	1975	1976 (estimate)
9,586,431	12,924,728	15,000,000

Main contributors:

The UPU has changed the contribution system, raising the maximum classes from 25 to 50 units. Up to 1976, this class consisted of the following countries:

Canada
China
Federal Republic of Germany
France
Japan
United Kingdom
United States

At present, the Union's expenses amount to 1,080 units, so that the Federal Republic's share is 4.5 %. In 1976, each unit was equivalent to approximately 12,000 SFR, which amounts to about 600,000 SFR for 50 units.

---

*) Budget amounts and contributions to UPU (in contrast to US dollar figures used with other UN Specialized Agencies) are stated in Swiss Francs on which the International Telecommunication Union bases its budgets; likewise, contributions have to be paid in Swiss Francs. Amounts have been stated exclusively in this currency, especially since a conversion into US dollars with its greatly changed value against the Swiss Franc, would not have presented a true picture of financial developments in recent years.

b. *German personnel:*

Absolute	Percentage	Germans in leading positions	Total UPU personnel	German financial contribution %
1	1.8	—	56	4.6

c. *Main areas of activity of the Federal Republic of Germany:*

The Federal Republic of Germany is both a member of the Executive Council and the Consultative Council for Postal Studies.

On the Executive Council, the Federal Republic of Germany participates in the work of all 10 Commissions (5 Commissions for the various postal services and 1 Commission each for Personnel, Finance, General Questions, Technical Co-operation, Documentation). The Federal Republic holds the chairmanship in the important Commission for General Questions (legal matters of the UPU and its statutes).

On the Consultative Council for Postal Studies, the Federal Republic participates in 35 out of 50 studies with special emphasis on technical and operational questions (mechanization and automation of postal services, delivery of letters and parcels, air mail, money orders and postal cheques). In six study groups, the Federal Republic acts as rapporteur.

d. *Competency in the Federal Republic of Germany:*

Federal Ministry of Posts and Telecommunications; Federal Foreign Office.

O. World Meteorological Organization WMO

A. The WMO was established as a Specialized Agency of the United Nations pursuant to A/Res. 531 (VI) of 20 December 1951. Headquarters: 41, Avenue Giuseppe Motta, Geneva.

Organs:

a. World Meteorological Congress, meets every four years.
   7th congress in Geneva from 28 April to 23 May 1975.

b. Executive Committee:

   24 members: the President, three Vice-Presidents, six Presidents of the Regional Associations, and fourteen directors of the Members' meteorological services.

   President:
   Mohammed Fathi Taha, Egypt (since 1971).

   Vice-Presidents:
   A. P. Navai, Iran
   Ju. A. Izrael, Soviet Union
   D. J. E. Echeveste, Argentina

   The 6 Regional Presidents come from:
   Brazil, Guatemala, Hungary, Nigeria, Philippines, Thailand.

   The 14 other members come from:
   Australia, Canada, China, Colombia, France, Federal Republic of Germany, Japan, Kenya, Mauritius, Pakistan, Senegal, Sweden, Tunisia, United States.

c. Six Regional Associations:

   Africa, Asia, South America, North and Central America, South-West Pacific, Europe.

d. Eight Technical Committees.

e. Secretariat.

Functions:

Worldwide co-operation in the development of networks of meteorological stations; promotion of the development and operation of central meteorological stations;

Promotion of the development and operation of a system for the speedy exchange of meteorological information;

Standardization of meteorological observations. Ensuring uniform publications of observations and statistics;

Encouragement of the use of meteorology in aviation, navigation, hydrological problems, agriculture and other human activities;

Promotion of the co-operation between meteorological and hydrological service systems in the field of hydrology;

Promotion of meteorological training and research and their international aspects and co-ordination.

145 member states and territories (1976, cf. p. 229)

Secretary-General:

David Arthur Davies, United Kingdom (since 1 January 1955).

B. Participation of the Federal Republic of Germany

The Federal Republic of Germany acceded to the WMO on 10 July 1954.

a. *Contributions of the Federal Republic of Germany — in US dollars:*

1969	1971	1973	1974	1975	1976
135,129	149,807	238,643	303,894	325,580	428,697

incl. payments for the Voluntary Assistance Programme

169,777	209,807	77,619	155,094	38,461

Total budget of the WMO — in mill. US dollars:

1969	1971	1973	1974	1975	1976
2.927	3.606	5.214	6.940	7.765	9.400

Main contributors — in US dollars:

	1969	1971	1973	1974	1975	1976
United States	698,595	860,400	1,233,745	1,577,878	1,683,187	2,216,287
Soviet Union	311,053	661,600	661,900	846,526	903,024	1,189,030
United Kingdom	175,923	216,700	310,688	397,349	423,868	558,116
Federal Republic of Germany	135,129	149,807	238,643	303,894	325,580	428,697

The contribution is calculated in contribution units, for the 7th financing period 1976—77 a total of 1,162 contribution units, the United States accounting for 274, the Soviet Union for 147, the United Kingdom for 69, and the Federal Republic of Germany for 53.

b. *German personnel:*

Absolute	Percentage	Germans in leading positions	Total WMO personnel	German financial contribution %
4	1.5	2	265	4.6

c. *Main areas of activity of the Federal Republic of Germany:*

The Federal Republic of Germany co-operates, via the WMO bodies — the Congress, the Executive Committee, the Regional Association for Europe and in all Technical Commissions — in the planning and implementation of technical programmes, particularly in the following:

1. Worldwide meteorological observations and separate components: global meteorological observation system, global meteorological and telecommunication system; global meteorological data-processing system. (The Federal Republic of Germany operates, within the framework of this programme, a meteorological telecommunications centre — address: Frankfurter Strasse 135, Offenbach — as a focal point between Eastern and Western Europe, and a regional meteorological forecasting station).

2. Global Atmospheric Research Programme (GARP).

   German co-operation mainly in the separate components:
   GATE (GARP Atlantic Tropical Experiment) and
   FGGE (First GARP Global Experiment).

3. Application of meteorological knowledge to human activities; co-operation mainly in the separate programmes: aeronautical meteorology, marine meteorology, climatology, agricultural meteorology, and hydrology. It also participates in the assistance programme for developing a world meteorological observation service in the developing countries and by training scholarship-holders from these countries with the German meteorological service.

d. *Competency in the Federal Republic of Germany:*

Federal Ministry of Transport; Federal Foreign Office.

Permanent Mission of the Federal Republic of Germany to the International Organizations; 28 D, Chemin du Petit-Saconnex, CH-1211 Geneva 19.

The Permanent Representative of the Federal Republic of Germany to the WMO is the President of the German Central Meteorological Office in Offenbach/Main.

P. International Atomic Energy Agency
IAEA

A. Establishment can be traced back to a suggestion made by President Eisenhower and took place pursuant to A/Res. 1145 (XII) of 14 November 1957. Headquarters: Kärntnerring 11, Vienna I.

Organs:

a. General Conference (annual):
   20th General Conference in Vienna (1976).

b. Board of Governors:

   34 members, divided into eight regional groups:

   1. North America, 2. Latin America, 3. Western Europe, 4. Eastern Europe, 5. Africa, 6. Middle East and Southern Asia, 7. South-East Asia and the Pacific, 8. Far East.

   The following nine states have permanent seats:

   Canada, Federal Republic of Germany, France, India, Italy, Japan, Soviet Union, United Kingdom and United States. The remaining 25 seats are non-permanent and are allocated, according to a complicated procedure, among the eight regional groups.

Functions:

Worldwide co-operation in nuclear research and nuclear technology. Assistance to developing countries.

IAEA is the agency for supervising the provisions of the Non-Proliferation Treaty.

109 member states (1976, cf. p. 229)

Director-General:
Arne Sigvard Eklund, Sweden (since 1 December 1961).

B. Participation of the Federal Republic of Germany

The Federal Republic of Germany acceded to IAEA on 1 October 1957.

a. *Contributions of the Federal Republic of Germany to the regular budget —
in US dollars:*

1969	1972	1973	1974	1975	1976
852,453	1,394,686	1,187,860	1,531,886	1,980,392	2,544,880

Net budget of IAEA — in US dollars:

1969	1972	1973	1974	1975	1976
11,251,000	15,392,000	18,258,757	23,474,491	26,660,000	34,237,000

Main contributors — in US dollars:

	1969	1973	1974	1975	1976	%
United States	3,041,235	5,724,974	7,382,611	7,452,741	9,545,897	27.88
Soviet Union	1,418,790	2,475,615	3,192,797	3,618,553	4,650,032	13.58
Japan		942,659	1,215,187	1,993,864	2,562,192	7.48
Federal Republic of Germany	852,453	1,187,860	1,531,886	1,980,392	2,544,880	7.43

b. *German personnel:*

Absolute	Percentage	Germans in leading positions	Total IAEA personnel	German financial contribution %
30	7.7	7	394	7.43

c. *Main areas of activity of the Federal Republic of Germany:*

Despatch of 660 German experts to conferences and of 30 experts to developing countries; 100 scholarships for studies in the Federal Republic; donations of equipment; research contracts of German research institutes with the IAEA; organization of conferences in the Federal Republic of Germany.

Joint research programmes for improving the protein content in vegetation, control of the tsetse fly, improvement of fertilizer yields by methods of nuclear technology.

d. *Competency in the Federal Republic of Germany:*

Federal Ministry of Research and Technology; Federal Foreign Office.

Permanent Mission of the Federal Republic of Germany to the International Organizations: Metternichgasse 3, Vienna.

3. Intergovernmental Organizations under the Aegis of the United Nations

A. General Agreement on Tariffs and Trade
GATT

A. Establishment: by Resolution 13 (I) of 18 February 1946, the Economic and Social Council convened an International Conference on Trade and Employment with a view to promoting production, exchange, and consumption of goods. The preparatory work led to the General Agreement on Tariffs and Trade (GATT) of 30 October 1947; the International Conference in Havana was submitted a draft international trade charter which, apart from the trade policy aspects dealt with by GATT, contained sections on economic development, full employment, international investment, international commodity agreements, restrictive trade practices, as well as the constitution, the method of work and the administration of an International Trade Organization (ITO); since not only the United States Congress but also many governments did not ratify the Havana Charter, the ITO did not come into being and since then GATT has been administered by a Secretariat called the Interim Commission of the International Trade Organization; GATT is currently valid in the version of the Final Act of the Protocol of Torquay of 21 April 1951, revised by protocols which entered into force on 7 February 1957 and 1 January 1968. Headquarters: Villa le Bocage, Palais des Nations, CH-1211 Geneva, Switzerland.

Organs:

a. Sessions of Contracting Parties:

These sessions, normally held annually, are the principal body of GATT; decisions are generally taken by consensus without a vote; if a vote has to be taken, each member country has one vote; for most decisions a simple majority is sufficient, but on matters of fundamental importance a two-thirds majority is necessary. Chairman: G. S. Maciel (since 1976).

b. Council of Representatives:

This council consists of representatives of all member countries, handles inter-session business, and usually meets every four to six weeks; it was established in May/June 1960 by the 16th session of the contracting parties. Chairman: Baron C. de Geer, Sweden.

c. Consultative Group of 18:

This high-ranking group was formed in 1975 on the basis of the IMF Group of 20. Its main function is to follow the development of world trade, prevent disturbances to trade, facilitate processes of international adjustments and coordination between GATT and IMF. Members: 7 industrial countries — including the European Community (including member states) — 9 developing countries, as well as Poland and Spain. Chairman: GATT Director General, Mr. Long.

d. Committee on Trade and Development:

A revision protocol which entered into force on 1 January 1968 added a Part IV to GATT concerning trade and development. At the same time the Committee on Trade and Development was established with the task of ensuring the observance of Part IV and communicating appropriate recommendations to the contracting parties. Chairman: M. A. B. Hanza, Egypt.

e. International Trade Centre:

The contracting parties set up this centre in May 1974 to provide information on export markets and advisory services for developing countries; since 1968 the centre has been operated jointly by GATT and UNCTAD. Director: V. E. Santiapillai, Sri Lanka.

Functions:

GATT has four basic elements:

1. Trade on the basis of non-discrimination; all contracting parties are obliged to apply the most favoured nation clause in connection with import and export duties and burdens, even if no corresponding bilateral agreement has been concluded with the GATT member concerned;

2. Domestic industry may only be protected through tariffs; accordingly, the introduction of import quotas as a protective measure are forbidden. However, such quotas may be introduced for certain other purposes, such as balance of payments deficits, but the circumstances are closely defined and consultations are compulsory to avoid any damage to others.

3. All the provisions of GATT are based on the concept of permanent consultations to ensure that the commercial interests of other contracting parties are not prejudiced.

4. GATT is the framework for negotiations to reduce tariffs and other trade barriers, and for transforming the results of such negotiations into legal instruments.

With tariff reductions totalling 23.8 % having been achieved between 1947 and 1951, further reductions amounting overall to 42 % were achieved in the Dillon Round and the Kennedy Round, which led to the preparation of similar proceedings (Tokyo Round).

86 member states (1976, cf. page 229)
83 full members
 3 provisional members
24 de facto members

Director-General:

Olivier Long, Switzerland (since May 1968).

B. Participation of the Federal Republic of Germany

The Federal Republic of Germany joined GATT on 1 October 1951.

a. *Contributions of the Federal Republic of Germany in Swiss Francs:*

1974	1975	1976	1977
2,657,600	3,081,200	3,823,400	4,005,000

Total GATT budget in Swiss Francs:

1974	1975	1976	1977
22,501,360	28,267,000	34,195,400	36,320,000

Main contributors in Swiss Francs:

	1976	1977
United States	4,817,000	5,065,900
Federal Republic of Germany	3,823,400	4,005,000
Japan	2,554,500	2,751,900
United Kingdom	2,588,100	2,694,900
France	2,410,200	2,563,200

b. *German personnel*

Absolute	Percentage	Germans in leading positions	Total GATT personnel	German financial contribution %
5	2.5	2	200	11.39

c. *Main areas of activity of the Federal Republic of Germany:*

As the second largest trading nation in the world, the Federal Government actively promotes the further liberalization of world trade through the progressive reduction of tariffs and non-tariff measures. Within the framework of the European Community, regular attendance at the 7th GATT round of multilateral trade negotiations (Tokyo Round).

d. *Official agencies of GATT in the Federal Republic of Germany:*

None

e. *Competency in the Federal Republic of Germany:*

Federal Ministry of Economics; Federal Foreign Office.
The Permanent Mission of the Federal Republic of Germany to the International Organizations in Geneva, 28 D, Chemin du Petit-Saconnex, P. O. Box 191, CH-1211 Geneva 19.

B. Regional Development Banks
1 African Development Fund
ADF

A. Establishment: by Convention of 29 November 1972, entered into force on 30 June 1973, began operations on 1 August 1973. Headquarters: Abidjan, Ivory Coast.

Organs:

a. Governing Council:

Each member of the ADF and of the African Development Bank (ADB) nominates a Governor and an alternate Governor; the Governing Council decides on all fundamental issues.

b. Directorate:

The Directorate consists of 6 regional and 6 non-regional directors; it determines the principles of business policy, decides on loans, and ensures the efficient use of funds.

Members:

Apart from the ADB (which currently has 42 African members), there are 16 non-regional members of the ADF; they follow in alphabetical order (capital subscription in mill. UA = 1.11111 US dollars/voting right in percentage): ADB (6.5/50) as well as Belgium (3.0/1.187), Brazil (3.0/1.187), Canada (22.5/8.9), Denmark (7.0/2.769), Finland (2.0/0.791), Federal Republic of Germany (15.0/5.933), Italy (10.0/3.956), Japan (15.0/5.933), Netherlands (6.0/2.373), Norway (7.5/2.967), Saudi Arabia (9.0/3.56), Sweden (9.0/3.56), Switzerland (6.19/2.448), Spain (3.0/1.187), United Kingdom (9.211/2.062), Yugoslavia (3.0/1.187).

Functions:

Supplements the activities of the ADB by granting loans on preferential terms to particularly needy regional member countries of the Bank. The fund is legally independent but uses the personnel and organization of the ADB.

Sectoral and regional distribution of funds (in mill. UA)

Sector	Central Africa	East Africa	North Africa	West Africa	Total commitments	Total commitments in %
Agriculture	17.70	10.85	4.48	20.00	53.03	42.2
Transport	4.45	14.58	4.00	9.67	33.70	26.8
Public utilities	7.00	5.35	3.60	5.00	20.95	16.7
Public health	—	4.50	—	8.50	13.00	10.3
Education	—	—	—	5.00	5.00	4.0
Total	30.15	35.28	12.08	48.17	125.68	100.0
	(8)	(12)	(4)	(16)	(40)	

President:

Kwame Fordwor, Ghana (since 1 September 1976).

B. Participation of the Federal Republic of Germany

The Federal Republic of Germany is a Founder Member.

a. *Contributions of the Federal Republic of Germany in UA*
(1 UA = 1.11111 US dollar):

From 1973 to 1975, the Federal Republic of Germany paid an original contribution of approx. 7.5 mill. UA. A selective capital replenishment of a further 7.5 mill. UA has increased its share to 15 mill. UA; the equivalent in DM (22.4 mill.) has been paid in three instalments from 1975 to 1977.

The share of the Federal Republic of Germany in the ADF replenishment agreed at the beginning of 1976 is 22.5 mill. UA (approx. 6.5 mill. DM), payable in three instalments between 1976 and 1978.

b. *German personnel:*

Up to now none.

c. *Competency in the Federal Republic of Germany:*

Federal Ministry for Economic Co-operation.

2 Asian Development Bank ADB

A. Establishment: by a Resolution adopted in March 1965, the UN Economic Commission for Asia and the Far East (ECAFE — converted in 1974 into the Economic and Social Commission for Asia and the Pacific — ESCAP) set up a Consultative Committee which drafted the ADB Convention which was signed in Manila on 14 December 1965 and entered into force on 22 August 1966. Headquarters: 2330 Roxas Boulevard, Passay City/Manila, Philippines.

Organs:

a. Governing Council:

Each member nominates a Governor and an alternative Governor; the Governing Council decides on all fundamental questions and meets annually.

b. Directorate:

The Directorate consists of eight regional and four non-regional Directors; the Federal Republic of Germany, the United Kingdom and Austria form a voting group: the present Executive Director of this group is Stanley Freyer of the United Kingdom. The Directorate lays down the principles of bank policy, decides on loans and ensures that funds are efficiently used.

c. Asian Development Fund (ADF):

Established by the Sixth Annual Assembly of the ADB in Manila; started business on 28 June 1974. The fund enables the bank to grant particularly needy members loans on preferential terms. The initial stock was 525 mill. US dollars (share of the Federal Republic of Germany 34.5 mill. US dollars). The replenishment of $ 809 mill. by 1978 is payable in three instalments (by the Federal Republic of Germany, $ 53.1 mill. or an alterable DM 123.5 mill.).

Members:

a. Regional (share of voting rights):

Afghanistan (0.808), Australia (6.372), Bangladesh (1.516), Burma (1.031), Cambodia (0.719), China/Taiwan (1.586), Cook Island (0.479), Fiji (0.545), Gilbert Island (0.480), Hongkong (1.031), India (6.927), Indonesia (6.025), Japan (14.348), South Korea (5.609), Laos (0.505), Malaysia (3.25), Nepal (0.626), New Zealand (2.041), Pakistan (2.696), Papua-New Guinea (0.572), Philippines (2.904), Singapore (0.823), Solomon Islands (0.483), Sri Lanka (1.067), Thailand (1.863), Tonga (0.48), Vietnam (1.308), Western Samoa (0.478). (Thus the regional votes totalled 66.572 %).

b. Regional contributors (in mill. US dollars/%):

Australia (41.6/5.1), Japan (272.6/33.7), New Zealand (5.359/0.7).

c. Non-regional contributors (in mill. US dollars/%/share of voting rights):

Austria (6.9/0.9/0.823), Belgium (7.3/0.9/0.823), Canada (76.4/9.4/5.806), Denmark (6.6/0.8/0.823), Finland (5.8/0.7/0.615), Federal Republic of Germany (53.1/6.6/2.834), France (42.4/5.2/21), Italy (30.8/3.8/1.863), Netherlands (12.9/1.6/1.239), Norway (6.1/0.8/0.823), Sweden (10.6/1.3/0.615), Switzerland (8.3/1.0/0.823), United Kingdom (42.4/5.2/2.557), United States (180.0/22.3/11.574). (The non-regional votes thus totalled 33.428 %).

Functions:

The ADB decides to promote the economic development of the developing countries of Asia, in so far as they are members of the ESCAP.

The funds are obtained by member subscriptions, the raising of loans, the sale of loans shares to other investors, the repayment of loans, and from net profits (up to now credit bonds for DM 275 mill. have been issued in the Federal Republic of Germany).

Lending activities:

I. Approved credits, cumulative	Number	Amount in mill. US $
1. from ordinary capital funds	161	2944.0
2. from special funds	104	738.0

II. Sectoral distribution of funds	
1968—1975	%
Agriculture	18.2
Industry	31.4
Public utilities	21.1
Transport and communications	1.6
Education and training	27.7

President:

Taroichi Yoshida, Japan (since 24 November 1976).

B. Participation of the Federal Republic of Germany

The Federal Republic of Germany became an original member of the ADB by law of 1 August 1966.

a. *Contributions of the Federal Republic of Germany:*
   As above

b. *German personnel*

Absolute	Percentage	Germans in leading positions	Total ADB personnel	German financial contribution %
10	3.7	5	736	3.05

c. *Competency in the Federal Republic of Germany:*
   Federal Ministry for Economic Co-operation.

3 Inter-American Development Bank IDB

A. Establishment: The convention on the establishment of the IDB was drafted on the proposal of the OAS Economic Conference, signed in Washington on 8 April 1959, and entered into force on 30 December 1959; the Bank started business in February 1961. Headquarters: 808 17th street, N. W. Washington, D. C. 20577, USA.

Organs:

a. Governing Council:

Each member nominates one Governor and one alternate Governor; the Governing Council decides on all fundamental matters.

b. Committee of the Governing Council:

The Committee has the same number of members as the Directorate (11). It is concerned primarily with matters of non-regional fund raising and the accession of non-regional countries. Since 1974 it has had an unlimited mandate and can thus handle all matters delegated to it by the Governing Council; these include, apart from general banking policy, basic aspects of development policy.

c. Directorate:

The Directorate consists of seven Directors of the Latin American members, one each from Canada and the United States, as well as two from non-regional members. (One of these non-regional Directors is nominated by the Federal Republic of Germany for the first period 1976/79; he represents at the same time the other members of the European Community who belong to the IDB, currently Belgium, Denmark and the United Kingdom; Italy and the Netherlands also intend to join this group after their accession). The Directorate lays down the principles of bank policy, decides on loans, and ensures that funds are used efficiently.

d. Special Fund:

This Fund was established in 1959 with a capital stock of US 150 mill. dollars to enable the IDB to promote economic and social projects in special circumstances with correspondingly generous terms: interest rates between one and four per cent p. a., maturity up to 40 years with 5–10 years of grace; for less developed member countries, the interest rate for the first ten years is one per cent p. a., afterwards two per cent.

Members:

According to the statutes, membership was originally confined to Members of the OAS; by an amendment of 27 March 1972, membership was opened to the Bahamas, Guyana and Canada and all non-regional member states of the IMF and all non-regional member states of the IMF as well as Switzerland; on 17 December 1974, the President of the IDB, together with representatives of 13 countries (Austria, Belgium, Federal Republic of Germany, Denmark, Israel, Italy, Japan, Netherlands, Portugal, Switzerland, Spain, United Kingdom, Yugoslavia) signed in Madrid the so-called Declaration of Madrid regarding their accession to the IDB and pledging total contributions of US dollars 755 mill; on 9 July 1976, Belgium, the Federal Republic of Germany, Denmark, Israel, Japan, Switzerland, Spain, the United Kingdom and Yugoslavia became full members; the others declared their intention to accede at a later date.

The distribution of votes is as follows: The Latin American members 53.5 %, the United States 34.5 %, Canada 4 %, and all non-regional members together 8 %.

a. Regional contributors (in mill. US $ taking the exchange rate of 18 February 1973; to the IDB/to the fund):

Argentina (1248/329), Barbados (14.9/1.1), Bolivia (100.3/29.3), Brazil (1249/336.7), Canada (488.6/124.6), Chile (342.9/93.7), Colombia (342.6/924.4), Costa Rica (50.1/13.6), Dominican Republic (66.9/18.2), Ecuador (66.9/17.8), El Salvador (50.11/13.23), Guatemala (66.9/18.025), Haiti (50.11/14.48), Honduras (50.11/14.32), Jamaica (66.9/17.62), Mexico (802.78/212.3), Nicaragua (50.11/14.091), Panama (50.11/13.7), Paraguay (50.11/15.3), Peru (167.3/45.3), Trinidad/Tobago (50.11/13.21), Uruguay (133.9/35.4), United States (3609.1/3640.4), Venezuela (669.1/192.2).

b. Non-regional contributors (in mill. US $ at the exchange rate valid on 18 February 1973):

This group pay 50 per cent of their contribution to the IDB itself, 50 per cent to the fund; in the following list, only one contribution is given, so that the total contribution is twice that amount:

Belgium 12.497, Denmark 5.392, Federal Republic of Germany 63.091, Israel 4.994, Japan 68.725, Spain 61.596, Switzerland 13.752, United Kingdom 61.595, Yugoslavia 5.504.

Functions:

The IDB promotes the ecomomic development of individual regional Member States and of the entire region by providing capital and technical assistance from the ordinary funds of the IDB and from the various special funds.

Funds are obtained from subscriptions and contributions by members, the raising of loans, the issue of bonds, sale of loan shares to other investors, repayment of loans, and net profits (up to now credit bonds for DM 760 million have been issued in the Federal Republic of Germany).

Lending activity of Bank and Fund:

I. Approved credits — cumulative

	Number		Amount in mill. US $	
1. From ordinary capital	290	(25)*)	3923.5	(646.2)
2. From funds for special projects	446	(37)	4076.5	(634.2)
3. From other funds	153	(8)	684.8	(94.6)
Total	889	(70)	8684.8	(1375.0)

II. Sectoral distribution of funds — cumulative

	in mill. US $		in % of total commitments	
Agriculture	1975.0	(332.0)	23	(24)
Industry and mining	1254.0	(185.0)	14	(14)
Energy supply	1856.0	(304.0)	21	(22)
Transport and communications	1592.0	(303.0)	18	(22)
Public health	838.0	(108.0)	10	(8)
Urban development	454.0	(38.0)	5	(3)
Education and training	375.0	(71.0)	4	(5)
Other sectors (e. g. tourism)	341.0	(34.0)	5	(2)
Total	8685.0	(1375.0)	100	(100)

The biggest borrowers of ordinary funds (mill. US $ and % of total commitments): Mexico 723.3 (17.7), Argentina 607.1 (14.09), Colombia 361.6 (8.8), Brazil 275.4 (6.7), Chile 231.6 (5.7).

The biggest borrowers of special funds (mill. US $ and % of total commitments): Brazil 650.5 (15.1), Mexico 445.1 (10.3), Argentina 395.7 (9.2), Colombia 276.6 (6.4) Chile 215.7 (5.0).

President:

Antonio Ortiz Mena, Mexico (since 1 March 1971).

---

*) The percentage given in brackets relates to the financial year 1975.

B. Participation of the Federal Republic of Germany

The Federal Republic of Germany acceded to the IDB on 9 July 1976.

a . *Contributions of the Federal Republic of Germany:*
As above.

b. *German personnel:*
Up to now none.

c. *Competency in the Federal Republic of Germany:*
Federal Ministry for Economic Co-operation.

Part IV

Documentation

1. Charter of the United Nations

WE THE PEOPLES OF THE UNITED NATIONS
DETERMINED

to save succeeding generations from the scourge of war, which twice in our lifetime has brought untold sorrow to mankind, and

to reaffirm faith in fundamental human rights, in the dignity and worth of the human person, in the equal rights of men and women and of nations large and small, and

to establish conditions under which justice and respect for the obligations arising from treaties and other sources of international law can be maintained, and
to promote social progress and better standards of life in larger freedom,

AND FOR THESE ENDS

to practise tolerance and live together in peace with one another as good neighbours, and

to unite our strength to maintain international peace and security, and

to ensure, by the acceptance of principles and the institution of methods, that armed force shall not be used, save in the common interest, and

to employ international machinery for the promotion of the economic and social advancement of all peoples,

HAVE RESOLVED TO COMBINE OUR EFFORTS TO ACCOMPLISH THESE AIMS.

Accordingly, our respective Governments, through representatives assembled in the city of San Francisco, who have exhibited their full powers found to be in good and due form, have agreed to the present Charter of the United Nations and do hereby establish an international organization to be known as the United Nations.

Chapter I — Purposes and Principles

Article 1

The Purposes of the United Nations are:

1. To maintain international peace and security, and to that end: to take effective collective measures for the prevention and removal of threats to the peace, and for the suppression of acts of aggression or other breaches of the peace, and to bring about by peaceful means, and in conformity with the principles of justice and international law, adjustment or settlement of international disputes or situations which might lead to a breach of the peace;

2. To develop friendly relations among nations based on respect for the principle of equal rights and self-determination of peoples, and to take other appropriate measures to strengthen universal peace;

3. To achieve international co-operation in solving international problems of an economic, social, cultural, or humanitarian character, and in promoting and encouraging respect for human rights and for fundamental freedoms for all without distinction as to race, sex, language, or religion; and

4. To be a centre for harmonizing the actions of nations in the attainment of these common ends.

Article 2

The Organization and its Members, in pursuit of the Purposes stated in Article 1, shall act in accordance with the following Principles.

1. The Organization is based on the principle of the sovereign equality of all its Members.

2. All Members, in order to ensure to all of them the rights and benefits resulting from membership, shall fulfil in good faith the obligations assumed by them in accordance with the present Charter.

3. All Members shall settle their international disputes by peaceful means in such a manner that international peace and security, and justice, are not endangered.

4. All Members shall refrain in their international relations from the threat or use of force against the territorial integrity or political independence of any state, or in any other manner inconsistent with the Purposes of the United Nations.

5. All Members shall give the United Nations every assistance in any action it takes in accordance with the present Charter, and shall refrain from giving assistance to any state against which the United Nations is taking preventive or enforcement action.

6. The Organization shall ensure that states which are not Members of the United Nations act in accordance with these principles so far as may be necessary for the maintenance of international peace and security.

7. Nothing contained in the present Charter shall authorize the United Nations to intervene in matters which are essentially within the domestic jurisdiction of any state or shall require the Members to submit such matters to settlement under the present Charter; but this principle shall not prejudice the application of enforcement measures under Chapter VII.

Chapter II — Membership

Article 3

The original Members of the United Nations shall be the states which, having participated in the United Nations Conference on International Organization at San Francisco, or having previously signed the Declaration by United Nations of January 1, 1942, sign the present Charter and ratify it in accordance with Article 110.

Article 4

1. Membership in the United Nations is open to all other peace-loving states which accept the obligations contained in the present Charter and, in the judgement of the

Organization, are able and willing to carry out these obligations.

2. The admission of any such state to membership in the United Nations will be effected by a decision of the General Assembly upon the recommendation of the Security Council.

Article 5

A Member of the United Nations against which preventive or enforcement action has been taken by the Security Council may be suspended from the exercise of the rights and privileges of membership by the General Assembly upon the recommendation of the Security Council. The exercise of these rights and privileges may be restored by the Security Council.

Article 6

A Member of the United Nations which has persistently violated the Principles contained in the present Charter may be expelled from the Organization by the General Assembly upon the recommendation of the Security Council.

Chapter III — Organs

Article 7

1. There are established as the principal organs of the United Nations: a General Assembly, a Security Council, an Economic and Social Council, a Trusteeship Council, an International Court of Justice, and a Secretariat.

2. Such subsidiary organs as may be found necessary may be established in accordance with the present Charter.

Article 8

The United Nations shall place no restrictions on the eligibility of men and women to participate in any capacity and under conditions of equality in its principal and subsidiary organs.

Chapter IV — The General Assembly

Composition

Article 9

1. The General Assembly shall consist of all the Members of the United Nations.

2. Each Member shall have not more than five representatives in the General Assembly.

Functions and Powers

Article 10

The General Assembly may discuss any questions or any matters within the scope of the present Charter or relating to the powers and functions of any organs provided for in the present Charter, and, except as provided in Article 12, may make recommendations to the Members of the United Nations or to the Security Council or to both on any such questions or matters.

Article 11

1. The General Assembly may consider the general principles of co-operation in the maintenance of international peace and security, including the principles governing disarmament and the regulation of armaments, and may make recommendations with regard to such principles to the Members or to the Security Council or to both.

2. The General Assembly may discuss any questions relating to the maintenance of international peace and security brought before it by any Member of the United Nations, or by the Security Council, or by a state which is not a Member of the United Nations in accordance with Article 35, paragraph 2, and, except as provided in Article 12, may make recommendations with regard to any such questions to the state or states concerned or to the Security Council or to both. Any such question on which action is necessary shall be referred to the Security Council by the General Assembly either before or after discussion.

3. The General Assembly may call the attention of the Security Council to situations which are likely to endanger international peace and security.

4. The powers of the General Assembly set forth in this Article shall not limit the general scope of Article 10.

Article 12

1. While the Security Council is exercising in respect of any dispute or situation the functions assigned to it in the present Charter, the General Assembly shall not make any recommendation with regard to that dispute or situation unless the Security Council so requests.

2. The Secretary-General, with the consent of the Security Council, shall notify the General Assembly at each session of any matters relative to the maintenance of international peace and security which are being dealt with by the Security Council and shall similarly notify the General Assembly, or the Members of the United Nations if the General Assembly is not in session, immediately the Security Council ceases to deal with such matters.

Article 13

1. The General Assembly shall initiate studies and make recommendations for the purpose of:

a. promoting international co-operation in the political field and encouraging the progressive development of international law and its codification;

b. promoting international co-operation in the economic, social, cultural, educational, and health fields, and assisting in the realization of human rights and fundamental freedoms for all without distinction as to race, sex, language, or religion.

2. The further responsibilities, functions, and powers of the General Assembly with respect to matters mentioned in paragraph 1 (b) above are set forth in Chapters IX and X.

Article 14

Subject to the provisions of Article 12, the General Assembly may recommend measures for the peaceful adjustment of any situation, regardless of origin, which it deems likely to impair the general welfare or friendly relations among nations, including situations resulting from a violation of the provisions of the present Charter setting forth the Purposes and Principles of the United Nations.

Article 15

1. The General Assembly shall receive and consider annual and special reports from the Security Council; these reports shall include an account of the measures that the Security Council has decided upon or taken to maintain international peace and security.

2. The General Assembly shall receive and consider reports from the other organs of the United Nations.

Article 16

The General Assembly shall perform such functions with respect to the international trusteeship system as are assigned to it under Chapters XII and XIII, including the approval of the trusteeship agreements for areas not designated as strategic.

Article 17

1. The General Assembly shall consider and approve the budget of the Organization.

2. The expenses of the Organization shall be borne by the Members as apportioned by the General Assembly.

3. The General Assembly shall consider and approve any financial and budgetary arrangements with specialized agencies referred to in Article 57 and shall examine the administrative budgets of such specialized agencies with a view to making recommendations to the agencies concerned.

Voting

Article 18

1. Each Member of the General Assembly shall have one vote.

2. Decisions of the General Assembly on important questions shall be made by a two-thirds majority of the Members present and voting. These questions shall include: recommendations with respect to the maintenance of international peace and security, the election of the non-permanent members of the Security Council, the election of the members of the Economic and Social Council, the election of the members of the Trusteeship Council in accordance with paragraph 1 (c) of Article 86, the admission of new Members to the United Nations, the suspension of the rights and privileges of membership, the expulsion of Members, questions relating to the operation of the trusteeship system, and budgetary questions.

3. Decisions on other questions, including the determination of additional categories of questions to be decided by a two-thirds majority, shall be made by a majority of the Members present and voting.

Article 19

A Member of the United Nations which is in arrears in the payment of its financial contributions to the Organization shall have no vote in the General Assembly if the amount of its arrears equals or exceeds the amount of the contributions due from it for the preceding two full years. The General Assembly may, nevertheless, permit such a Member to vote if it is satisfied that the failure to pay is due to conditions beyond the control of the Member.

Procedure

Article 20

The General Assembly shall meet in regular annual sessions and in such special sessions as occasion may require. Special sessions shall be convoked by the Secretary-General at the request of the Security Council or of a majority of the Members of the United Nations.

Article 21

The General Assembly shall adopt its own rules of procedure. It shall elect its President for each session.

Article 22

The General Assembly may establish such subsidiary organs as it deems necessary for the performance of its functions.

Chapter V — The Security Council

Composition

Article 23

1. The Security Council shall consist of fifteen Members of the United Nations. The Republic of China, France, the Union of Soviet Socialist Republics, the United Kingdom of Great Britain and Northern Ireland, and the United States of America shall be permanent members of the Security Council. The General Assembly shall elect ten other Members of the United Nations to be non-permanent members of the Security Council, due regard being specially paid, in the first instance to the contribution of Members of the United Nations to the maintenance of international peace and security and to the other purposes of the Organization, and also to equitable geographical distribution.

2. The non-permanent members of the Security Council shall be elected for a term of two years. In the first election of the non-permanent members after the increase of the membership of the Security Council from eleven to fifteen, two of the four additional members shall be chosen for a term of one year. A retiring member shall not be eligible for immediate re-election.

3. Each member of the Security Council shall have one representative.

Functions and Powers

Article 24

1. In order to ensure prompt and effective action by the United Nations, its Members confer on the Security Council primary responsibility for the maintenance of international peace and security, and agree that in carrying out its duties under this responsibility the Security Council acts on their behalf.

2. In discharging these duties the Security Council shall act in accordance with the Purposes and Principles of the United Nations. The specific powers granted to the Security Council for the discharge of these duties are laid down in Chapters VI, VII, VIII, and XII.

3. The Security Council shall submit annual and, when necessary, special reports to the General Assembly for its consideration.

Article 25

The Members of the United Nations agree to accept and carry out the decisions of the Security Council in accordance with the present Charter.

Article 26

In order to promote the establishment and maintenance of international peace and security with the least diversion for armaments of the world's human and economic resources, the Security Council shall be responsible for formulating, with the assistance of the Military Staff Committee referred to in Article 47, plans to be submitted to the Members of the United Nations for the establishment of a system for the regulation of armaments.

Voting

Article 27

1. Each member of the Security Council shall have one vote.

2. Decisions of the Security Council on procedural matters shall be made by an affirmative vote of nine members.

3. Decisions of the Security Council on all other matters shall be made by an affirmative vote of nine members including the concurring votes of the permanent members; provided that, in decisions under Chapter VI, and under paragraph 3 of Article 52, a party to a dispute shall abstain from voting.

Procedure

Article 28

1. The Security Council shall be so organized as to be able to function continuously. Each member of the Security Council shall for this purpose be represented at all times at the seat of the Organization.

2. The Security Council shall hold periodic meetings at which each of its members may, if it so desires, be represented by a member of the government or by some other specially designated representative.

3. The Security Council may hold meetings at such places other than the seat of the Organization as in its judgment will best facilitate its work.

Article 29

The Security Council may establish such subsidiary organs as it deems necessary for the performance of its functions.

Article 30

The Security Council shall adopt its own rules of procedure, including the method of selecting its President.

Article 31

Any Member of the United Nations which is not a member of the Security Council may participate, without vote, in the discussion of any question brought before the Security Council whenever the latter considers that the interests of that Member are specially affected.

Article 32

Any Member of the United Nations which is not a member of the Security Council or any state which is not a Member of the United Nations, if it is a party to a dispute under consideration by the Security Council, shall be invited to participate, without vote, in the discussion relating to the dispute. The Security Council shall lay down such conditions as it deems just for the participation of a state which is not a Member of the United Nations.

Chapter VI — Pacific Settlement of Disputes

Article 33

1. The parties to any dispute, the continuance of which is likely to endanger the maintenance of international peace and security, shall, first of all, seek a solution by negotiation, enquiry, mediation, conciliation, arbitration, judicial settlement, resort to regional agencies or arrangements, or other peaceful means of their own choice.

2. The Security Council shall, when it deems necessary, call upon the parties to settle their dispute by such means.

Article 34

The Security Council may investigate any dispute, or any situation which might lead to international friction or give rise to a dispute, in order to determine whether the continuance of the dispute or situation is likely to endanger the maintenance of international peace and security.

Article 35

1. Any Member of the United Nations may bring any dispute, or any situation of the nature referred to in Article 34, to the attention of the Security Council or of the General Assembly.

2. A state which is not a Member of the United Nations may bring to the attention of the Security Council or of the General Assembly any dispute to which it is a party if it accepts in advance, for the purposes of the dispute, the obligations of pacific settlement provided in the present Charter.

3. The proceedings of the General Assembly in respect of matters brought to its attention under this Article will be subject to the provisions of Articles 11 and 12.

Article 36

1. The Security Council may, at any stage of a dispute of the nature referred to in Article 33 or of a situation of like nature, recommend appropriate procedures or methods of adjustment.

2. The Security Council should take into consideration any procedures for the settlement of the dispute which have already been adopted by the parties.

3. In making recommendations under this Article the Security Council should also take into consideration that legal disputes should as a general rule be referred by the parties to the International Court of Justice in accordance with the provisions of the Statute of the Court.

Article 37

1. Should the parties to a dispute of the nature referred to in Article 33 fail to settle it by the means indicated in that Article, they shall refer it to the Security Council.

2. If the Security Council deems that the continuance of the dispute is in fact likely to endanger the maintenance of international peace and security, it shall decide whether to take action under Article 36 or to recommend such terms of settlement as it may consider appropriate.

Article 38

Without prejudice to the provisions of Articles 33 to 37, the Security Council may, if all the parties to any dispute so request, make recommendations to the parties with a view to a pacific settlement of the dispute.

Chapter VII — Action with Respect to Threats to the Peace, Breaches of the Peace, and Acts of Aggression

Article 39

The Security Council shall determine the existence of any threat to the peace, breach of the peace, or act of aggression and shall make recommendations, or decide what measures shall be taken in accordance with Articles 41 and 42, to maintain or restore international peace and security.

Article 40

In order to prevent an aggravation of the situation, the Security Council may, before making the recommendations or deciding upon the measures provided for in Article 39, call upon the parties concerned to comply with such provisional measures as it deems necessary or desirable. Such provisional measures shall be without prejudice to the rights, claims, or positions of the parties concerned. The Security Council shall duly take account of failure to comply with such provisional measures.

Article 41

The Security Council may decide what measures not involving the use of armed force are to be employed to give effect to its decisions, and it may call upon the Members of the United Nations to apply such measures. These may include complete or partial interruption of economic relations and of rail, sea, air, postal, telegraphic, radio, and other means of communication, and the severance of diplomatic relations.

Article 42

Should the Security Council consider that measures provided for in Article 41 would be inadequate or have proved to be inadequate, it may take such action by air, sea, or land forces as may be necessary to maintain or restore international peace and security. Such action may Include demonstrations, blockade, and other operations by air, sea, or land forces of Members of the United Nations.

Article 43

1. All Members of the United Nations, in order to contribute to the maintenance of international peace and security, undertake to make available to the Security Council, on its call and in accordance with a special agreement or agreements, armed forces, assistance, and facilities, including rights of passage, necessary for the purpose of maintaining international peace and security.

2. Such agreement or agreements shall govern the numbers and types of forces, their degree of readiness and general location, and the nature of the facilities and assistance to be provided.

3. The agreement or agreements shall be negotiated as soon as possible on the initiative of the Security Council. They shall be concluded between the Security Council and Members or between the Security Council and groups of Members and shall be subject to ratification by the signatory states in accordance with their respective constitutional processes.

Article 44

When the Security Council has decided to use force it shall, before calling upon a Member not represented on it to provide armed forces in fulfilment of the obligations assumed under Article 43, invite that Member, if the Member so desires, to participate in the decisions of the Security Council concerning the employment of contingents of that Member's armed forces.

Article 45

In order to enable the United Nations to take urgent military measures, Members shall hold immediately available national air-force contingents for combined international enforcement action. The strength and degree of readiness of these contingents and plans for their combined action shall be determined, within the limits laid down in the special agreement or agreements referred to in Article 43, by the Security Council with the assistance of the Military Staff Committee.

Article 46

Plans for the application of armed force shall be made by the Security Council with the assistance of the Military Staff Committee.

Article 47

1. There shall be established a Military Staff Committee to advise and assist the Security Council on all questions relating to the Security Council's military requirements for the maintenance of international peace and security, the employment and command of forces placed at its disposal, the regulation of armaments, and possible disarmament.

2. The Military Staff Committee shall consist of the Chiefs of Staff of the permanent members of the Security Council or their representatives. Any Member of the United Nations not permanently represented on the Committee shall be invited by the Committee to be associated with it when the efficient discharge of the Committee's responsibilities requires the participation of that Member in its work.

3. The Military Staff Committee shall be responsible under the Security Council for the strategic direction of any armed forces placed at the disposal of the Security Council. Questions relating to the command of such forces shall be worked out subsequently.

4. The Military Staff Committee, with the authorization of the Security Council and after consultation with appropriate regional agencies, may establish regional sub-committees.

Article 48

1. The action required to carry out the decisions of the Security Council for the maintenance of international peace and security shall be taken by all the Members of the United Nations or by some of them, as the Security Council may determine.

2. Such decisions shall be carried out by the Members of the United Nations directly and through their action in the appropriate international agencies of which they are members.

Artikel 49

The Members of the United Nations shall join in affording mutual assistance in carrying out the measures decided upon by the Security Council.

Article 50

If preventive or enforcement measures against any state are taken by the Security Council, any other state, whether a Member of the United Nations or not, which finds itself confronted with special economic problems arising from the carrying out of those measures shall have the right to consult the Security Council with regard to a solution of those problems.

Article 51

Nothing in the present Charter shall impair the inherent right of individual or collective self-defence if an armed attack occurs against a Member of the United Nations, until the Security Council has taken the measures necessary to maintain international peace and security. Measures taken by Members in the exercise of this right of self-defence shall be immediately reported to the Security Council and shall not in any way affect the authority and responsibility of the Security Council under the present Charter to take at any time such action as it deems necessary in order to maintain or restore international peace and security.

Chapter VIII — Regional Arrangements

Article 52

1. Nothing in the present Charter precludes the existence of regional arrangements or agencies for dealing with such matters relating to the maintenance of international peace and security as are appropriate for regional action, provided that such arrangements or agencies and their activities are consistent with the Purposes and Principles of the United Nations.

2. The Members of the United Nations entering into such arrangements or constituting such agencies shall make every effort to achieve pacific settlement of local disputes through such regional arrangements or by such regional agencies before referring them to the Security Council.

3. The Security Council shall encourage the development of pacific settlement of local disputes through such regional arrangements or by such regional agencies either on the initiative of the states concerned or by reference from the Security Council.

4. This Article in no way impairs the application of Articles 34 and 35.

Article 53

1. The Security Council shall, where appropriate, utilize such regional arrangements or agencies for enforcement action under its authority. But no enforcement action shall be taken under regional arrangements or by regional agencies without the

authorization of the Security Council, with the exception of measures against any enemy state, as defined in paragraph 2 of this Article, provided for pursuant to Article 107 or in regional arrangements directed against renewal of aggressive policy on the part of any such state, until such time as the Organization may, on request of the Governments concerned, be charged with the responsibility for preventing further aggression by such a state.

2. The term enemy state as used in paragraph 1 of this Article applies to any state which during the Second World War has been an enemy of any signatory of the present Charter.

Article 54

The Security Council shall at all times be kept fully informed of activities undertaken or in contemplation under regional arrangements or by regional agencies for the maintenance of international peace and security.

Chapter IX — International Economic and Social Co-operation

Article 55

With a view to the creation of conditions of stability and well-being which are necessary for peaceful and friendly relations among nations based on respect for the principle of equal rights and self-determination of peoples, the United Nations shall promote:

a. higher standards of living, full employment, and conditions of economic and social progress and development;

b. solutions of international economic, social, health, and related problems; and international cultural and educational co-operation; and

c. universal respect for, and observance of, human rights and fundamental freedoms for all without distinction as to race, sex, language, or religion.

Article 56

All Members pledge themselves to take joint and separate action in co-operation with the Organization for the achievement of the purposes set forth in Article 55.

Article 57

1. The various specialized agencies, established by intergovernmental agreement and having wide international responsibilities, as defined in their basic instruments, in economic, social, cultural, educational, health, and related fields, shall be brought into relationship with the United Nations in accordance with the provisions of Article 63.

2. Such agencies thus brought into relationship with the United Nations are hereinafter referred to as specialized agencies.

Article 58

The Organization shall make recommendations for the co-ordination of the policies and activities of the specialized agencies.

Article 59

The Organization shall, where appropriate, initiate negotiations among the states concerned for the creation of any new specialized agencies required for the accomplishment of the purposes set forth in Article 55.

Article 60

Responsibility for the discharge of the functions of the Organization set forth in this Chapter shall be vested in the General Assembly and, under the authority of the General Assembly, in the Economic and Social Council, which shall have for this purpose the powers set forth in Chapter X.

Chapter X — The Economic and Social Council

Composition

Article 61

1. The Economic and Social Council shall consist of fifty-four Members of the United Nations elected by the General Assembly.

2. Subject to the provisions of paragraph 3, nine members of the Economic and Social Council shall be elected each year for a term of three years. A retiring member shall be eligible for immediate re-election.

3. At the first election after the increase in the membership of the Economic and Social Council from eighteen to twenty-seven members, in addition to the members elected in place of the six members whose term of office expires at the end of that year, nine additional members shall be elected. Of these nine additional members, the term of office of three members so elected shall expire at the end of one year, and of three other members at the end of two years, in accordance with arrangements made by the General Assembly.

4. Each member of the Economic and Social Council shall have one representative.

Functions and Powers

Article 62

1. The Economic and Social Council may make or initiate studies and reports with respect to international economic, social, cultural, educational, health, and related matters and may make recommendations with respect to any such matters to the General Assembly, to the Members of the United Nations, and to the specialized agencies concerned.

2. It may make recommendations for the purpose of promoting respect for, and observance of, human rights and fundamental freedoms for all.

3. It may prepare draft conventions for submission to the General Assembly, with respect to matters falling within its competence.

4. It may call, in accordance with the rules prescribed by the United Nations, international conferences on matters falling within its competence.

Article 63

1. The Economic and Social Council may enter into agreements with any of the agencies referred to in Article 57, defining the terms on which the agency concerned shall be brought into relationship with the United Nations. Such agreements shall be subject to approval by the General Assembly.

2. It may co-ordinate the activities of the specialized agencies through consultation with and recommendations to such agencies and through recommendations to the General Assembly and to the Members of the United Nations.

Article 64

1. The Economic and Social Council may take appropriate steps to obtain regular reports from the specialized agencies. It may make arrangements with the Members of the United Nations and with the specialized agencies to obtain reports on the steps taken to give effect to its own recommendations and to recommendations on matters falling within its competence made by the General Assembly.

2. It may communicate its observations on these reports to the General Assembly.

Article 65

The Economic and Social Council may furnish information to the Security Council and shall assist the Security Council upon its request.

Article 66

1. The Economic and Social Council shall perform such functions as fall within its competence in connection with the carrying out of the recommendations of the General Assembly.

2. It may, with the approval of the General Assembly, perform services at the request of Members of the United Nations and at the request of specialized agencies.

3. It shall perform such other functions as are specified elsewhere in the present Charter or as may be assigned to it by the General Assembly.

Voting

Article 67

1. Each member of the Economic and Social Council shall have one vote.

2. Decisions of the Economic and Social Council shall be made by a majority of the members present and voting.

Procedure

Article 68

The Economic and Social Council shall set up commissions in economic and social fields and for the promotion of human rights, and such other commissions as may be required for the performance of its functions.

Article 69

The Economic and Social Council shall invite any Member of the United Nations to participate, without vote, in its deliberations on any matter of particular concern to that Member.

Article 70

The Economic and Social Council may make arrangements for representatives of the specialized agencies to participate, without vote, in its deliberations and in those of the commissions established by it, and for its representatives to participate in the deliberations of the specialized agencies.

Article 71

The Economic and Social Council may make suitable arrangements for consultation with non-governmental organizations which are concerned with matters within its competence. Such arrangements may be made with international organizations and, where appropriate, with national organizations after consultation with the Member of the United Nations concerned.

Article 72

1. The Economic and Social Council shall adopt its own rules of procedure, including the method of selecting its President.

2. The Economic and Social Council shall meet as required in accordance with its rules, which shall include provision for the convening of meetings on the request of a majority of its members.

Chapter XI — Declaration regarding Non-Self-Governing Territories

Article 73

Members of the United Nations which have or assume responsibilities for the administration of territories whose peoples have not yet attained a full measure of self-government recognize the principle that the interests of the inhabitants of these territories are paramount, and accept as a sacred trust the obligation to promote to the utmost, within the system of international peace and security established by the present Charter, the well-being of the inhabitants of these territories, and, to this end:

a. to ensure, with due respect for the culture of the peoples concerned, their political, economic, social, and educational advancement, their just treatment, and their protection against abuses;

b. to develop self-government, to take due account of the political aspirations of the peoples, and to assist them in the progressive development of their free political institutions, according to the particular circumstances of each territory and its peoples and their varying stages of advancement;

c. to further international peace and security;

d. to promote constructive measures of development, to encourage research, and to co-operate with one another and, when and where appropriate, with specialized international bodies with a view to the practical achievement of the social, economic, and scientific purposes set forth in this Article; and

e. to transmit regularly to the Secretary-General for information purposes, subject to such limitation as security and constitutional considerations may require, statistical and other information of a technical nature relating to economic, social, and educational conditions in the territories for which they are respectively responsible other than those territories to which Chapters XII and XIII apply.

Article 74

Members of the United Nations also agree that their policy in respect of the territories to which this Chapter applies, no less than in respect of their metropolitan areas, must be based on the general principle of goodneighbourliness, due account being taken of the interests and wellbeing of the rest of the world, in social, economic, and commercial matters.

Chapter XII — International Trusteeship System

Article 75

The United Nations shall establish under its authority an international trusteeship system for the administration and supervision of such territories as may be placed thereunder by subsequent individual agreements. These territories are hereinafter referred to as trust territories.

Article 76

The basic objectives of the trusteeship system, in accordance with the Purposes of the United Nations laid down in Article 1 of the present Charter, shall be:

a. to further international peace and security;

b. to promote the political, economic, social, and educational advancement of the inhabitants of the trust territories, and their progressive development towards self-government or independence as may be appropriate to the particular circumstances of each territory and its peoples and the freely expressed wishes of the peoples concerned, and as may be provided by the terms of each trusteeship agreement;

c. to encourage respect for human rights and for fundamental freedoms for all without distinction as to race, sex, language, or religion, and to encourage recognition of the interdependence of the peoples of the world; and

d. to ensure equal treatment in social, economic, and commercial matters for all Members of the United Nations and their nationals, and also equal treatment for the latter in the administration of justice, without prejudice to the attainment of the foregoing objectives and subject to the provisions of Article 80.

Article 77

1. The trusteeship system shall apply to such territories in the following categories as may be placed thereunder by means of trusteeship agreements:

a. territories now held under mandate;

b. territories which may be detached from enemy states as a result of the Second World War; and

c. territories voluntarily placed under the system by states responsible for their administration.

2. It will be a matter for subsequent agreement as to which territories in the foregoing categories will be brought under the trusteeship system and upon what terms.

Article 78

The trusteeship system shall not apply to territories which have become Members of the United Nations, relationship among which shall be based on respect for the principle of sovereign equality.

Article 79

The terms of trusteeship for each territory to be placed under the trusteeship system, including any alteration or amendment, shall be agreed upon by the states directly concerned including the mandatory power in the case of territories held under mandate by a Member of the United Nations, and shall be approved as provided for in Articles 83 and 85.

Article 80

1. Except as may be agreed upon in individual trusteeship agreements, made under Articles 77, 79, and 81, placing each territory under the trusteeship system, and until such agreements have been concluded, nothing in this Chapter shall be construed in or of itself to alter in any manner the rights whatsoever of any states or any peoples or the terms of existing international instruments to which Members of the United Nations may respectively be parties.

2. Paragraph 1 of this Article shall not be interpreted as giving grounds for delay or postponement of the negotiation and conclusion of agreements for placing mandated and other territories under the trusteeship system as provided for in Article 77.

Article 81

The trusteeship agreement shall in each case include the terms under which the trust territory will be administered and designate the authority which will exercise the administration of the trust territory. Such authority, hereinafter called the administering authority, may be one or more states or the Organization itself.

Article 82

There may be designated, in any trusteeship agreement, a strategic area or areas which may include part or all of the trust territory to which the agreement applies, without prejudice to any special agreement or agreements made under Article 43.

Article 83

1. All functions of the United Nations relating to strategic areas, including the approval of the terms of the trusteeship agreements and of their alteration or amendment, shall be exercised by the Security Council.

2. The basic objectives set forth in Article 76 shall be applicable to the people of each strategic area.

3. The Security Council shall, subject to the provisions of the trusteeship agreements and without prejudice to security considerations, avail itself of the assi-

stance of the Trusteeship Council to perform those functions of the United Nations under the trusteeship system relating to political, economic, social, and educational matters in the strategic areas.

Article 84

It shall be the duty of the administering authority to ensure that the trust territory shall play its part in the maintenance of international peace and security. To this end the administering authority may make use of volunteer forces, facilities, and assistance from the trust territory in carrying out the obligations towards the Security Council undertaken in this regard by the administering authority, as well as for local defence and the maintenance of law and order within the trust territory.

Article 85

1. The functions of the United Nations with regard to trusteeship agreements for all areas not designated as strategic, including the approval of the terms of the trusteeship agreements and of their alteration or amendment, shall be exercised by the General Assembly.

2. The Trusteeship Council, operating under the authority of the General Assembly, shall assist the General Assembly in carrying out these functions.

Chapter XIII — The Trusteeship Council

Composition

Article 86

1. The Trusteeship Council shall consist of the following Members of the United Nations:

a. those Members administering trust territories;

b. such of those Members mentioned by name in Article 23 as are not administering trust territories; and

c. as many other Members elected for three-year terms by the General Assembly as may be necessary to ensure that the total number of members of the Trusteeship Council is equally divided between those Members of the United Nations which administer trust territories and those which do not.

2. Each member of the Trusteeship Council shall designate one specially qualified person to represent it therein.

Functions and Powers

Article 87

The General Assembly and, under its authority, the Trusteeship Council, in carrying out their functions, may:

a. consider reports submitted by the administering authority;

b. accept petitions and examine them in consultation with the administering authority;

c. provide for periodic visits to the respective trust territories at times agreed upon with the administering authority; and

d. take these and other actions in conformity with the terms of the trusteeship agreements.

Article 88

The Trusteeship Council shall formulate a questionnaire on the political, economic, social, and educational advancement of the inhabitants of each trust territory, and the administering authority for each trust territory within the competence of the General Assembly shall make an annual report to the General Assembly upon the basis of such questionnaire.

Voting

Article 89

1. Each member of the Trusteeship Council shall have one vote.

2. Decisions of the Trusteeship Council shall be made by a majority of the members present and voting.

Procedure

Article 90

1. The Trusteeship Council shall adopt its own rules of procedure, including the method of selecting its President.

2. The Trusteeship Council shall meet as required in accordance with its rules, which shall include provision for the convening of meetings on the request of a majority of its members.

Article 91

The Trusteeship Council shall, when appropriate, avail itself of the assistance of the Economic and Social Council and of the specialized agencies in regard to matters with which they are respectively concerned.

Chapter XIV — The International Court of Justice

Article 92

The International Court of Justice shall be the principal judicial organ of the United Nations. It shall function in accordance with the annexed Statute, which is based upon the Statute of the Permanent Court of International Justice and forms an integral part of the present Charter.

Article 93

1. All Members of the United Nations are ipso facto parties to the Statute of the International Court of Justice.

2. A state which is not a Member of the United Nations may become a party to the Statute of the International Court of Justice on conditions to be determined in each case by the General Assembly upon the recommendation of the Security Council.

Article 94

1. Each Member of the United Nations undertakes to comply with the decision of the International Court of Justice in any case to which it is a party.

2. If any party to a case fails to perform the obligations incumbent upon it under a judgment rendered by the Court, the other party may have recourse to the Security Council, which may, if it deems necessary, make recommendations or decide upon measures to be taken to give effect to the judgment.

Article 95

Nothing in the present Charter shall prevent Members of the United Nations from entrusting the solution of their differences to other tribunals by virtue of agreements already in existence or which may be concluded in the future.

Article 96

1. The General Assembly or the Security Council may request the International Court of Justice to give an advisory opinion on any legal question.

2. Other organs of the United Nations and specialized agencies, which may at any time be so authorized by the General Assembly, may also request advisory opinions of the Court on legal questions arising within the scope of their activities.

Chapter XV — The Secretariat

Article 97

The Secretariat shall comprise a Secretary-General and such staff as the Organization may require. The Secretary-General shall be appointed by the General Assembly upon the recommendation of the Security Council. He shall be the chief administrative officer of the Organization.

Article 98

The Secretary-General shall act in that capacity in all meetings of the General Assembly, of the Security Council, of the Economic and Social Council, and of the Trusteeship Council, and shall perform such other functions as are entrusted to him by these organs. The Secretary-General shall make an annual report to the General Assembly on the work of the Organization.

Article 99

The Secretary-General may bring to the attention of the Security Council any matter which in his opinion may threaten the maintenance of international peace and security.

Article 100

1. In the performance of their duties the Secretary-General and the staff shall not seek or receive instructions from any government or from any other authority external to the Organization. They shall refrain from any action which might reflect on their position as international officials responsible only to the Organization.

2. Each Member of the United Nations undertakes to respect the exclusively international character of the responsibilities of the Secretary-General and the staff and not to seek to influence them in the discharge of their responsibilities.

Article 101

1. The staff shall be appointed by the Secretary-General under regulations established by the General Assembly.

2. Appropriate staffs shall be permanently assigned to the Economic and Social Council, the Trusteeship Council, and, as required, to other organs of the United Nations. These staffs shall form a part of the Secretariat.

3. The paramount consideration in the employment of the staff and in the determination of the conditions of service shall be the necessity of securing the highest standards of efficiency, competence, and integrity. Due regard shall be paid to the importance of recruiting the staff on as wide a geographical basis as possible.

Chapter XVI — Miscellaneous Provisions

Article 102

1. Every treaty and every international agreement entered into by any Member of the United Nations after the present Charter comes into force shall as soon as possible be registered with the Secretariat and published by it.

2. No party to any such treaty or international agreement which has not been registered in accordance with the provisions of paragraph 1 of this Article may invoke that treaty or agreement before any organ of the United Nations.

Article 103

In the event of a conflict between the obligations of the Members of the United Nations under the present Charter and their obligation under any other international agreement, their obligations under the present Charter shall prevail.

Article 104

The Organization shall enjoy in the territory of each of its Members such legal capacity as may be necessary for the exercise of its functions and the fulfilment of its purposes.

Article 105

1. The Organization shall enjoy in the territory of each of its Members such privileges and immunities as are necessary for the fulfilment of its purposes.

2. Representatives of the Members of the United Nations and officials of the Organization shall similarly enjoy such privileges and immunities as are necessary for the independent exercise of their functions in connection with the Organization.

3. The General Assembly may make recommendations with a view to determining the details of the application of paragraphs 1 and 2 of this Article or may propose conventions to the Members of the United Nations for this purpose.

Chapter XVII — Transitional Security Arrangements

Article 106

Pending the coming into force of such special agreements referred to in Article 43 as in the opinion of the Security Council enable it to begin the exercise of its responsibilities under Article 42, the parties to the Four-Nation Declaration, signed at Moscow, October 30, 1943, and France, shall, in accordance with the provisions of paragraph 5 of that Declaration, consult with one another and as occasion requires with other Members of the United Nations with a view to such joint action on behalf of the Organization as may be necessary for the purpose of maintaining international peace and security.

Article 107

Nothing in the present Charter shall invalidate or preclude action, in relation to any state which during the Second World War has been an enemy of any signatory to the present Charter, taken or authorized as a result of that war by the Governments having responsibility for such action.

Chapter XVIII — Amendments

Article 108

Amendments to the present Charter shall come into force for all Members of the United Nations when they have been adopted by a vote of two thirds of the members of the General Assembly and ratified in accordance with their respective constitutional processes by two thirds of the Members of the United Nations, including all the permanent members of the Security Council.

Article 109

1. A General Conference of the Members of the United Nations for the purpose of reviewing the present Charter may be held at a date and place to be fixed by a two-thirds vote of the members of the General Assembly and by a vote of any nine members of the Security Council. Each Member of the United Nations shall have one vote in the conference.

2. Any alteration of the present Charter recommended by a two-thirds vote of the conference shall take effect when ratified in accordance with their respective constitutional processes by two thirds of the Members of the United Nations including all the permanent members of the Security Council.

3. If such a conference has not been held before the tenth annual session of the General Assembly following the coming into force of the present Charter, the proposal to call such a conference shall be placed on the agenda of that session of the General Assembly, and the conference shall be held if so decided by a majority vote of the members of the General Assembly and by a vote of any seven members of the Security Council.

Chapter XIX — Ratification and Signature

Article 110

1. The present Charter shall be ratified by the signatory states in accordance with their respective constitutional processes.

2. The ratifications shall be deposited with the Government of the United States of America, which shall notify all the signatory states of each deposit as well as the Secretary-General of the Organization when he has been appointed.

3. The present Charter shall come into force upon the deposit of ratifications by the Republic of China, France, the Union of Soviet Socialist Republics, the United Kingdom of Great Britain and Northern Ireland, and the United States of America, and by a majority of the other signatory states. A protocol of the ratifications deposited shall thereupon be drawn up by the Government of the United States of America which shall communicate copies thereof to all the signatory states.

4. The states signatory to the present Charter which ratify it after it has come into force will become original Members of the United Nations on the date of the deposit of their respective ratifications.

Article 111

The present Charter, of which the Chinese, French, Russian, English, and Spanish texts are equally authentic, shall remain deposited in the archvies of the Government of the United States of America. Duly certified copies thereof shall be transmitted by that Government to the Governments of the other signatory states.

IN FAITH WHEREOF the representatives of the Governments of the United Nations have signed the present Charter.

DONE at the city of San Francisco the twenty-sixth day of June, one thousand nine hundred and forty-five.

2. Statute of the International Court of Justice

Article 1

The International Court of Justice established by the Charter of the United Nations as the principal judicial organ of the United Nations shall be constituted and shall function in accordance with the provisions of the present Statute.

Chapter I — Organization of the Court

Article 2

The Court shall be composed of a body of independent judges, elected regardless of their nationality from among persons of high moral character, who possess the qualifications required in their respective countries for appointment to the highest judicial offices, or are jurisconsults of recognized competence in international law.

Article 3

1. The Court shall consist of fifteen members, no two of whom may be nationals of the same state.

2. A person who for the purposes of membership in the Court could be regarded as a national of more than one state shall be deemed to be a national of the one in which he ordinarily exercises civil and political rights.

Article 4

1. The members of the Court shall be elected by the General Assembly and by the Security Council from a list of persons nominated by the national groups in the Permanent Court of Arbitration, in accordance with the following provisions.

2. In the case of Members of the United Nations not represented in the Permanent Court of Arbitration, candidates shall be nominated by national groups appointed for this purpose by their governments under the same conditions as those prescribed for members of the Permanent Court of Arbitration by Article 44 of the Convention of The Hague of 1907 for the pacific settlement of international disputes.

3. The conditions under which a state which is a party to the present Statute but is not a Member of the United Nations may participate in electing the members of the Court shall, in the absence of a special agreement, be laid down by the General Assembly upon recommendation of the Security Council.

Article 5

1. At least three months before the date of the election, the Secretary-General of the United Nations shall address a written request to the members of the Permanent Court of Arbitration belonging to the states which are parties to the present Statute, and to the members of the national groups appointed under Article 4, paragraph 2, inviting them to undertake, within a given time, by national groups, the nomination of persons in a position to accept the duties of a member of the Court.

2. No group may nominate more than four persons, not more than two of whom shall be of their own nationality. In no case may the number of candidates nominated by a group be more than double the number of seats to be filled.

Article 6

Before making these nominations, each national group is recommended to consult its highest court of justice, its legal faculties and schools of law, and its national academies and national sections of international academies devoted to the study of law.

Article 7

1. The Secretary-General shall prepare a list in alphabetical order of all the persons thus nominated. Save as provided in Article 12, paragraph 2, these shall be the only persons eligible.

2. The Secretary-General shall submit this list to the General Assembly and to the Security Council.

Article 8

The General Assembly and the Security Council shall proceed independently of one another to elect the members of the Court.

Article 9

At every election, the electors shall bear in mind not only that the persons to be elected should individually possess the qualifications required, but also that in the body as a whole the representation of the main forms of civilization and of the principal legal systems of the world should be assured.

Article 10

1. Those candidates who obtain an absolute majority of votes in the General Assembly and in the Security Council shall be considered as elected.

2. Any vote of the Security Council, whether for the election of judges or for the appointment of members of the conference envisaged in Article 12, shall be taken without any distinction between permanent and non-permanent members of the Security Council.

3. In the event of more than one national of the same state obtaining an absolute majority of the votes both of the General Assembly and of the Security Council, the eldest of these only shall be considered as elected.

Article 11

If, after the first meeting held for the purpose of the election, one or more seats remain to be filled, a second and, if necessary, a third meeting shall take place.

Article 12

1. If, after the third meeting, one or more seats still remain unfilled, a joint conference consisting of six members, three appointed by the General Assembly and three by the Security Council, may be formed at any time at the request of either the General Assembly or the Security Council, for the purpose of choosing by the vote of an absolute majority one name for each seat still vacant, to submit to the General Assembly and the Security Council for their respective acceptance.

2. If the joint conference is unanimously agreed upon any person who fulfils the required conditions, he may be included in its list, even though he was not included in the list of nominations referred to in Article 7.

3. If the joint conference is satisfied that it will not be successful in procuring an election, those members of the Court who have already been elected shall, within a period to be fixed by the Security Council, proceed to fill the vacant seats by selection from among those candidates who have obtained votes either in the General Assembly or in the Security Council.

4. In the event of an equality of votes among the judges, the eldest judge shall have a casting vote.

Article 13

1. The members of the Court shall be elected for nine years and may be re-elected; provided, however, that of the judges elected at the first election, the terms of five judges shall expire at the end of three years and the terms of five more judges shall expire at the end of six years.

2. The judges whose terms are to expire at the end of the above-mentioned initial periods of three and six years shall be chosen by lot to be drawn by the Secretary-General immediately after the first election has been completed.

3. The members of the Court shall continue to discharge their duties until their places have been filled. Though replaced, they shall finish any cases which they may have begun.

4. In the case of the resignation of a member of the Court, the resignation shall be addressed to the President of the Court for transmission to the Secretary-General. This last notification makes the place vacant.

Article 14

Vacancies shall be filled by the same method as that laid down for the first election, subject to the following provision: the Secretary-General shall, within one month of the occurence of the vacancy, proceed to issue the invitations provided for in Article 5, and the date of the election shall be fixed by the Security Council.

Article 15

A member of the Court elected to replace a member whose term of office has not expired shall hold office for the remainder of his predecessor's term.

Article 16

1. No member of the Court may exercise any political or administrative function, or engage in any other occupation of a professional nature.

2. Any doubt on this point shall be settled by the decision of the Court.

Article 17

1. No member of the Court may act as agent, counsel, or advocate in any case.

2. No member may participate in the decision of any case in which he has previously taken part as agent, counsel, or advocate for one of the parties, or as a member of a national or international court, or of a commission of enquiry, or in any other capacity.

3. Any doubt on this point shall be settled by the decision of the Court.

Article 18

1. No member of the Court can be dismissed unless, in the unanimous opinion of the other members, he has ceased to fulfil the required conditions.

2. Formal notification thereof shall be made to the Secretary-General by the Registrar.

3. This notification makes the place vacant.

Article 19

The members of the Court, when engaged on the business of the Court, shall enjoy diplomatic privileges and immunities.

Article 20

Every member of the Court shall, before taking up his duties, make a solemn declaration in open court that he will exercise his powers impartially and conscientiously.

Article 21

1. The Court shall elect its President and Vice-President for three years; they may be re-elected.

2. The Court shall appoint its Registrar and may provide for the appointment of such other officers as may be necessary.

Article 22

1. The seat of the Court shall be established at The Hague. This, however, shall not prevent the Court from sitting and exercising its functions elsewhere whenever the Court considers it desirable.

2. The President and the Registrar shall reside at the seat of the Court.

Article 23

1. The Court shall remain permanently in session, except during the judicial vacations, the dates and duration of which shall be fixed by the Court.

2. Members of the Court are entitled to periodic leave, the dates and duration of which shall be fixed by the Court, having in mind the distance between The Hague and the home of each judge.

3. Members of the Court shall be bound, unless they are on leave or prevented from attending by illness or other serious reasons duly explained to the President, to hold themselves permanently at the disposal of the Court.

Article 24

1. If, for some special reason, a member of the Court considers that he should not take part in the decision of a particular case, he shall so inform the President.

2. If the President considers that for some special reason one of the members of the Court should not sit in a particular case, he shall give him notice accordingly.

3. If in any such case the member of the Court and the President disagree, the matter shall be settled by the decision of the Court.

Article 25

1. The full Court shall sit except when it is expressly provided otherwise in the present Statute.

2. Subject to the condition that the number of judges available to constitute the Court is not thereby reduced below eleven, the Rules of the Court may provide for allowing one or more judges, according to circumstances and in rotation, to be dispensed from sitting.

3. A quorum of nine judges shall suffice to constitute the Court.

Article 26

1. The Court may from time to time form one or more chambers, composed of three or more judges as the Court may determine, for dealing with particular categories of cases; for example, labour cases and cases relating to transit and communications.

2. The Court may at any time form a chamber for dealing with a particular case. The number of judges to constitute such a chamber shall be determined by the Court with the approval of the parties.

3. Cases shall be heard and determined by the chambers provided for in this Article if the parties so request.

Article 27

A judgment given by any of the chambers provided for in Articles 26 and 29 shall be considered as rendered by the Court.

Article 28

The chambers provided for in Articles 26 and 29 may, with the consent of the parties, sit and exercise their functions elsewhere than at The Hague.

Article 29

With a view to the speedy dispatch of business, the Court shall form annually a chamber composed of five judges which, at the request of the parties, may hear and determine cases by summary procedure. In addition, two judges shall be selected for the purpose of replacing judges who find it impossible to sit.

Article 30

1. The Court shall frame rules for carrying out its functions. In particular, it shall lay down rules of procedure.

2. The Rules of the Court may provide for assessors to sit with the Court or with any of its chambers without the right to vote.

Article 31

1. Judges of the nationality of each of the parties shall retain their right to sit in the case before the Court.

2. If the Court includes upon the Bench a judge of the nationality of one of the parties, any other party may choose a person to sit as judge. Such person shall be chosen preferably from among those persons who have been nominated as candidates as provided in Articles 4 and 5.

3. If the Court includes upon the Bench no judge of the nationality of the parties, each of these parties may proceed to choose a judge as provided in paragraph 2 of this Article.

4. The provisions of this Article shall apply to the case of Articles 26 and 29. In such cases, the President shall request one or, if necessary, two of the members of the Court forming the chamber to give place to the members of the Court of the nationality of the parties concerned, and, failing such, or if they are unable to be present, to the judges specially chosen by the parties.

5. Should there be several parties in the same interest, they shall, for the purpose of the preceding provisions, be reckoned as one party only. Any doubt upon this point shall be settled by the decision of the Court.

6. Judges chosen as laid down in paragraphs 2, 3, and 4 of this Article shall fulfil the conditions required by Articles 2, 17 (paragraph 2), 20, and 24 of the present Statute. They shall take part in the decision on terms of complete equality with their colleagues.

Article 32

1. Each member of the Court shall receive an annual salary.

2. The President shall receive a special annual allowance.

3. The Vice-President shall receive a special allowance for every day on which he acts as President.

4. The judges chosen under Article 31, other than members of the Court, shall receive compensation for each day on which they exercise their functions.

5. These salaries, allowances, and compensation shall be fixed by the General Assembly. They may not be decreased during the term of office.

6. The salary of the Registrar shall be fixed by the General Assembly on the proposal of the Court.

7. Regulations made by the General Assembly shall fix the conditions under which retirement pensions may be given to members of the Court and to the Registrar, and the conditions under which members of the Court and the Registrar shall have their travelling expenses refunded.

8. The above salaries, allowances, and compensation shall be free of all taxation.

Article 33

The expenses of the Court shall be borne by the United Nations in such a manner as shall be decided by the General Assembly.

Chapter II — Competence of the Court

Article 34

1. Only states may be parties in cases before the Court.

2. The Court, subject to and in conformity with its Rules, may request of public international organizations information relevant to cases before it, and shall receive such information presented by such organizations on their own initiative.

3. Whenever the construction of the constituent instrument of a public international organization or of an international convention adopted thereunder is in question in a case before the Court, the Registrar shall so notify the public international organization concerned and shall communicate to it copies of all the written proceedings.

Article 35

1. The Court shall be open to the states parties to the present Statute.

2. The conditions under which the Court shall be open to other states shall, subject to the special provisions contained in treaties in force, be laid down by the Security Council, but in no case shall such conditions place the parties in a position of inequality before the Court.

3. When a state which is not a Member of the United Nations is a party to a case, the Court shall fix the amount which that party is to contribute towards the expenses of the Court. This provision shall not apply if such state is bearing a share of the expenses of the Court.

Article 36

1. The jurisdiction of the Court comprises all cases which the parties refer to it and all matters specially provided for in the Charter of the United Nations or in treaties and conventions in force.

2. The states parties to the present Statute may at any time declare that they recognize as compulsory ipso facto and without special agreement, in relation to any other state accepting the same obligation, the jurisdiction of the Court in all legal disputes concerning:

a. the interpretation of a treaty;
b. any question of international law;
c. the existence of any fact which, if established, would constitute a breach of an international obligation;
d. the nature or extent of the reparation to be made for the breach of an international obligation.

3. The declarations referred to above may be made unconditionally or on condition of reciprocity on the part of several or certain states, or for a certain time.

4. Such declarations shall be deposited with the Secretary-General of the United Nations, who shall transmit copies thereof to the parties to the Statute and to the Registrar of the Court.

5. Declarations made under Article 36 of the Statute of the Permanent Court of International Justice and which are still in force shall be deemed, as between the parties to the present Statute, to be acceptances of the compulsory jurisdiction of the International Court of Justice for the period which they still have to run and in accordance with their terms.

6. In the event of a dispute as to whether the Court has jurisdiction, the matter shall be settled by the decision of the Court.

Article 37

Whenever a treaty or convention in force provides for reference of a matter to a tribunal to have been instituted by the League of Nations, or to the Permanent Court of International Justice, the matter shall, as between the parties to the present Statute, be referred to the International Court of Justice.

Article 38

1. The Court, whose function is to decide in accordance with international law such disputes as are submitted to it, shall apply:

a. international conventions, whether general of particular, establishing rules expressly recognized by the contesting states:

b. international custom, as evidence of a general practice accepted as law;

c. the general principles of law recognized by civilized nations;

d. subject to the provisions of Article 59, judicial decisions and the teachings of the most highly qualified publicists of the various nations, as subsidiary means for the determination of rules of law.

2. This provision shall not prejudice the power of the Court to decide a case ex aequo et bono, if the parties agree thereto.

Chapter III — Procedure

Article 39

1. The official languages of the Court shall be French and English. If the parties agree that the case shall be conducted in French, the judgment shall be delivered in French. If the parties agree that the case shall be conducted in English, the judgment shall be delivered in English.

2. In the absence of an agreement as to which language shall be employed, each party may, in the pleadings, use the language which it prefers; the decision of the Court shall be given in French and English. In this case the Court shall at the same time determine which of the two texts shall be considered as authoritative.

3. The Court shall, at the request of any party, authorize a language other than French or English to be used by that party.

Article 40

1. Cases are brought before the Court, as the case may be, either by the notification of the special agreement or by a written application addressed to the Registrar. In either case the subject of the dispute and the parties shall be indicated.

2. The Registrar shall forthwith communicate the application to all concerned.

3. He shall also notify the Members of the United Nations through the Secretary-General, and also any other states entitled to appear before the Court.

Article 41

1. The Court shall have the power to indicate, if it considers that circumstances so require, any provisional measures which ought to be taken to preserve the respective rights of either party.

2. Pending the final decision, notice of the measures suggested shall forthwith be given to the parties and to the Security Council.

Article 42

1. The parties shall be represented by agents.

2. They may have the assistance of counsel or advocates before the Court.

3. The agents, counsel, and advocates of parties before the Court shall enjoy the privileges and immunities necessary to the independent exercise of their duties.

Article 43

1. The procedure shall consist of two parts: written and oral.

2. These written proceedings shall consist of the communication to the Court and to the parties of memorials, counter-memorials and, if necessary, replies; also all papers and documents in support.

3. These communications shall be made through the Registrar, in the order and within the time fixed by the Court.

4. A certified copy of every document produced by one party shall be communicated to the other party.

5. The oral proceedings shall consist of the hearing by the Court of witnesses, experts, agents, counsel, and advocates.

Article 44

1. For the service of all notices upon persons other than the agents, counsel, and advocates, the Court shall apply direct to the government of the state upon whose territory the notice has to be served.

2. The same provision shall apply whenever steps are to be taken to procure evidence on the spot.

Article 45

The hearing shall be under the control of the President or, if he is unable to preside, of the Vice-President; if neither is able to preside, the senior judge present shall preside.

Article 46

The hearing in Court shall be public, unless the Court shall decide otherwise, or unless the parties demand that the public be not admitted.

Article 47

1. Minutes shall be made at each hearing and signed by the Registrar and the President.

2. These minutes alone shall be authentic.

Article 48

The Court shall make orders for the conduct of the case, shall decide the form and time in which each party must conclude its arguments, and make all arrangements connected with the taking of evidence.

Article 49

The Court may, even before the hearing begins, call upon the agents to produce any document or to supply any explanations. Formal note shall be taken of any refusal.

Article 50

The Court may, at any time, entrust any individual, body, bureau, commission, or other organization that it may select, with the task of carrying out an enquiry or giving an expert opinion.

Article 51

During the hearing any relevant questions are to be put to the witnesses and experts under the conditions laid down by the Court in the rules of procedure referred to in Article 30.

Article 52

After the Court has received the proofs and evidence within the time specified for the purpose, it may refuse to accept any further oral or written evidence that one party may desire to present unless the other side consents.

Article 53

1. Whenever one of the parties does not appear before the Court, or fails to defend its case, the other party may call upon the Court to decide in favour of its claim.

2. The Court must, before doing so, satisfy itself, not only that it has jurisdiction in accordance with Articles 36 and 37, but also that the claim is well founded in fact and law.

Article 54

1. When, subject to the control of the Court, the agents, counsel, and advocates have completed their presentation of the case, the President shall declare the hearing closed.

2. The Court shall withdraw to consider the judgment.

3. The deliberations of the Court shall take place in private and remain secret.

Article 55

1. All questions shall be decided by a majority of the judges present.
2. In the event of an equality of votes, the President or the judge who acts in his place shall have a casting vote.

Article 56

1. The judgment shall state the reasons on which it is based.

2. It shall contain the names of the judges who have taken part in the decision.

Article 57

If the judgment does not represent in whole or in part the unanimous opinion of the judges, any judge shall be entitled to deliver a separate opinion.

Article 58

The judgment shall be signed by the President and by the Registrar. It shall be read in open court, due notice having been given to the agents.

Article 59

The decision of the Court has no binding force except between the parties and in respect of that particular case.

Article 60

The judgment is final and without appeal. In the event of dispute as to the meaning or scope of the judgment, the Court shall construe it upon the request of any party.

Article 61

1. An application for revision of a judgment may be made only when it is based upon the discovery of some fact of such a nature as to be a decisive factor, which fact was, when the judgment was given, unknown to the Court and also to the party claiming revision, always provided that such ignorance was not due to negligence.

2. The proceedings for revision shall be opened by a judgment of the Court expressly recording the existence of the new fact, recognizing that it has such a character as to lay the case open to revision, and declaring the application admissible on this ground.

3. The Court may require previous compliance with the terms of the judgment before it admits proceedings in revision.

4. The application for revision must be made at latest within six months of the discovery of the new fact.

5. No application for revision may be made after the lapse of ten years from the date of the judgment.

Article 62

1. Should a state consider that it has an interest of a legal nature which may be affected by the decision in the case, it may submit a request to the Court to be permitted to intervene.

2. It shall be for the Court to decide upon this request.

Article 63

1. Whenever the construction of a convention to which states other than those concerned in the case are parties is in question, the Registrar shall notify all such states forthwith.

2. Every state so notified has the right to intervene in the proceedings; but if it uses this right, the construction given by the judgment will be equally binding upon it.

Article 64

Unless otherwise decided by the Court, each party shall bear its own costs.

Chapter IV — Advisory Opinions

Article 65

1. The Court may give an advisory opinion on any legal question at the request of whatever body may be authorized by or in accordance with the Charter of the United Nations to make such a request.

2. Questions upon which the advisory opinion of the Court is asked shall be laid before the Court by means of a written request containing an exact statement of the question upon which an opinion is required, and accompanied by all documents likely to throw light upon the question.

Article 66

1. The Registrar shall forthwith give notice of the request for an advisory opinion to all states entitled to appear before the Court.

2. The Registrar shall also, by means of a special and direct communication, notify any state entitled to appear before the Court or international organization considered by the Court, or, should it not be sitting, by the President, as likely to be able to furnish information on the question, that the Court will be prepared to receive, within a time limit to be fixed by the President, written statements, or to hear, at a public sitting to be held for the purpose, oral statements relating of the question.

3. Should any such state entitled to appear before the Court have failed to receive the special communication referred to in paragraph 2 of this Article, such state may express a desire to submit a written statement or to be heard; and the Court will decide.

4. States and organizations having presented written or oral statements or both shall be permitted to comment on the statements made by other states or organizations in the form, to the extent, and within the time limits which the Court, or, should it not be sitting, the President, shall decide in each particular case. Accordingly, the Registrar shall in due time communicate any such written statements to states and organizations having submitted similar statements.

Article 67

The Court shall deliver its advisory opinions in open court, notice having been given to the Secretary-General and to the representatives of Members of the United Nations, of other states and of international organizations immediately concerned.

Article 68

In the exercise of its advisory functions the Court shall further be guided by the provisions of the present Statute which apply in contentious cases to the extent to which it recognizes them to be applicable.

Chapter V — Amendment

Article 69

Amendments to the present Statute shall be effected by the same procedure as is provided by the Charter of the United Nations for amendments to that Charter, subject however to any provisions which the General Assembly upon recommendation of the Security Council may adopt concerning the participation of states which are parties to the present Statute but are not Members of the United Nations.

Article 70

The Court shall have power to propose such amendments to the present Statute as it may deem necessary, through written communications to the Secretary-General, for consideration in conformity with the provisions of Article 69.

3. Law Relating to the Accession of the Federal Republic of Germany to the Charter of the United Nations of 6 June 1973*)

The German Bundestag has adopted the following Law:

Article 1

The accession of the Federal Republic of Germany to the Charter of the United Nations is approved.

The Charter of the United Nations and the Statute of the International Court of Justice, which forms an integral part of the Charter, are appended in the currently applicable versions.

Article 2

This Law also applies in the *Land* Berlin, provided that the *Land* Berlin decides on the application of this Law, in which the rights and responsibilities of the Allied authorities, including those which relate to matters security and status, are unaffected.

Article 3

(1) This Law enters into force on the day following its proclamation.

(2) The date on which the Charter of the United Nations enters into force in the Federal Republic of Germany will be announced in the Federal Law Gazette.

The constitutional rights of the Bundesrat are observed. The above Law is herewith proclaimed.

Bonn, 6 June 1973

The Federal President

Heinemann

The Federal Chancellor

Brandt

The Federal Minister for Foreign Affairs

Scheel

The Bundestag took the final vote on the above bill on 11 May 1973, and voted as follows:

364 delegates and 13 delegates (with limited voting rights) from Berlin voted in favour of the proposed law relating to the accession. Among those in favour were 99 delegates from the CDU/CSU opposition.

121 delegates from the CDU/CSU opposition and nine CDU delegates from Berlin voted against the proposed law.

The Bundesrat adopted the proposed law on 25 May 1973.

---

*) Federal Law Gazette No. 25/1973, Part II, page 430, of 6 June 1973.

4. Memorandum
Concerning the Law Relating to the Accession of the
Federal Republic of Germany
to the Charter of the United Nations*)

General Part

I.

The Federal Republic of Germany has a considerable political interest in co-operating in the World Organization of the United Nations as a Member. Only thus can it take care of its own interests within the world-wide framework and furnish the contribution to international co-operation that is commensurate with its importance and possibilities.

For a long time now the Federal Republic of Germany has been making use of such possibilities of collaborating in the UN system as are open to it under the given political situation through accession to all Specialized Agencies and co-operation in the subsidiary organs of the UN to which, thanks to its political and economic weight, it was admitted. In numerous agreements it has recognized the competence of the International Court of Justice, to which it has submitted two important cases at issue for decision. In its policy statement of October 28, 1969, the Federal Government again emphasized its intention to strengthen its co-operation in the United Nations and other international organizations.

All Federal Governments have made the purposes and principles of the Charter of the United Nations — the renunciation of force, the maintenance of peace, and the strengthening of international co-operation — the guideline of their policy. In connection with the accession to NATO, the Federal Government, on October 3, 1954, undertook to conduct its policy in harmony with the principles of the Charter of the United Nations and to assume the obligations embodied in Article 2 of the Charter; in Article 3 of the Bonn Conventions the Federal Republic of Germany undertook to adhere to those principles. In the Moscow and Warsaw Treaties it reconfirmed its intention to be guided by the principles embodied in the Charter of the United Nations, these including, in particular, the renunciation of the threat or use of force in international relations.

However, notwithstanding the multifarious relations and ties the Federal Republic of Germany long ago established with the UN system, accession to the United Nations Organization itself was not yet possible in view of the situation in Germany and the attitude of the Soviet Union, which, as a Permanent Member of the Security Council, would have refused the accession of the Federal Republic of Germany without the simultaneous accession of the German Democratic Republic. Only in the course of her policy directed towards an adjustment of relations with the East and the settlement of the intra-German relationship on the lines of a modus vivendi did it become possible for the Federal Government to open the way to accession to the United Nations Organization. This presupposed, however, that admittance to the United Nations would be made simultaneously possible for the German Democratic Republic.

---

*) Federal Law Gazette No. 25/1973, Part II, page 430, of 6 June 1973.

In Point 20 of the Kassel Declaration of May 21, 1970, the Federal Government proposed to the German Democratic Republic the regulation of the membership and co-operation of the two states in Germany in international organizations on the basis of a treaty with the Federal Republic of Germany. This proposal was converted into reality with the Basic Treaty, and the preconditions were created for the membership of both states in the United Nations.

II.

The Basic Treaty regulates the relationship between the two German states for the duration of the partition on the basis of equal rights and non-discrimination. It represents a modus videndi and takes account of Germany's peculiar situation. This situation is determined, above all, by the fact that a freely agreed settlement for Germany in a peace treaty is still outstanding and that, until this comes about, the above-mentioned rights and responsibilities of the Four Powers relating to Berlin and Germany as a whole remain unchanged.

The Four Powers, in a declaration proclaimed in the four capitals on November 9, 1972, stated that the accession of the two German states to the United Nations does not affect the rights and responsibilities of the the the Four Powers. This makes it clear that the accession of the two German states to the United Nations does not involve any change in the situation in Germany. This declaration was notified to the Federal Government by the Three Powers and to the Government of the German Democratic Republic by the Soviet Union on November 9, 1972. The two German states have also agreed to deposit their applications for membership in the United Nations at approximately the same time.

The membership of the two German states in the United Nations effected under these circumstances does not prejudice the peculiar situation in Germany. The Charter of the United Nations involves no legal effects as a result of which the division of Germany is rendered permanent. A reunification brought about by means of a policy of peace is consonant with the Charter of the United Nations; the Charter confirms that the right of self-determination of peoples is one of the fundamental principles governing international relations. A policy directed towards a peaceful state of affairs in Europe in which the German nation achieves its unity in free self-determination is, therefore, consonant with the Charter of the United Nations.

III.

The Federal Republic of Germany has already, within the framework of the United Nations, rendered important contributions to the extent that it was able to assist in United Nations activities. However, the policy of the Federal Government within the scope of the United Nations was complicated by the unresolved relationship with the German Democratic Republic.

Following the accession of the two German states to the United Nations, the Federal Republic of Germany will be able to extend its participation to cover the whole domain of the United Nations and to co-operate in all its bodies. As a full Member of the World Organization enjoying equal rights, the Federal Republic of Germany will, in partnership with all other UN Member states, support the efforts of the United Nations to maintain peace and will continue, on a strengthened scale, its collaboration in the UN's far-ranging efforts in the field of international co-operation. It considers the development aid which, in a great variety of ways, it has already for a long time been providing within the framework of the United Nations and the importance of which will increase even more in the future, as a contribution towards the promotion of economic and social advancement in the Third World, above all in the poorer regions, and towards reducing antagonisms and tensions threatening universal peace. The Federal Republic of Germany will also pay special attention to the promotion and encouragement of respect for human rights and the right of self-determination, to the combating racial discrimination, to disarmament efforts, and to the UN's newly planned programme for the protection of the human environment. It will continue to grant humanitarian assistance within the framework of the United Nations to mitigate the effects of acute emergencies and disasters.

The Federal Government will take steps to see that, in the matter of personnel, the representation of the Federal Republic of Germany in the United Nations will, in accordance with the UN regulations currently applicable, be commensurate with the importance and size of its contribution, also where it has not so far been represented. It will take the necessary measures to place suitable personnel at the disposal of the Secretariats.

Also within the framework of the United Nations the Federal Government will continue and intensify the close co-operation with its allies. It will seek co-operation with other Member states wherever this is possible.

Special Part

I.

Pursuant to the Law on the Accession of the Federal Republic of Germany to the United Nations, the application for membership is being submitted to the UN Secretary-General. Subjoined will be the necessary formal declaration, in compliance with Rule 135 of the UN General Assembly's Rules of Procedure and with Rule 58 of the Security Council's Rules of Procedure, that the Federal Republic of Germany accepts the obligations on a UN Member embodied in the Charter.

The German Democratic Republic will submit its application for membership in the United Nations at approximately the same time. In connection with the Basic Treaty there was an exchange of letters concerning the application for membership in the United Nations (see Annexes 1 a and 1 b to this Memorandum) as well as the statements on record concerning the application for membership in the United Nations made on the occasion of the initialling of the Basic Treaty on November 8, 1972 (see Annex 2 to this Memorandum). In connection with the application of the two German states for admission, the notice of the United Nations will be drawn to the Declaration of the Four Powers of November 9, 1972 (see Annex 3 to this Memorandum).

Then, the UN Secretary-General will forward the applications of the two German states to the Security Council, which will decide whether or not it can recommend to the General Assembly the admission of the two states. If the Security Council makes such a recommendation, the General Assembly can decide by a two thirds majority to admit the two German states. The next session of the General Assembly is on September 18, 1973.

II.

A. The Charter of the United Nations takes the form of a Preamble and 19 Chapters.

The Chapters cover, respectively:

I. Purposes and Principles (Articles 1 and 2)

II. Membership (Articles 3 to 6; the admission of new Members is dealt with in Article 4)

III. Organs (Articles 7 and 8)

IV. The General Assembly (Article 9: composition; Articles 10 to 17: functions and powers; Articles 18 and 19: voting; Articles 20 to 22: procedure)

V. The Security Council (Article 23: composition; Articles 24 to 26: functions and powers; Article 27: voting; Articles 28 to 32: procedure)

VI. Pacific Settlement of Disputes (Articles 33 to 38; Article 33 contains the provision concerning the fundamental obligation to seek a solution by peaceful means)

VII. Action with respect to Threats to the Peace, Breaches of the Peace and Acts of Aggression (Articles 39 to 51; together with Chapter VI, this Chapter contains the most important provisions for the maintenance of peace and security, such as provisional measures, peaceful and military measures, obligation on all UN Members to render assistance, etc.)

VIII. Regional Arrangements (Articles 52 to 54)

IX. International Economic and Social Co-operation (Articles 55 to 60; besides the function of maintaining peace, herein lies one of the UN's primary purposes)

X. The Economic and Social Council (Article 61: composition; Articles 62 to 66: functions and powers; Article 67: voting; Articles 68 to 72: procedure)

XI. Declaration regarding Non-self-governing Territories (Articles 73 and 74; herein is embodied the principle of decolonization)

XII. International Trusteeship System (Articles 75 to 85)

XIII. The Trusteeship Council (Articles 86 to 88; composition, functions and powers, voting and procedure)

XIV. The International Court of Justice (Articles 92 to 96)

XV. The Secretariat (Articles 97 to 101; functions and powers of the Secretary-General, etc.)

XVI. Miscellaneous Provisions (Article 102: obligation to register all treaties and international agreements with the Secretariat; Article 103: precedence of the Charter; Articles 104 and 105: legal capacity of the UN and privileges)

XVII. Transitional Security Arrangements (Article 106: reservations; Article 107: enemy states clause)

XVIII. Amendments (Articles 108 and 109: requirement of two thirds majority and reviewing procedure)

XIX. Ratification and Signature (Articles 110 and 111: requirements and ruling on authentic texts).

B. The Statute of the International Court of Justice, which, in accordance with Article 92, forms an integral part of the Charter of the United Nations, is divided into five Chapters covering, respectively, the following:

I. Organization of the Court (Article 1: establishment of the Court; Articles 2 to 33: organization)

II. Competence of the Court (Articles 34 to 38)

III. Procedure (Articles 39 to 64)

IV. Advisory Opinions (Articles 65 to 68)

V. Amendments (Articles 69 and 70).

III.

As a Member of the United Nations, the Federal Republic of Germany is liable to the following obligations embodied in the Charter:

1. The Federal Republic of Germany is bound to uphold the Purposes and Principles of the UN enunciated in Articles 1 and 2; these are directed towards the maintenance of peace and the strengthening of international co-operation. Before becoming a Member of the United Nations, the Federal Republic of Germany had already undertaken to uphold these Purposes and Principles.

2. The Security Council, to which is assigned the primary responsibility for the maintenance of international peace and security, can, within the framework of its competence on the authority of Chapter VII, decide measures for the maintenance of peace which, in accordance with Article 25 of the Charter, are binding upon the Members of the United Nations. This has already taken place in two cases.

3. As a Member of the United Nations, the Federal Republic of Germany will be called upon to pay contributions to the budget of the United Nations. In accordance with Article 17, the expenses of the Organization are borne by the Members as apportioned by the General Assembly. Since the Federal Republic of Germany has already been a Member of some of the subsidiary organs whose expenses are covered out of general UN budget, the size of the Federal Republic of Germany's contribution has already been fixed; for the period 1971 to 1973 it amounts to 6.8 per cent. If this apportionment is taken as a basis, and if it is assumed that the UN's present budgetary structure continues to hold good, the Federal Republic of Germany will have to reckon with an additional annual contribution to the UN budget of approximately 50 million DM.

4. In accordance with Article 104 of the Charter, the United Nations enjoys in the territory of each of its Members such legal capacity as may be necessary for the exercise of its functions and the fulfilment of its purposes. According to Article 105 of the Charter, the Organization enjoys in the territory of each of its Members such privileges and immunities as are necessary for the exercise of its

functions. Similarly, the Member's representatives and the Organization's officials enjoy such privileges and immunities as are necessary for the independent exercise of their functions in connection with the Organization.

The General Assembly, on February 13, 1946, approved an Arrangement concerning the privileges and immunities of the United Nations and recommended that each Member should accede to it. The Federal Republic of Germany has already embodied the provisions of this Arrangement in domestic law through the 'Ordinance on the Granting of Privileges and Immunities to the United Nations' of June 16, 1970 (Federal Law Gazette II, pages 669 *et seq.*).

IV.

As a Member of the United Nations, the Federal Republic of Germany is *ipso facto* a party to the Statute of the International Court of Justice (Article 93 of the UN Charter).

5. Exchange of Letters
between the Federal Republic of Germany and the German Democratic Republic in Connection with the Basic Treaty, Concerning the Application for Membership of the United Nations

Annex 1 a to the Memorandum*)

The Federal Chancellery
The State Secretary

Bonn, November 8, 1972

To the
State Secretary to the Council of Ministers
of the German Democratic Republic,
Dr. Michael Kohl
Berlin.

Dear Herr Kohl,

I have the honour to inform you of the following: The Government of the Federal Republic of Germany has noted that the Government of the German Democratic Republic is initiating the necessary steps in accordance with the domestic legislation of the German Democratic Republic to achieve membership of the United Nations Organization.

The two Governments will inform each other of the date on which the application will be made.
(Formal close)

Annex 1 b to the Memorandum

State Secretary to the Council of Ministers
of the German Democratic Republic

Berlin, November 8, 1972

To the
State Secretary in the
Chancellery of the
Federal Republic of Germany,

Herr Egon Bahr

Bonn.

Dear Herr Bahr,

I have the honour to inform you of the following: The Government of the German Democratic Republic has noted that the Government of the Federal Republic of Germany is initiating the necessary steps in accordance with the domestic legislation of the Federal Republic of Germany to achieve membership of the United Nations Organization.

The two Goverments will inform each other of the date on which the application will be made.
(Formal close)

---

*) Application and three Annexes: see pages 168 et seq.

Annex 2 to the Memorandum

6. Statements on Record
Concerning Application for Membership of the United Nations

Statement on Record of the Federal Republic of Germany:

> The Government of the Federal Republic of Germany will, after the Bundestag has assembled, initiate the necessary steps to create the domestic prerequisites for the Federal Republic of Germany to apply for membership of the United Nations.

Statement on Record by the two Heads of Delegation:

The mutual information is to ensure that the applications will be made on approximately the same date.

Annex 3 to Memorandum

7. Declaration of the Four Powers

The Embassies of France, the United Kingdom and the United States transmitted to the Federal Government on November 9, 1972, the following Declaration of the Governments of France, the United Kingdom, the Soviet Union and the United States issued on the same day in London, Moscow, Paris and Washington:

"The Governments of the French Republic, the Union of Soviet Socialist Republics, the United Kingdom of Great Britain and Northern Ireland, and the United States of America, having been represented by their Ambassadors, who held a series of meetings in the building formerly occupied by the Allied Control Council, are in agreement that they will support the applications of the Federal Republic of Germany and the German Democratic Republic, and affirm in this connection that this membership shall in no way affect the rights and responsibilities of the Four Powers and the corresponding related Quadripartite agreements, decisions, and practices."

8. Letter of the Allied Kommandatura

to the Governing Mayor concerning
the representation of Berlin
BKC/L (73) 1
April 13, 1973

Subject: Accession of the Federal Republic of Germany to the United Nations Charter

To: The Governing Mayor, Berlin

Dear Mr. Governing Mayor,

The Allied Kommandatura refers to Senat Letter No. 16 of 2 February 1973 which transmits to the Allied Kommandatura the draft law providing for adherence by the Federal Republic to the United Nations Charter. This draft law contains a Berlin clause.

In accordance with the arrangements referred to in Annex IV A of the Quadripartite Agreement of September 3, 1971, and in particular with the exception of matters concerning security and status:

(a) The Allied Kommandatura has no objection to the acceptance by the Federal Republic of Germany of the rights and obligations contained in the United Nations Charter with respect also to the Western Sectors of Berlin;

(b) The Allied Kommandatura approves the representation of the interests of the Western Sectors of Berlin in the United Nations and its subsidiary organs by the Federal Republic.

Yours sincerely,
Cathcart
Major General
Chairman Commandant

9. Application of the Federal Republic of Germany for Membership of the United Nations

Press Announcement of the Federal Foreign Office of June 15, 1973
The Foreign Office announces:

Today, June 15, 1973, at 10 a.m. local time, the Federal Republic of Germany's Observer at the United Nations, Ambassador Dr. Walter Gehlhoff, handed to UN Secretary-General Dr. Kurt Waldheim in New York the application of the Federal Republic of Germany for membership of the United Nations.

The application consists of a Letter of Application, signed by the Federal Minister for Foreign Affairs Walter Scheel, and a Deed of Accession bearing the signature of Federal President Dr. Gustav Heinemann. In the Deed of Accession it is made clear that the Federal Republic of Germany accepts the obligations contained in the Charter of the United Nations and solemnly undertakes to carry them out.

The Deed of Accession also mentions that the Charter of the United Nations, the text of which, together with a German translation, is attached, has received parliamentary assent in due legal form.

The Federal Republic of Germany, as a member of all the Specialized Agencies of the United Nations, has for many years displayed its readiness and capability to promote the aims of the United Nations. The Federal Republic of Germany is determined, as a Full Member of the United Nations, to render an even more active contribution to the efforts of the United Nations, to support international cooperation, and to strengthen world peace.

The Federal Republic of Germany will, except in questions of security and status, represent the interests of Berlin (West) in the United Nations and indeed in conformity with the authorization given by the Three Powers who exercise supreme authority over this part of the city. The Secretary-General has been notified accordingly.

ANNEX 1

Letter of the Federal Minister for Foreign Affairs to the Secretary-General of the United Nations

Bonn, June 13, 1973

Mr. Secretary-General,

I have the honour to inform you that the Government of the Federal Republic of Germany herewith applies for the admission of the Federal Republic of Germany to the United Nations.

In accordance with Rule 58 of the Security Council's provisional Rules of Procedure, I have the honour to enclose a declaration made in accordance with that Rule. I should be grateful if you would place this application for admission before the Security Council as soon as possible.

Walter Scheel
Minister for Foreign Affairs
of the Federal Republic of Germany

ANNEX 2

Bonn, June 12, 1973

Deed of Accession of the Federal Republic of Germany to the Charter
of the United Nations

Now that the Charter of the United Nations, signed in San Francisco on June 26,
1945, and the text of which is enclosed as an Annex, has received constitutional
assent in due legal form, I declare that the Federal Republic of Germany accepts
the obligations contained in the Charter of the United Nations and solemnly undertakes to carry them out.

The Federal President
Heinemann

The Federal Minister for Foreign Affairs
Scheel

Letter of the Federal Minister for Foreign Affairs to the UN Secretary-General
concerning the Representation of the Interests of Berlin (West)
in the United Nations

Bonn, June 13, 1973

Mr. Secretary-General,

In connection with the application of the Federal Republic of Germany made today
for membership of the United Nations, I have the honour to state that, respecting
the validity of the Charter of the United Nations for Berlin (West), the Federal Republic of Germany will, from the day on which it is admitted as a Member of the
United Nations, assume, except in questions of security and status, for Berlin (West)
also the rights and obligations arising out of the Charter of the United Nations and
will represent the interests of Berlin (West) in the United Nations and its subsidiary
organs.

I have the honour to request that this Note be circulated as an official document
of the United Nations.

Walter Scheel
Minister for Foreign Affairs
of the Federal Republic of Germany

10. Letter dated 16 June 1973
sent to the Secretary-General by the Permanent Representative
of the United States of America to the United Nations

United Nations
Security Council

General Distribution
S/10955
June 18, 1973

I have the honour to transmit herewith, in connection with the applications for membership in the United Nations submitted by the Federal Republic of Germany (A/9070-S/10949) and by the German Democratic Republic (A/9069-S/10945), the text of a declaration of the French Republic, the Union of Soviet Socialist Republics, the United Kingdom of Great Britain and Northern Ireland and the United States of America, issued on November 9, 1972, and to inform you that a copy of this declaration has been transmitted by the United States Embassy in the Federal Republic of Germany to the Ministry of Foreign Affairs of the Federal Republic of Germany, which acknowledged receipt thereof on 10 November 1972.

I have the honour to request that this letter and its enclosure be circulated as an official document of the Security Council.

(Signed) John A. Scali

Permanent Representative
of the United States of America
to the United Nations

ANNEX

Declaration of the Governments

of the United States of America, the French Republic, the Union of Soviet Socialist Republics and the United Kingdom of Great Britain and Northern Ireland.

(Corresponding letters with a similarly worded annex were sent on the same day by the Permanent Representatives of France, the Soviet Union and the United Kingdom to the Secretary-General of the United Nations.)

The Governments of the United States of America, the French Republic, the Union of Soviet Socialist Republics and the United Kingdom of Great Britain and Northern Ireland, having been represented by their Ambassadors, who held a series of meetings in the building formerly occupied by the Allied Control Council, are in agreement that they will support the applications for membership in the United Nations when submitted by the Federal Republic of Germany and the German Democratic Republic, and affirm in this connection that this membership shall in no way affect the rights and responsibilities of the Four Powers and the corresponding related Quadripartite agreements, decisions, and practices.

**11. Report of the Security Council Committee
on the Admission of New Members Concerning the Application
of the German Democratic Republic
and the Application of the Federal Republic of Germany
for Admission to Membership in the United Nations**

June 21, 1973

United Nations
Security Council

1. At its 1729th meeting, held on 21 June 1973, the Security Council considered the application of the German Democratic Republic and the application of the Federal Republic of Germany for the admission of each to membership in the United Nations (S/10945 and S/10949). In accordance with Rule 59 of the provisional Rules of Procedure and with the decision taken by the Council at its 1729th meeting, the President of the Security Council referred the two applications to the Committee on the Admission of New Members, requesting it to examine the applications and report its conclusions.

2. At its 42nd meeting, held on 21 June 1973, the Committee considered the application of the German Democratic Republic and the application of the Federal Republic of Germany and unanimously decided to recommend to the Security Council the admission of the German Democratic Republic and of the Federal Republic of Germany to membership in the United Nations.

3. Accordingly, the Committee decided to recommend that the Security Council adopt the following draft resolution:

    "The Security Council,

    Having considered separately the application of the German Democratic Republic (S/10945) and the application of the Federal Republic of Germany (S/10949) for admission to membership in the United Nations,

    1. Recommends to the General Assembly that the German Democratic Republic be admitted to membership in the United Nations;

    2. Recommends to the General Assembly that the Federal Republic of Germany be admitted to membership in the United Nations."

The Security Council unanimously approved the above Recommendation on June 22, 1973.

12. Resolution of the Twenty-eighth Session
of the General Assembly of the United Nations
on the Admission of the Federal Republic of Germany to the United Nations

September 18, 1973

United Nations
General Assembly
Twenty-eighth Session
Item 27 of the provisional agenda

Admission of New Members to the United Nations

Proposers:

Afghanistan, Argentina, Australia, Austria, Barbados, Belgium, Bhutan, Bolivia, Botswana, Bulgaria, Burundi, Byelorussian Soviet Socialist Republic, Cameroon, Canada, Colombia, Costa Rica, Cyprus, Czechoslovakia, Democratic Yemen, Dahomey, Denmark, Ecuador, Egypt, El Salvador, Ethiopia, Fiji, Finland, France, Honduras, Hungary, Iceland, India, Indonesia, Iran, Ireland, Italy, Ivory Coast, Japan, Lebanon, Lesotho, Luxembourg, Malaysia, Mali, Malta, Mauritania, Mauritius, Mexico, Mongolia, Netherlands, New Zealand, Norway, Pakistan, Panama, Peru, Philippines, Poland, Romania, Singapore, Spain, Sri Lanka, Sudan, Sweden, Syrian Arab Republic, Thailand, Togo, Tunisia, Ukrainian Soviet Socialist Republic, Union of Soviet Socialist Republics, United Kingdom of Great Britain and Northern Ireland, United States of America, Uruguay, Venezuela, Yemen, Yugoslavia and Zaire;

Draft Resolution:

Admission of the German Democratic Republic
and the Federal Republic of Germany
to membership in the United Nations

The General Assembly,

Having received the recommendation of the Security Council of 22 June 1973 that the German Democratic Republic and the Federal Republic of Germany should be admitted to membership in the United Nations,

Having considered separately the application for membership of the German Democratic Republic and the application for membership of the Federal Republic of Germany,

1. Decides to admit the German Democratic Republic to membership in the United Nations;

2. Decides to admit the Federal Republic of Germany to membership in the United Nations.

This Draft Resolution was approved by the General Assembly without adverse vote by acclamation on September 18, 1973.

13. Speech by the Federal Minister for Foreign Affairs, Herr Walter Scheel, before the Twenty-eighth Session of the General Assembly of the United Nations, New York, 19 September 1973

I.

Mr. President,

Almost to the day 47 years ago Germany became a member of the League of Nations. Eight years had passed since the First World War. The German Foreign Minister, Gustav Stresemann, was welcomed by his French colleague, Aristide Briand, with the words: "Finished is the series of agonising and bloody encounters with which all pages of history are stained ... No more wars, no more brutal and bloody solving of our differences ...". Stresemann replied: "... If we want to emerge from the abyss, we cannot do so by fighting each other, but only by co-operating with each other ...".

A dialogue of expectation and hope borne on the best of will. A fleeting chance for peace. But a few years later it was thrown away.

This time, 28 years have passed since the end of the war. Now, two German Foreign Ministers appear before the delegates. This illustrates the fate of my people: origin and victim of war, divided without its own doing, now living in two states and uncertain as to a common future.

Do you realize why we hesitated to cross the threshold to the United Nations? It is painful to face up to the political reality of the division of one's own country. We were afraid such a step might convey the impression as though we had given up, abandoned hope of unity. We were anxious lest the barriers between the people in Germany would become even higher through membership of both parts of the country.

Now we have a new starting point. The two states in Germany have regulated their mutual relations by the Basic Treaty of December 21, 1972. As regards Berlin, the Quadripartite Agreement came about with the participation of the two states in Germany on September 3, 1971. In particular, this Agreement has also opened the way for Berlin (West) to be able to share in our co-operation in the United Nations. Our aim remains clear: the Federal Republic of Germany will continue to work for a state of peace in Europe in which the German nation will recover its unity in free self-determination.

II.

Gustav Stresemann addressed an organization comprising 53 States. The League of Nations centre of gravity lay in Europe and European was its measure.

The United Nations countenance is different: 135 members from all over the world, many of them exercising their right of self-determination. Could I address you with an easy conscience without welcoming a development of such historic significance on behalf of my Government, on behalf of my country? To us the right of self-determination is indivisible. Whoever, in accordance with the principles of the Charter, takes his destiny into his own hands, whoever seeks his freedom by peaceful means, will find us on his side.

I say this as a European, a member of a state which seeks its future in a European union. The old continent, its problems and its disputes, have been the source of conflicts which have brought immeasurable suffering on the whole world. Now for the first time nine European states have resolved to form through their co-operation an element of stability, of economic and social development in the world. The Federal Republic of Germany regards its participation in this huge task of unification as the very core of its policy.

III.

Not only was the principle of self-determination as a universal right alien to the League of Nations. Its aims were more limited. The prime objective of its members was to give governments a guideline for their conduct.

The United Nations stands for more ambitious goals: to promote and strengthen respect for human rights and for fundamental freedoms for all. This means more than the mere security of states, more than the mere regulation of their diplomatic relations. It concerns the beginning and the objective of any rational policy; it concerns man.

"The dignity of man is inviolable. To respect it and protect it is the duty of all state authority", says the Basic Law of the Federal Republic of Germany.

That is how we see our co-operation in your activities. Specifically speaking, this means for us that before any decision in any body of this organization is taken we shall first ask ourselves: what does this mean for the individual?

Every individual has the right freely to develop his personality and to live free from oppression. We therefore reject all racial discrimination and colonial rule. Just as of racial discrimination, the international covenants on economic, social and leged to lead a life in dignity.

The United Nations has already done much work in this field. The Universal Declaration of Human Rights, the international convention on the elimination of all forms of racial discrimination, the international covenants on economic, social and cultural rights and on civil and political rights are milestones for the realization of human rights. The Federal Republic of Germany has not hesitated to sign them.

But declarations and covenants are not enough in themselves. Having agreed on the texts and signed them, we cannot rest on our laurels. So long as human rights continue to be trampled underfoot, so long will we be bound by Article 1 of the Charter, which requires us to promote and encourage respect for human rights and for fundamental freedoms. This means doing everything in our power to ensure that these rights and freedoms are exercised in practice.

IV.

To many people this may seem utopian. You will ask what is freedom if all it means is the freedom to sleep under bridges? What is the use of the right of information where not even reading and writing can be taught, indeed where day in and day out millions of people have to struggle for a handful of rice? You are right. We cannot be content simply with fighting for rights and freedoms. This battle will be lost wherever we fail to secure man's material existence.

It is no coincidence that the Charter mentions international co-operation in solving problems of an economic, social or humanitarian character in one breath with respect for human rights. Universality means also universality of obligations. Only if we accept this can we remove the tensions which have their origin in social and economic disparities.

The United Nations employs over two thirds of its financial resources and its personnel to fight hunger, disease and ignorance. From the very beginning, we have been an ally in that battle, the only form of battle we can support. And I therefore assure you that wherever a battle is fought to liberate man from physical want and in defence of his right to worthy existence, there you will find the Federal Republic of Germany in the vanguard.

One constantly hears about the one, the other, the third world. I am not able to perceive the deeper meaning of such a distinction. Should we not rather declare our solidarity in the fight against poverty, together as citizens of one world?

If there is a policy which can achieve this, then it is the policy of détente. My Government has taken an active part in it. Détente is not meant to be exclusive; it is to benefit all. The reduction of confrontation can set free energies. These are to be used to overcome economic and social injustice.

V.

The League of Nations and the United Nations were both born of the suffering caused by two world catastrophes which claimed millions of innocent victims. "Never again war" was the general outcry after the First World War. This was the dominating theme of the dialogue between Briand and Stresemann.

War as a tool of national policies was renounced by more than 50 countries in the Briand-Kellogg Pact of 1928. But in spite of that, the Second World War broke out 11 years later. Does this mean that those endeavours to eradicate war were superfluous?

Article 1 of the United Nations Charter sets us the aim "to maintain international peace and security". Yet since its adoption many armed conflicts have taken place. True, there exists a precarious nuclear balance between the Great Powers. The threat of a Third World War does not hang over us. These days one speaks only of local conflicts, of minor wars. It is pointed out that destruction was not so widespread and the number of deaths smaller. But you will agree that this is cold comfort for those concerned. Wounds, loss of families, flight and expulsion — must they forever remain the fate of tens of thousands, indeed millions of people? Are they to be mankind's ever-present companions?

We must nip violence in the bud. With the Charter we have together renounced force while recognizing the right to self-defence. We must take that oath seriously. We must say clearly what we mean by the renunciation of force. And we should have the courage and strength to solve all our problems without force.

To us this is not just an empty phrase. The Federal Republic of Germany has renounced the use of force, not only in its own interest but from its sense of international responsibility, and it has done so particularly as regards the solution of its national problem. No political objective can justify force: no nationalism, no class warfare, no colonial or racial struggles, no utopia, no ideology.

In the United Nations we must work out that minimum of mutual understanding on this question and draw the practical consequences. Our world is imperfect. The Golden Age remains a beautiful dream. This does not mean resignation, nor the abandonment of our duty to do all that is necessary and possible every day in order to improve the state of our world. But it does mean recognizing the limits of human ability and not indulging in illusions which in the history of mankind have proved often enough to be the germ of violence.

Peace takes first place. The times have gone when the family of nations allowed a single state, or a political group, to upset the coexistence of the world family through the use of force. In our time, there is no longer any room for the law of the jungle.

Universality means both interdependence and mutual restriction. But let us not misunderstand that. Interdependence does not mean dependence on this or that Great Power or indeed on both. It is everyone's dependence on everyone, even dependence of the industrial countries on the developing countries.

Would anyone still maintain that he can measure all the consequences of a conflict? Who is still in a position to guarantee the local confinement of an armed conflict? In the past hundred years the world has taken a leap bigger than ever before. We must at long last recognize this fact, also in the world of politics. We shall have to find systems for the peaceful settlement of disputes if we wish to remain at that level of civilization which we are otherwise apt to speak of so proudly.

Only the United Nations can be the place where the now rampant use of force can be stopped. Only this Organization can by and by develop the formulas and take the decisions that will **ban force**.

Some will think this picture is too good to come true, that the United Nations could not or not yet fulfil this task. I can only repeat what President Kennedy said from this rostrum 12 years ago: "In the development of this Organization rests the only true alternative to war."

VI.

Mr. President,

The accession of the Federal Republic of Germany to the United Nations does not in itself make history. Yet to us Germans it is a historic day, especially as it has not been an easy step to take. I wish therefore all the more to express my warm thanks to you, Mr. President, and to all those who have welcomed us here today.

We do not come to you as strangers. The Federal Republic of Germany has for many years played a constructive part in all the Specialized Agencies of the United Nations. Its co-operation in the full organization will be borne by the same spirit. Where it is a question of international co-operation, of preserving peace, and of protecting the rights of man, there we shall always be found.

If there is anything we have learned from our own bitter experience then it is this: Man is the measure of all things.

14. Speech by the Federal Chancellor, Herr Willy Brandt, before the General Assembly of the United Nations, New York, 26 September 1973

I.

I speak to you as a German and as a European. To be more exact: my people live in two states, but they have not ceased to regard themselves as one nation. At the same time our part of Europe is as yet not much more than an economic community, but before the end of this decade it will grow into a European union.

We — the representatives of the Federal Republic of Germany — are no strangers here. We have long participated in the work of the Specialized Agencies. We maintain good relations with nearly all Member States. Here, at United Nations headquarters in New York, we have been shown much understanding in past years.

I wish to take this opportunity to thank our friends who have spoken up for us in this forum when we were not in a position to speak for ourselves. We shall not forget on whom we were able to rely.

But I would add that we have not come here to use the United Nations as a wailing-wall for the German problems or to make claims which we know cannot be met here in any case. Rather have we come to assume a share in the responsibility for world affairs on the basis of our convictions and within the framework of our possibilities.

The foundation of the United Nations and the deepest cut in German history were events which coincided in a dismal, though at the same time encouraging, manner. The recent history of my people is truly closely linked with the genesis of this world organization.

Since 1945, my people and the two German States have put a considerable distance behind them. And yet, our gratification over the fact that we have been given a friendly welcome here is mitigated by the division of Europe, which is glaringly manifest in Germany and which, almost three decades after the end of the war, still claims its victims.

Certainly, starting from that part of Europe which has been the source of so many tensions, we have initiated and developed a policy of understanding which was, and still is, to fill in the rifts left behind by the cold war.

We have, I feel, seen in the meantime that not only tension but also détente can be contagious.

As the Federal Republic of Germany we shall — as our Foreign Minister emphasized here last week in internationally binding terms — seek to create a state of peace in Europe in which the German people also can regain their unity in free self-determination. I say this knowing very well — with all respect — that the United Nations cannot really help us in this matter.

The two German states have learned that their inter-relationship, belonging as they do to different political groupings, and the problems resulting therefrom are today of greater importance than what is known as the "national question".

This applies to Europe in general.

In spite of their different social and political systems, bound by treaty and conviction to different alliances, the two German states have resolved to embark on a policy of peaceful neighbourhood, coexistence, and, we hope, co-operation.

We shall therefore try to spell out peaceful coexistence German-style. But in view of the thoroughness which is said to be a German characteristic, I cannot promise that this will always be easy.

More important: the consistent renunciation of force as a means of achieving aims, of furthering one's interests, and of settling differences, was the decisive factor needed to sow the seed of détente in the heart of Europe. The Treaties of Moscow and Warsaw, the Treaty on the basis of our relations with the GDR, the Quadripartite Agreement on Berlin, and soon, I hope, the treaty with Czechoslovakia, which has already been negotiated, are based on the renunciation of force.

Berlin, in particular, displays constructive opportunities. It no longer needs to be a source of tension in the heart of Europe. Berlin (West) can bank on its interests being looked after by the Federal Republic of Germany and on its protection being insured by the Three Powers who, being the supreme authority, remain directly responsible for the city's security and status. If there is anyone to appreciate what this change means it is most certainly the one who carried responsibility as Governing Mayor of Berlin during a critical phase of its history.

Renunciation of force was the first element of our peace policy, acceptance of the realities the other. Accepting things as they are has been a bitter pill for some, but it was necessary for the sake of peace, for the renunciation of force and the right attitude to reality are the two basic elements of concrete efforts to safeguard the peace.

This prepared the way for the next step. A new foundation is to be laid for security and co-operation in Europe.

The bilateral renunciation of force encourages us to enter a second, multilateral phase of European diplomacy, the purpose of which will be to produce a real change in the relationship between the European states on the basis of what has come about: it will do so through growing security from military threat, through intensive economic and technological exchanges, through human contacts, through better knowledge of each other. In other words, through a state of every-day peace.

It would indeed be a good thing if the work done in Helsinki and now being continued in Geneva could soon end with a conference convened at a level that is commensurate with the results achieved.

What I am talking about here will one day be understood as a significant experiment — how states can learn to master conflicts and eliminate the use of force. And if we even succeed, by means of confidence-building measures, in reducing the tremendous wastage that has been the outcome of mistrust between antagonistic systems we should then have set a historic example.

II.

Security cannot ensue from trust alone. This, too, is a reality. The reverse is also true. Confidence ensues from security.

A distinguished American spoke in this city of the impending "nuclear death dance". Well, the two superpowers who have in their hands by far the most powerful means of destruction recently signed an agreement which some are still trying to fathom but which is quite certainly intended to obviate the death dance.

That agreement between the United States and the Soviet Union is oriented to the principle of renunciation of force and the recognition of realities. It is, as I understand it, a piece of active coexistence and surely also a response to the demands made by the non-nuclear-weapon states at the Conference in Geneva in 1968.

On that occasion, the nuclear-weapon states were called upon to assume concrete obligations of their own. I still hold the view today that those who have power, particularly nuclear power, do not on that account have morality on their side, nor wisdom. Big dangers to mankind emanate from the big powers, not from the small.

A code of responsibilities should be defined to which the nuclear powers should subject themselves.

But if the two superpowers do not guarantee peace, who could do so in their place? The responsibility of neither of the two I have mentioned can today be assumed by anyone else, and neither of them can relinquish that responsibility.

Thus our world today finds its balance. But it cannot achieve that delicate balance without the specific weight of the People's Republic of China, Japan and the European Community. In such a system the specific rôle of Latin America, of the African countries, of the Asian subcontinent and the other partners in Asia becomes effective.

Power cannot be quantified at will. There is a limit to its expansion — a limit where power becomes transformed into impotence. But détente is not synonymous with disengagement, and it must by no means turn into disinterest if fresh tensions are not to be created.

At the end of the cold war there can in my view be neither conquerors nor conquered. Truly, peace, if it is to be secured, must not call for victory of the one and defeat of the other, but only the one victory of reason and moderation.

Incidentally, the use or threat of force should be renounced by all states — regardless of whether they possess nuclear weapons or not. If we have the determination and the luck, this can be achieved by means of an appropriate system of international agreements.

The only legitimate exception would remain the right to individual and collective self-defence as embodied in Article 51 of the United Nations Charter.

My Government is willing — and I wish to state this clearly — to help bring about an agreement which is being prepared in the Atlantic Alliance in order to make possible a balanced reduction of forces and weapons systems. This will not be possible overnight, but we must get down to the job seriously and consistently.

It is not only a question of giving Europe an opportunity. It is a question of giving the world an opportunity to create conditions which will permit us to turn our attention and to devote our national energies to the massive problems of tomorrow. If I may pose the question: If the world does not succeed in quelling force and violence and effectively proscribing it, how will it then be capable of resolving the problems of peace which — free and remote from force — will demand the employment of all our energies?

III

In a world in which we are all increasingly dependent on each other, a policy for peace must not stop on our own doorstep. Small steps can, as experience has shown, take us quite a long way.

To mediation and conciliation in disputes we attach special importance. The strengthening of international jurisdiction, the consolidation and further development of international law, require in our opinion the active attention of this Assembly.

The world is going through a process of rapid change. Many of its explosive problems and conflicts spread like epidemics owing to the increasing proximity of states and continents. Conflicts can, as shown by the terrorism of the present time which either does not want to use or is incapable of using political means, have unforeseeable consequences owing to the vulnerability of highly developed societies.

The catchphrase "preventive conflict research" — the prerequisite to "preventive diplomacy" — is born of the realization that it is no longer sufficient to investigate the so-called classical motives of disputes — territorial claims, ideological domination, nationalistic ambitions, the temptations of imperialist dominance, the flaws in security systems, disturbances of the balance of power.

I am not preaching an existence free from conflict and free from tension. That would be an anaemic illusion. What I have in mind are the fruitless negative conflicts which confirm to us every day that man, afraid of man, is capable of destroying himself. This opens up new and deeper areas of responsibility for conflict research. I wish to state in all due clarity that human distress is conflict. Where hunger prevails, there can be no peace in the long run. Where bitter poverty prevails, there can be no justice. Where a man's very existence is threatened for want of basic daily needs it is not permissible to speak of security. There must not be resignation in the face of destitution.

"Non-violence" is a concept we owe to the man who awakened a great member country of this Assembly; the force of that doctrine has not diminished. But the realities of today require it to be complemented by an opposite statement of fact, namely that there is violence through tolerance, intimidation through indolence, threat through passiveness, manslaughter through immobility. We must not stop on this threshold, for it may be the threshold between survival and decline.

I did not make the personal acquaintance of the President of that Latin American country who lost his life through the recent coup, but I wish to emphasize most strongly: this is not the answer. Or, if you like, unfortunately it can be. But then one day it will be said that reform could only come from revolution because changes were not otherwise accepted.

We are becoming more and more conscious of the limits of the globe. We must not ruthlessly exhaust its resources lest we condemn ourselves to slow suicide. We must not allow the globe's biological cycles to be poisoned any further.

It is surely no coincidence that man today, having seen his planet from out of the depth of space, is becoming conscious of the material and biological dependence of the inhabitants of this so very small "spaceship" Earth. Not only within individual countries but also on a world basis we shall — if we want to live in freedom and security — in future have to go without some things which, though economically profitable, are of questionable social value. And some of the things which appear to be economically unprofitable have become indispensable to the existence of a modern society.

I know that there is a tendency in some developing countries to regard the dearth of raw materials as a special kind of political opportunity, for it may here and there swing the pendulum in highly industrialized countries from surplus to shortage. But I say this: this is no ground for satisfaction; these are problems which concern us all — and not just those who come after us.

We must soberly appreciate that the resources of this world will only suffice to give posterity an existence worthy of the modern concept of the quality of life, if we keep population growth within responsible limits and unless we achieve a larger measure of social justice in the world.

The depressing food situation in many parts of the world requires us to draft a world food plan so that, if in any way possible, catastrophes can be prevented by means of an integrating strategy for the production of food and its distribution.

Let me emphasize: we must not only establish, and very quickly, what food is needed to keep large sections of mankind from hunger, but also whether states are prepared to accept the rules required to that end, and — at the same time — what raw materials are needed in order to guarantee the quality of our civilization and to improve it where possible.

Let me say quite frankly: morally it makes no difference whether a man is killed in war or is condemned to starve to death by the indifference of others. We shall have to decide to break with the ritualistic traditions; who proscribes war also has to proscribe hunger.

IV

The United Nations — built in response to the challenge of an almost total world war — is the mirror of an age-old dream of mankind. That dream closely matches the hopes of eternal peace cherished by the nations.

But the members having some thirty years of UN training here know at least as well as we newcomers that 1945 did not see the start of the millennium; unfortunately the United Nations has not — at least not yet — crystallized into the nucleus of a world government.

And yet, mankind has brought into this Assembly of Nations not only its good will but also many of its problems. There is not a member nation that left its history at home when it came here, indeed did not find its identity confirmed to some extent in this unwieldy design for a republic of nations.

I perceive here a convergence of the perspectives of all continents. To comprehend and to respect the diversity of life and its systems, to enable it to present itself freely, to set up standards to that end which are binding for all — this seems to me the mandate of the United Nations for civilization. That is our hope.

It is this very diversity which gives us the right to speak of a 'world society'. It is bound up in the tension between equal sovereignty and mutual dependence in this one, troubled world.

Some of the criticism directed at the United Nations sounds bitter and cynical, is filled with almost jubilant pessimism, as if it stemmed from a secret hope that the weaknesses of the Organization would refute the idea and the purpose. But setbacks in pursuit of an ideal do not necessarily prove that that ideal is wrong but often merely that the road to it could be better.

In this respect, many of the goals the Organization has set itself have not been achieved. I want to say this in all frankness. But we also know that this Organization was able to prevent a great deal of misery, misfortune and death.

Here in this institution arguments of reason and morality have time and again and untiringly been proclaimed, arguments which have prohibited a step into the abyss. The United Nations is not a clinic where our peoples can be cured of their neuroses by patient world doctors. Yet it can help to create more solidarity among nations.

That solidarity is the fundamental requirement of a world society, and it is the prerequisite to its survival.

I am not speaking of the utopian realm of the equality of all nations and of all men. But anyone who has never dreamt this dream of equality knows little of the will for justice which, beyound all barriers of continents, race and religion, is perhaps the true binding power among us humans.

There is solidarity, but not enough of it. I ask for more sympathy for the victims of armed conflicts that threaten to break out anew in this or that corner of the world. But neither should we forget the victims of non-war which sometimes can be just as brutal.

On the road to world citizenship we must practise solidarity. We shall not be able to speak of a humane world order until the principle of justice is universally understood.

Permit me to say on behalf of the Federal Republic of Germany that we shall support United Nations resolutions aimed at liquidating the anachronistic remnants of colonialism. This applies not least to our neighbouring continent of Africa.

Without any addition and without any reservation I declare that we condemn racism as inhuman and as the cause of the most terrible crimes. Our own history has been a bitter experience on that score.

Moreover, those who take their place in this Assembly must also adopt a position on the moral aspects of international coexistence even when their own national interests are not directly affected. In this process they come face to face with two recognised principles both of which serve the cause of peace:

The first is the principle of non-interference in the internal affairs of others. The other is the principle of the universality of human rights. Not only states but also individual citizens can invoke the fundamental rights embodied in the United Nations Charter. It is peace that benefits if people and information can move as freely as possible across boundaries.

I would add that if we speak our mind on violations of individual human rights, on the suppression of the freedom to express critical opinions, on the artificial barriers at national frontiers to the exchange of people and information, the decisive criterion for that attitude will not be whether the offender is an ally or one with whom we have friendly contractual ties, or whether it is a less friendly power. What matters is that we do not remain indifferent on these questions — even if some details should be hard to assess.

A policy of peace, solidarity and renunciation of force is indivisible. The conflict in South East Asia has not yet burnt itself out, the smouldering conflict in the Middle East has not yet been diffused. In both cases the main thing is that those concerned should talk, not shoot.

I wish to stress our interest in a peaceful settlement of the conflict in the Middle East.

My Government shares the hope that the international community will not relinquish the possibilities of mediation. It also feels that it is primarily direct peace talks between the Arab countries concerned and Israel that will best secure a balance of the elementary interests of both sides.

The struggle for peace, the fight against misery require us to recognize that in the one world we live in our fate is after all indivisible. Here, too, mankind is therefore under compulsion to establish solidarity. Where else than in this United Nations Organization should we be able to discuss freely new forms of vital co-operation?

No nation should live at the expense of another. Anyone who refuses to accept this principle is instrumental in our having to pay dearly for it.

National egoism is no shield. On the contrary, it is an obstacle to that very solidarity which, in the last resort, is the best guardian of natural and legitimate national interests as well.

We should not speak of "young" and "old" nations. It is more realistic to distinguish between young and old nationalisms.

Ours, in Europe, are old, although a century or two are only a couple of short breaths in history. But believe me, the wild dream that the destiny of a nation can be fulfilled only in unbridled nationalism has in our case completely faded away. We learnt from painful experience that there have to be more rational, more reliable forms for the lives of nations — and that such forms actually exist: the system of good-neighbourliness.

The countries of Western Europe have resolved to establish the first regional community that is more than a classical alliance and at the same time does not imply that its members subject themselves to a set of ideological rules. Our aim is to achieve in this decade the union of our economies, our currencies, our social systems and our foreign policies, and — as dictated by the signs of our time — of our security.

The membership of the Federal Republic which I represent also strengthens the presence of Europe in the United Nations. We are sure it will also be of benefit to others.

The Western European Community can become an example of economic achievement and social balance. It establishes itself as a power without imperial pretensions. The European Union will be a power of peace and will be outward-looking.

The Federal Republic of Germany had declared in its constitution its willingness to transfer sovereign rights to supra-national organizations and it has placed international law above national law and made it directly applicable. This expresses the realization that the sovereignty of the individual and of nations can only be secured in larger communities, that the meaning and fulfilment of history can no longer be attributed to the nation-state.

Thus I end my speech with a plea: let us all together be on our guard against making a taboo of a concept which I regard as perhaps the most dubious legacy of European history: nationalism, which has claimed millions and millions of human lives, and under whose banner fertile country has been devastated, thriving cities destroyed, peoples exterminated, and a whole civilization — our own — nearly swept away.

Europe has ceased to pretend that it is the measure of things for the rest of the world. But it has occasion to warn the nations of the world about the great error which almost brought about its destruction: negative nationalism. We have to a large extent shaken off that hypnosis.

The nation no longer finds its security in isolated sovereignty. In actual fact isolation creates dependencies which have ceased to have anything to do with enlightened sovereignty. We need the larger community which gives us peace, security and hence freedom.

That is perhaps not yet "the world free from war", not yet "the worldwide rule of reason" enunciated by the President of the United States on 26 June 1945 after the proclamation of the United Nations Convention in San Francisco's opera house. But mankind must not allow itself to become paralyzed in the face of gigantic, seemingly insoluble problems. What we need now is a programme of new confidence in man's abilities.

This is my plea:

1. Let us courageously and jointly venture forth on a new road to the great goals of eliminating conflicts, bringing armaments under control, making peace safer.

2. Let us courageously and jointly fight for universal recognition of the renunciation of force as a principle for the solution of political problems.

3. Let us courageously and jointly — and I hope we will be many — work untiringly to ensure that human rights and fundamental freedoms are respected and may be exercised all over the world.

4. Let us courageously and jointly — and I hope we will be many — fight to defend the right of nations freely to decide their own destiny, to ensure that the remnants of colonialism are removed and all forms of racism banned.

5. Let us courageously and jointly promote the further development of international law — also by an effective convention against terrorism.

6. Let us courageously and jointly do what is necessary to sustain the viability of the world we live in by protecting the natural environment and — partly by intensifying and widening scientific exchanges — securing for mankind conditions of a quality that will make life worth living.

7. Let uns courageously and jointly — in addition to our endeavours to foster the further development of world trade — make fresh efforts to intensify economic co-operation and development, and above all, let us in this way combine all our energies and declare war irrevocably on hunger around the world.

Distinguished delegates, colleagues and friends,

man's ability to apply his faculty of reason has made the United Nations possible. Man's propensity for being irrational makes it necessary. Reason will have won the field if one day all states and regions come to live and work together as world neighbours in accordance with the principles of the United Nations.

That will not be in my lifetime, but I want to do what I can to make that possible. And I exhort us all to give every assistance we can, progressing step by step, to ease the task of future generations.

15. Speech by the Federal Minister for Foreign Affairs, Herr Hans-Dietrich Genscher, during an Official Visit to the Federal Republic of Germany by the UN Secretary-General, Mr. Kurt Waldheim

The Federal Minister for Foreign Affairs delivered the following speech at a dinner at Schloss Gymnich on 4 February 1975 in honour of the UN Secretary-General and Mrs. Waldheim:

Madam, Mr. Secretary-General,

It is a special honour for me to be able to welcome you here in Bonn together with the members of your party following the two meetings we had in New York last year. Your visit affords us an opportunity to continue our exchange of views on a number of major international problems and events, on the participation of the Federal Republic of Germany in the work of the United Nations, and on problems concerning the United Nations itself.

Since our last meeting in New York major developments and events have taken place which require careful analysis and discussion. We shall have an opportunity for this tomorrow. The first official visit by the Secretary-General of the United Nations to the Federal Republic of Germany is an outstanding political event. It is taking place almost 30 years after the establishment of the United Nations.

When the Federal Republic of Germany became a member of the World Organization just under 18 months ago, the necessary inner-German and international requirements had been met. Above all, the Federal Governments right to represent Berlin-West in international organizations, especially the United Nations, was reaffirmed.

But the Federal Republic has long been associated with the United Nations in many ways. It has based its constitution on principles that are embodied in the United Nations Charter and form the basis of every democratic system. We can state that these principles hare become more than mere declarations in the Federal Republic of Germany; they are constitutional reality.

The Federal Republic of Germany has made the purposes and principles of the United Nations the objectives of its policies. It has played an active part in nearly all spheres where this has been possible without membership of the UN organization, and can therefore claim to have felt at home within the United Nations system for a very long time.

The United Nations arose out of the debris of a world-wide catastrophe which was the result of nationalistic arrogance. It was more than a new international organization. It brought forward the idea of international co-operation based on peace, renunciation of force, and respect for human rights.

The United Nations has made a major contribution to the safeguarding of peace and the promotion of international co-operation. But we realise that the great ideas that inspired the organization's founders have not been achieved. Organizing international co-operation world-wide remains a permanent task which still faces us today and the solution of which has become more urgent than ever before.

Mr. Secretary-General, at the beginning of your introduction to the last annual report you spoke of an aptitude test which should also be applied to the United Nations. You said that one of the most important tests of a political institution's attitude was its ability to accept challenges and changes without relinquishing its fundamental principles and aims.

The World Organization has succeeded in adopting a pragmatic approach to the far-reaching changes of the post-war era and in adapting itself where this has been necessary on account of the growth in the number of Members and the emergence of new tasks.

The United Nations of 1975 is no longer the United Nations of the founder nations, but it remains pledged to its purposes and principles.

Today, the United Nations faces a new test. The imbalance of economic development, the underdevelopment of large sections of the world population, the supply of energy and food, are among the most acute problems which the community of nations has to solve.

The United Nations is today trying to find the solutions to these problems, and today in particular the United Nations must remain capable of meeting new challenges. But at the same time it must not leave its basic foundations. The proven fundamental rules of co-operation between sovereign states in an interdependent world must be respected in the world organization.

We should see the dangers which would arise for the organization's ability to act effectively if the United Nations forum were no longer to be governed by the spirit of conciliation but by the will to assert aims unilaterally.

The Federal Republic of Germany has excellent bilateral relations with the Third World. And it is the spirit of bilateral relations that influences our will for co-operation within the United Nations. Both sides should invest the capital of bilateral relations in constructive co-operation within the United Nations.

It is a question of the United Nations itself, of the realization that in a world in which we are all dependent upon one another, it can only render its contribution to the solution of common problems if the will for co-operation, for negotiation and fair compromise, remains intact on all sides.

Mr. Secretary-General, you pointed out recently, and rightly so, that we should not only see the flaws of the World Organization but must at the same time admit that there is no alternative to the international co-operation which the United Nations makes possible.

And I am glad that we have you, Mr. Secretary-General, the determined champion of international co-operation, with us here this evening. We admire and respect your untiring work and unqualified commitment to the common task.

Mr. Secretary-General, I hope that your work will continue to bring success and extend to you my best wishes for your personal well-being.

16. Speech by Herr Hans-Dietrich Genscher,
Federal Minister for Foreign Affairs
before the Seventh Special Session
of the General Assembly of the United Nations, New York,
2 September 1975

I

The Seventh Special Session of the General Assembly of the United Nations on Development and International Economic Co-operation assembles against the background of the gravest economic recession since 1930. For the first time in the postwar era international economic growth has lost its momentum and world trade and the world social product will probably decline. For the first time the development process in many developing countries threatens to be brought to a standstill owing to the pressure of mounting balance-of-payments deficits.

Lack of growth and unemployment put a strain on many industrialized countries. They are the result of worldwide inflation which to no small degree is due to the fact that it was preceded, especially in the industrialized countries, by an inflation of demand on the social product. We spent more than we earned.

It will require close co-operation of all countries to achieve continuous real growth for the international economy again. Federal Chancellor Schmidt has repeatedly emphasized the need for a co-ordinated approach and co-ordinated action to overcome the recession and has made proposals to this end: suggestions and proposals which refer not only to the efforts within the European Community but aim at worldwide co-ordinated action. Last week the Federal Government adopted a programme which combines additional public expenditure for investments with structural budgetary improvements on the revenue and expenditure side.

We all know what it will mean if we fail to master the recession: growth and development are the foundation not only of our economic stability but also of the stability of our social and political structures, and in the final analysis of the stability of international peace.

The recession has brought home to all of us the extent of the economic interdependence of states. Here we see a consequence of the unparalleled growth of the world economy: the equally unparalleled increase in the dependence of individual national economies on developments and decisions beyond their borders.

Today, interdependence also marks the relations between industrialized and developing countries: If the industrialized countries need the commodities and the oil of the developing countries, they for their part need the capital, the technology and the grain of the industrialized countries. And they need each other's markets for their products.

Out of the total exports of the developing countries 75 percent are absorbed by the OECD countries alone; 20 percent constitute exchanges among the developing countries themselves; 5 percent go to countries with centrally planned economies. This means: The growth rates of the industrialized countries with free market economies and those of the developing countries are inseparably linked with each other. Deceleration of growth in the OECD countries cuts back imports from the developing countries and thus automatically slows down their rate of economic growth. If any evidence of this were required then the present situation is a perfect case in point. So both sides can either expand together or they must stagnate together. If one side ignores the other side's chances of growth, it jeopardizes its own growth as well. And if one side, by the policy it pursues, were even to impair the other side's growth, it would finish by harming itself.

Translated into practical politics, this means that no side can gain by asserting claims that are incompatible with the aim of continuous world economic growth. A redistribution of existing wealth in a stagnating economy will not get us any farther; in the long term, development can be speeded up with lasting effect only within an expanding world economy.

In an interdependent world the inevitable outcome of confrontation and selfish unilateral action is that in the end all will be the losers. Interdependence therefore compels us to co-operate and to accept the common responsibility. But at the same time it holds out one big chance: by co-operation we can today achieve together economic growth and social progress for all. Therefore, today and in the future, co-operation must be the basis of human co-existence.

The most hopeful aspect of the current situation is that, unlike in 1930, governments are aware of these implications. This has been amply proved by the unbroken succession of international discussions and conferences on economic affairs over the past two years. Economics have moved to the forefront of international diplomacy. The reconciliation of conflicting economic interests has become the test of statesmanship in foreign affairs.

The OECD countries have worked out rules for co-operative action in the recession. They have undertaken in particular not to resort to trade restrictions in spite of grave balance-of-payments difficulties.

The two years of the recession have produced a first forward-looking example for co-operation between industrialized and developing countries in a spirit of interdependence: the Convention of Lomé between the European Community and 46 African, Caribbean and Pacific states. Never before have such a large group of industrialized and developing countries launched an attempt, on the basis of complete equality, to lay down the framework for future co-operation.

The Convention translates into reality new concepts:

— It gives the ACP states practically free access to the European market, while the European Community itself will forego reverse preferences. This concept of a "unilateral free trade area", which the Federal Republic of Germany has strongly advocated from the very beginning, makes allowance for the different levels of development of the two sides.

— Furthermore, it sets up a stabilization scheme for commodity export earnings of the contracting parties from Africa, the Caribbean and the Pacific.

— And finally, it embarks on new roads in the promotion of industrial co-operation.

The task now ahead of us is to transfer the spirit of common responsibility, as expressed in the Convention of Lomé, to the worldwide negotiations on co-operation between industrialized and developing countries. The task before us is to create a more balanced and more equitable structure for co-operation in an interdependent world economy.

189

Signor Rumor, the Italian Foreign Minister, speaking yesterday on behalf of the nine member states of the European Community, identified himself with this objective and promised the active and constructive support of the Community in achieving it.

The Government ot the Federal Republic of Germany will stand by that promise.

Co-operation between industrialized and developing countries has a twofold objective: For one thing we must lead the world economy out of the recession and back onto the path of real growth. National efforts alone are no longer enough. The synchronization of business cycles rather means that growth for one's own national economy and for the world economy as a whole can now only be achieved through joint efforts and close co-ordination. Secondly, and this is of decisive importance, we will have to map out that path in such a way that it will take the developing countries more rapidly than in the past to higher levels of development. The world economy must not merely grow, it must grow in such a way that the gap between industrialized and developing countries will steadily diminish. Bridging that gap is the big task of our time. Today and tomorrow we will be judged by our readiness and ability to tackle and master that task.

Whether or not we shall solve that task will depend in the final analysis also on whether the developing countries themselves make every effort to mobilize their productive forces and make efficient use of them. But the industrialized countries as well can, and must provide assistance in all fields and, together with the developing countries, mould the world economic system in such a way that it will help speed up development as much as possible.

Our debate centres on the further development of the world economic order. Its aim is an equitable balance of interests, an order which fully integrates the developing countries into the world economy and finally gives them the place which is due to them.

Further development presupposes the preservation of what has been achieved. Nobody should overlook one thing: the order which emerged in the early post-war years formed the basis for an unparalleled growth of world production and trade, and what is more, it has enabled not only the industrialized countries but also the developing countries to achieve that growth. Between 1960 and 1974, that is, since the beginning of the first Development Decade, the developing countries achieved an annual growth rate of almost 6 percent, higher, that is, than the growth rate of the industrialized countries in that period.

But the aim of reducing the gap in per-capita incomes as between rich countries and poor has not been achieved. The ground that was made up by the more vigorous growth of the Third World has been overcompensated by the population explosion. The efforts of many developing countries to slow down the population growth will surely have a positive effect in the medium term. At the same time, however, we will have to make every effort to bring about an even faster economic growth in the developing countries.

Furthermore, the growth rate of 6 percent represents an average rate which hides the huge disparities between the rates of individual developing countries. The least developed countries in particular have been unable to make the best possible use of the opportunities for growth. This, too, must change. However, the solution of these tasks lies in the improved functioning of market mechanisms, not in the flight to worldwide, bureaucratic dirigism.

It is the task of the world economic order to co-ordinate the division of labour among more than one hundred and fifty states — sovereign states with different economic systems. This complex task can only be solved with the help of the steering principle of the free market. It would therefore be utopian, and dangerous at that, to try and solve it by international dirigism. Any attempt to do so could only end up in paralysis and a wastage of resources.

When we were faced in the Federal Republic of Germany with the task of rebuilding the economy out of the debris of war, there was also a discussion whether we should take the road of the free market economy or whether, in view of the desperate conditions at the time, dirigistic solutions were to be preferred. The fact that we have today a highly developed economy and a balanced social structure is not least due to the decision we then took in favour of a free market economy. It is largely as a result of that experience that the Federal Government is without qualification in favour of reforming the world economic system, but it warns against paralyzing the efficiency of the world economy by dirigistic experiments. That would deal a blow to both industrialized and developing countries.

Reform of the existing free market system: This alone can be the common denominator for our endeavours, irrespective of the economic systems the member countries of the United Nations have accepted at home. For this order alone respects the sovereignty of all countries and this order alone makes worldwide partnership on a basis of equality possible. The reform task is to preserve the efficiency of the market, but at the same time to link it with effective help for the weak. We must prevent abuse of the market by the powerful and provide greater opportunities for the weak.

What we must achieve is a world market economy which meets the requirements of a just reconciliation of interests. To get there we need a coherent programme of reforms which are in line with market requirements. What does this programme look like? I mention the most important elements:

1. We must open the markets of the industrialized countries more than in the past to products of the developing countries; this applies in particular to processed products.

2. We must stabilize the commodity export earnings of the individual developing countries; this applies in particular to the least developed countries and those most seriously affected by the crisis.

3. We must prevent excessive commodity price fluctuations.

4. We must, in the interest of the smooth functioning and the growth of the world economy, ensure a continuous commodity supply.

5. We must accelerate the process of industrialization in the developing countries by means of industrial and technological co-operation.

6. We must facilitate and improve the transfer of technology from the industrialized to the developing countries.

7. We must vigorously increase food production in the developing countries.

8. We must increase with all means available to us the flow of capital to the developing countries particularly to the poorest among them.

9. We must shape the international monetary system in such a way that it can be conducive to the growth of world trade and the world economy and to the preservation of monetary value.

II

With your permission, Mr. President, I would like to enlarge a little on these points.

Opening of the markets

The objective of opening up the markets of the industrialized countries is to secure for the developing countries an increasing share in world trade.

The Federal Government therefore advocates the reduction of tariff and non-tariff barriers to trade, and, within the framework of the European Community, is seeking at the current GATT negotiations still better access for developing countries to the import markets of industrialized countries. I would point out in this connection that in terms of per-capita imports from developing countries, my country is among the leading market economy countries, and that its imports are ten times greater than the corresponding per-capita imports of the countries with centrally planned economies.

The most dynamic sector of world trade is the exchange of industrial goods. This, therefore, is where the developing countries have the greatest opportunities for increasing their exports, and it is here in particular that the markets of the industrialized countries should be made even more accessible to the developing countries. It is no longer justifiable that the existing tariffs in the industrialized countries are, in spite of many improvements, generally lower for commodities than for manufatcures and semi-manufactures. This hampers particularly the export of manufactured products from the developing countries. One of our primary objectives, therefore, must be to reduce these progressively graded tariffs. At the same time the preferences for imports of industrial goods from developing countries will have to be further extended and improved.

The Federal Republic of Germany was, and still is, a driving force for opening markets to processed products from the developing countries. Having a dynamic economy it sees the intensification of the international division of labour as being in its own interest as well. That is why the Federal Republic of Germany has always tried to set an example in creating openings for industrial goods from the developing countries. In 1973, for instance, its imports of manufactures and semi-manufactures from the developing countries increased by no less than 56 percent. They at the same time increased much faster than the corresponding imports from industrialized countries. The share of the developing countries in the Federal Republic of Germany's total imports of manufactured goods doubled bettween 1972 and 1974. Opening up the markets in this fashion not only for commodities but particularly for manufactured goods from the Third World, is, in the Federal Government's view, one of the most effective ways in which the industrialized countries can help the developing countries. All industrialized countries, irrespective of the economic system to which they belong, should make every possible effort to achieve this aim. The European Community was the first economic region to introduce a system of general tariff preferences for processed goods from developing countries, a system which it has constantly expanded and improved. The Community is resolved to continue this policy consistently and feels that the system of preferences should be extended beyond 1980.

Stabilization of commodity export earnings

Most developing countries depend on commodity exports for their foreign exchange earnings and their revenue. Thus stability of and increases in commodity export earnings are vital to these countries. The Federal Republic of Germany appreciates the importance of this aim and supports it.

The Federal Government considers it necessary to assist especially the least developed and the most seriously affected countries in achieving more stable export earnings. During a special meeting of the Federal Cabinet on June 9, 1975, it submitted therefore a proposal, which in the meantime has been accepted by the International Monetary Fund, that part of the gold reserves of the Fund be sold and the proceeds used to provide these countries with low-cost loans in case of a decline in their earnings from commodity exports. The Federal Government regards the provision of one sixth of the IMF gold as a first step in the right direction. In view of the problems facing us it does not yet consider this volume to be sufficient and will therefore advocate its expansion.

Flexibility in using this instrument would increase its effectiveness. This applies both to the terms and the maturity of loans and to the possibility under special circumstances to waive the debt altogether.

Measures designed to stabilize earnings have the advantage with regard to commodities exported by both developing and industrialized countries of permitting a selective application. They benefit the developing countries exclusively, thus avoiding the paradoxical effect of commodity-exporting industrialized countries receiving additional income at the expence of commodity-importing countries, whether industrialized or developing.

In addition, the Federal Government advocates quantitative and qualitative improvements of the present system of compensatory financing operated by the International Monetary Fund.

Prevention of excessive price fluctuations

Apart from the stabilization of commodity earnings the Federal Government also supports the aim of preventing excessive commodity price fluctuations. This is in the interest of consumers and producers alike. The Federal Government is therefore willing to envisage international commodity agreements in cases where

— they are capable of avoiding excessive price fluctuations in a commodity market,

— they keep prices at levels apt to balance supply and demand in the longer term, and

— there is a reasonable cost/benefit ratio.

The Federal Republic of Germany is a member of all existing commodity agreements and has played an active part in all negotiations leading to them. My Government will continue to do so. It feels that such agreements should be made as effective as possible and therefore welcomes it that there is now hope of a larger number of states acceding to them.

The objective of our efforts is to arrive at prices that are remunerative to producers and reasonable to consumers, thus making for long-term equilibrium between expanding supply and expanding demand. The Federal Government accepts rising price trends in the long term provided they are in line with developments of supply and demand. But it would be sceptical about any attempt of fixing commodity prices artificially above long-term equilibrium prices. Such excessive prices imply overproduction and can therefore only be maintained by restricting production and exports. In worldwide economic terms such a non-utilization, indeed dismantling, of capacities makes no sense considering the world shortage.

With most of the commodities under consideration it also seems doubtful whether excessive prices would in any case be worthwhile for producers in the longer term, for they would mean: a slackening of demand, replacement by substitute products, and the appearance of new producers in the market—and this often means new producers from the industrialized countries in particular. The outcome for the original producers could then be falling instead of rising export earnings, and for the world's economy as a whole a transition from low-cost to high-cost production.

And finally the developing countries, too, import commodities, directly or indirectly in the form of manufactures. Conversely, in the case of many commodities industrialized countries are also exporters, indeed sometimes the principal exporters. Consequently, a transfer of resources by means of excessively high commodity prices would also be a burden on developing countries, whilst at the same time considerably benefiting some industrialized countries.

These problems would also arise in all their intensity with regard to plans for tying commodity prices to the prices developing countries have to pay for their imports, in other words by means of an index. For, after all, this, too, would be an attempt to fix prices independently of the long-term market equilibrium price. And on top of this we would have additional problems: the task of finding a fair index formula is, even in theory, insoluble. In practice any attempt to enforce the index price would be followed by a flood of government controls.

Furthermore, a global index formula would cement the relative prices of individual commodities irrespective of the development of productivity.

Taking all these points into consideration, the Federal Government is convinced that the aim of increasing the commodity export earnings of developing countries should be achieved not by administered prices but via the workings of the free market: in other words, by increasing productivity and hence profits, by boosting sales, by playing a bigger part in marketing processes, by entering the initial processing stages, and ultimately by means of a determined diversification policy where the producer country, because of the cost, can no longer produce goods at market equilibrium prices.

Here lie considerable, still unused opportunities for many developing countries. The Federal Government is prepared to help them effectively in making use of them. It will in particular encourage the local processing of commodities.

Securing the commodity supply

Even in the present situation of stagnation and declining commodity consumption we must not lose sight of the problem of ensuring commodity supplies. For the expanding world economy and rapid population growth lead to increasing commodity consumption. We must, therefore, plan well ahead in order to ensure the availability of adequate production capacities. This includes exploration of new raw material resources, developing these resources and establishing an infrastructure to bring these commodities to the market. This task of ensuring a continuous commodity supply can only be solved by co-operation between industrialized and developing countries. Co-operation means partnership. Co-operation prevents commodities of a developing country from being exploited by another country without the country of origin thereby being actually promoted in its development.

For a number of commodities, and not only grain, the problem of continuous commodity supplies could indeed become the crucial problem of the future. The question of how to finance and organize the necessary co-operation between industrialized and developing countries and of finding new and appropriate forms of co-operation should, in the opinion of the Federal Government, receive due attention in the discussions on commodities between industrialized and developing countries. Another topic of such talks must be the question of how a parallel development of commodity production and industrialization can be attained in the developing countries. Without such a parallel development those countries are constantly faced with the danger of serious economic setbacks, especially when their raw material resources dry up or when technological developments make their particular commodity superfluous.

Accelerating the process of industrialization

At the second UNIDO conference in Lima, the Federal Government supported the aim of speeding up the process of industrialization in the developing countries. It will play an active part in the pursuit of that objective.

The industrialization of developing countries involves changes in the structure of the world economy. For structurally weak branches in the industrialized countries this often means a painful process of adaptation. Every government must try to ensure that it takes place in an orderly fashion. My Government has always been convinced that structural changes brought about by the market situation should not be held up by subsidies to keep ailing industries alive. The process should rather be eased by helping manpower and investors to transfer from structurally weak branches to those that have good future prospects. I need not emphasize the fact that this task is much easier for an expanding economy than for a recessive one. Here, too, the growth of the industrialized countries and achieving the aims of the developing countries are closely connected.

Improved transfer of technology

As regards the industrialization of the Third World and the acceleration of the development process, the Federal Government is conscious of the major role which science and technology will have to assume in order to achieve these objectives.

The Federal Government is therefore endeavouring to strengthen the scientific-technological infrastructure of the developing countries on the basis of partnership within a bilateral and multilateral framework. The purpose of these measures is to give the developing countries a greater capacity to absorb technology and in particular to enable them to develop it creatively and to adapt it to their own economic situation. In many spheres it will be necessary to replace the capital-intensive production methods of the industrialized countries with equally modern but labour-intensive methods.

The Federal Government is also seeking to improve the general conditions for the transfer of technology. Within the framework of UNCTAD it will play a constructive part in the elaboration of an international code of conduct for the transfer of technology.

195

Frequently, the speed-up of both the process of industrialization and of the transfer of technology can be brought about solely through industrial co-operation between developing countries and companies from industrialized countries with a market economy. In some cases the developing countries, too, will want such firms to have a financial interest in joint ventures. The Federal Government is promoting industrial co-operation by granting financial assistance and offering tax concessions, and also by assuming guarantees. But what really matters in the final analysis are the conditions which the developing countries themselves create for such co-operation. The two crucial requirements are mutual trust and the long-term assurance that such co-operation has the backing of law, and that means both sides must be able to bank on the safeguards of international law. Creating forms of industrial co-operation which meet both these conditions is of decisive importance for the aim of development.

I recall in this connection a proposal which Helmut Schmidt, who was at the time Federal Minister of Finance and is now Federal Chancellor, made as early as 1974: he proposed the elaboration of guidelines for the activities of multinational corporations and for their co-operation with the governments of the host countries. The necessary work on these guidelines should be taken up soon.

Increase of food production

Raising food production in the developing countries must be a priority aim especially for countries with a food deficit.

According to estimates put before the World Food Conference, the food requirements of the developing countries will increase by 3.6 percent a year, whereas their agricultural production will increase by only 2.6 percent a year. In view of this alarming prospect, industrialized and developing countries must co-operate intensively to ensure, as a short-term aim, that the present already inadequate food supply situation in the Third World at least does not grow worse. The food problems of the deficit countries can only be resolved with lasting effect by helping them expand their own food production. The Federal Government therefore gives priority to aid designed to boost food production. In addition, it will continue to provide food aid.

The Federal Government also identifies itself with the principles, proposed by the FAO, for an International Undertaking for World Food Security. It therefore advocates the co-ordination within the framework of international arrangements of national grain stocks already existing or to be created in order to help meet foreseeable major shortages of supply. An essential prerequisite for world food security is that the expected harvests and the import requirements of staple foods are known in good time, for only then can specific steps be taken to prevent supply bottlenecks. For this reason the Federal Government has agreed to participate in the world-wide information and early-warning system for food and agriculture. It would like to see the Seventh Special Session of the General Assembly call upon all nations to do the same, and also to sign the International Undertaking for World Food Security.

Increase in the transfer of capital

Even if future development strategy attaches even greater importance to trade than in the past, direct transfers of capital will continue to be an indispensable and central element of co-operation between industrial and developing countries.

The Federal Government realizes that an increased flow of capital — from both official and private sources — is absolutely essential if the developing countries are to achieve the necessary growth rates. This applies quite particularly to the least developed countries which, as a rule, will derive less value from improvements in the field of trade than those countries that are richly endowed with major commodities or who already have an industrial basis.

The official aid afforded by the Federal Republic also increases in 1974, which was a difficult year. The Federal Government will also in future live up to its responsibilities. But we must all realize that both for the Federal Republic of Germany and the other industrialized countries, this largely depends on our overcoming the world recession.

The value of the aid commitments of the Federal Republic of Germany, thanks to the Federal Government's determined efforts to maintain economic stability, has remained stable. This is indicated by the index of German export prices, which this year has risen only little. Thus the steps we have taken to maintain stability benefit the developing countries as well. In the past two years the oil-producing countries have emerged as new, major donors. The mobilization of investment capital from these countries can play an essential part in the efforts to increase overall aid. Co-operation between oil-producing and industrialized countries embracing the joint financing, planning and implementation of projects could increase the effectiveness of that contribution. In some countries initial formulas for such triangular co-operation have already been elaborated and we would like to see co-operation in this respect intensified.

Apart from increasing the volume of capital transfers we must also improve the terms. Loans made available by the Federal Republic of Germany carried an average interest rate of 1.85 percent in 1974. The money made available to the countries most seriously affected by the economic crisis is provided by the Federal Government on IDA terms, in other words at an interest rate of 0.75 percent for a period of 50 years.

Restructuring of the international monetary system

As seen by the Government of the Federal Republic of Germany, the restructuring of the international monetary system is a major problem. It would like to see the special drawing rights within the framework of the International Monetary Fund become more the focal point of the monetary system and the role of national currencies and gold as reserve currencies correspondingly reduced.

International monetary co-operation must be based on a balanced distribution of rights and responsibilities of all states. The Federal Government therefore welcomes the proposed doubling of the oil countries quota of the International Monetary Fund from five to ten per cent. This corresponds to the considerably increased importance and responsibility of these countries for the world monetary system.

The increase of that quota would be accompanied by a reduction of the quota of the industrialized countries; the influence of the developing countries as a whole in the International Monetary Fund will thus increase.

Moreover, the Federal Government will contribute towards subsidizing interests under the IMF oil facility. To the oil facility itself the *Deutsche Bundesbank* is contributing 300 million special drawing rights.

III

Mr. President, more balanced and more equitable economic relations between developing and industrialized countries cannot be achieved at one full swoop at one conference. This is a process which will continue to dominate international politics in the years ahead.

The Federal Government participates in this process with the sincere readiness for partnership and co-operation. It welcomes and promotes the dialogue between industrialized countries and countries of the Third World with the aim of achieving an equitable balance of interests. We want to proceed beyond this dialogue to joint practical action. Let us make use of all our possibilities, our bilateral relations, let us make use of the co-operation in international organizations, let us use all contacts between our peoples in order to overcome the errors of the past and to bring about world-wide a better order of economic relations. Within the framework of that order we must all consider ourselves as equal partners. Let us realize, above all, that in a state of mutual dependence what is important is not only one's own advantage and one's own prosperity but the advantage and the prosperity of others as well.

Economic power has again and again been abused just as political and military power has been abused. It is the task of the United Nations to overcome such abuse in all its forms. He who possesses power must not also be at liberty to use it unrestrictedly. Therefore a world economic order based on fair co-operation requires clear rules and above all the possibilities for enforcing them.

The economic capacity of all states on earth taken together, no matter how big it may be, is still not unlimited. Perhaps it is just big enough to solve the severe problems of mankind at the end of the 20th century, that means to overcome underdevelopment, hunger, disease and poverty. But one thing is certain: Our combined economic strenght will not be enough if the individual states use their economic potential against each other instead of for each other's benefit and for a joint peaceful development. In this Special General Assembly we hold the key for better co-operation. We must not let that chance go by unused.

17. Statement on Disarmament and Arms Control

The Permanent Representative of the Federal Republic of Germany to the United Nations, Ambassador Rüdiger von Wechmar, made the following statement on disarmament and arms control on November 5, 1975, to the First Committee of the General Assembly of the United Nations.

The First Committee is once again required to take stock of endeavours in the field of disarmament and arms control and to put forward constructive proposals for achieving further progress. Obviously we shall not achieve that aim by eloquent speeches, largely oriented towards propaganda goals. On the contrary, what is needed is a sober analysis of the situation, and the ability to perceive what is possible in the existing political circumstances and to pursue it resolutely.

We cannot be satisfied with the progress achieved so far.

True, it has been possible to conclude a number of important multilateral and bi-lateral agreements and to give effect to them. For instance, certain regions have been spared from the arms race. The ban on the use of bacteriological and chemical weapons established by the Geneva Protocol of 1925 has been considerably reinforced by the prohibition of the manufacture of bacteriological weapons. The horizontal proliferation of nuclear weapons has been rendered more difficult and the radio-active contamination of the atmosphere substantially restricted. Communication between the United States and the Soviet Union has been further developed In order to prevent nuclear wars. All those measures have helped to safeguard international peace.

On the other hand, there is no denying that the arms race and the development of weapons technology are continuing on many levels and in almost every region.

In the introduction to his annual report, the Secretary-General, Mr. Waldheim, said and I quote:

"In a world increasingly pre-occupied with the problems of social justice, hunger, poverty, development and an equitable sharing of resources, global expenditures on armaments are approaching $ 300,000 million a year. Never before in peacetime has the world witnessed such a flow of weapons of war. Some $ 20,000 million worth of arms are now sold annually in the international arms trade.

"To the perils inherent in the massive nuclear and conventional armouries of the greatest Powers are now added growing and competitive military establishments in some of the most sensitive areas of the world . . ."

Alarming as these facts are, we must not see in them a cause for resignation. We must rather show endurance and imagination in the search for new ways of reducing political tensions, of checking the arms race and substantially reducing armaments. It really goes without saying, but I cannot help mentioning it all the same: the task is to concentrate the scarce resources of the nations on meeting mankind's urgent humanitarian and social requirements.

However, there is one point that must not be forgotten. Disarmament must serve to safeguard peace. Disarmament policies can have dangerous consequences if they are not aimed at a global and regional balance of forces, of maximum stability. Furthermore, eliminating the causes of political tension must go hand in hand with the elimination of military confrontation. Mutual confidence in the observance of agreements in these fields should be strengthened by adequate verification.

Through its consistent policy of renunciation of force, the Federal Government has promoted détente in Europe and thus laid the foundations for fruitful co-operation. The Conference on Security and Co-operation in Europe has created a good basis for the continuation of a policy of peace in Europe. Its results must now be translated into action. The nations of Europa and North America, aware of their common responsibility, have tried to span the gulf by mutual co-operation. My country has strongly supported these efforts from the very beginning. No nation in Europe senses more than the German nation the dangers ensuing from the division of our continent.

There is still a great deal of mismust and fear to get rid of. That is why the Federal Government has immediately set about implementing the confidence-building measures adopted in Helsinki. It has notified military manoeuvres to all the States who participated in the Conference and has invited them to send observers. The willingness of all parties to give effect to these concrete agreements in the field of military security will have a bearing on efforts to achieve more far-reaching agreements with the aim of reducing the dangers of military confrontation in Europe.

Uppermost in our minds in this connexion are the Vienna negotiations on mutual and balanced force reductions. We hope that perseverance and patience will assert at regional level the principle of parity that governs the Strategic Arms Limitation Talks (SALT). The establishment of a stable balance of power in Central Europe would constitute a substantial contribution to the elimination of tensions in Europe and to the consolidation of world peace.

The nuclear Powers, but especially the two world Powers, carry a high responsibility for checking the nuclear arms race and maintaining peace and security. The Strategic Arms Limitation Talks are of major significance for world-wide stability. We have welcomed the results produced so far. Between the United States and the Soviet Union there should be no insurmountable obstacles on the way to the successful conclusion of the Vladivostok agreements.

The fixing of common ceilings for the central offensive strategic systems would then at least have secured a quantitative stop and created a basis for the reduction of such weapons. We understand the impatience of world opinion, and especially of the non-aligned countries, over the sluggish progress and therefore we appeal to the world Powers not to relax their negotiating efforts and thus meet their obligations under the Non-Proliferation Treaty.

Even more difficult than quantitative restrictions and quantitative reductions of nuclear arsenals appears to be the task of calling a halt in qualitative terms. Up to now the problem of ensuring that the inevitable advancement of technology is not aimed at the achievement of military perfection appears to be hardly soluble. Non-verifiable prohibitions with vague definitions of what is actually banned would at any rate not suffice.

As regards the nuclear arms race, however, the conclusion of a sufficiently verifiable comprehensive test-ban treaty and the cessation of all nuclear weapon tests would represent a decisive advancement and are therefore strongly recommended. We realize that in the final analysis this calls for political decisions at the highest level. All the same, we do not think that this makes a further study of the complex technical and scientific problems superfluous.

After all, scientists are still not in agreement as to how far it is possible to distinguish, without the necessity of on-site inspections, between low-yield nuclear tests and earthquakes by means of the present methods of teleseismic detection, even if these were to be further developed. In particular we shall have to continue our search for ways and means of ensuring that substantial knowledge derived from peaceful nuclear explosions (PNEs) is not diverted to the development of nuclear weaponry.

Debates in the Geneva Conference of the Committee on Disarmament (CCD) have confirmed that a nuclear explosive device intended for peaceful purposes can also be used as a weapon. That is why separate PNE development by non-nuclear-weapon states is at least a potential contributor to horizontal proliferation. But PNEs can also be used by nuclear-weapon States for testing new weapons technologies and hence promote vertical proliferation. In order to make sure that the resulting complex verification problems do not delay the conclusion of a comprehensive test-ban treaty, it has been proposed that a moratorium on PNEs be agreed at the same time. We think such a proposal is worth considering if it will remove a major obstacle to a comprehensive test-ban treaty.

In any event tests for PNEs or their practical application should only be carried out under a non-discriminatory international régime of the IAEA. The Agency's work in this connexion, including the elaboration of a model agreement, is in the interest of a consistent non-proliferation policy and therefore deserves our full support.

The Federal Republic of Germany ratified the Non-Proliferation Treaty last spring, together with four other Euratom countries. It considers that Treaty, to which so far 96 states have acceded, to be an indispensable instrument of the policy of non-proliferation, and it repeats its appeal to those countries which have not yet done so to accede to the Treaty, or at least observe its principles. As the Geneva Review Conference has shown, however, the Treaty will only become more attractive if the nuclear-weapon states, too, meet their obligations to the full and if they voluntarily subject their civilian nuclear installations to international control. The Review Conference also underlined the role of the Non-Proliferation Treaty as a basis for intensive international co-operation in the use of nuclear energy for peaceful purposes. The shortage of conventional energy sources and rising energy requirements are leading to a rapid expansion of peaceful nuclear technologies, and hence to a growing production of plutonium and other fissionable material. In the plenary of the General Assembly, Foreign Minister Genscher and other speakers pointed out that it was one of the most pressing tasks of our time to promote the peaceful uses of nuclear energy while preventing its misuse for weapons purposes.

We understand the developing countries' desire to possess modern technologies and are ready to co-operate with them without discrimination while observing the Non-Proliferation Treaty in letter and spirit. The Final Declaration of the Review Conference contains valuable recommendations for ensuring the use of nuclear energy for peaceful purposes. It would serve the goal of non-proliferation and facilitate nuclear exports if all non-nuclear-weapon states were to subject their entire fuel cycle to international safeguards. For economic and security considerations the proposals to examine the question of establishing regional and multi-national nuclear fuel cycle centres also deserve our full support. Surely it would be easier to put them into practice if the countries participating in such installations were given a guarantee that they will be supplied with nuclear fuel. The Federal Government also endorses the request made by the Review Conference that uniform standards, covering physical protection as well, be evolved for the export of fissionable material and nuclear equipment. Both supplier and recipient countries should understand that this is necessary in the interest of a consistent non-proliferation policy.

Ideas and suggestions to set up nuclear-weapon-free zones in various regions of the globe met with a considerable response at the last session of the General Assembly. Following the Finnish proposal which we supported, a comprehensive study was elaborated by government experts under the auspices of the CCD, which we feel is a useful compendium. We think that the following aspects should be given particular attention. Nuclear-weapon-free zones must serve to supplement the world-wide system of a constistent non-proliferation policy, which means that they must not conflict with the provisions of the Non-Proliferation Treaty and should make allowance for the fact that a nuclear explosive device designed for peaceful purposes can also be put to military use. Furthermore, plans for nuclear-weapon-free zones should be considered in the light of the specific characteristics of any one region and examined as to whether they are capable of strengthening international security and stability and are consistent with the accepted rules of international law. If these requirements are met, we welcome the initiatives put forward by some groups of countries to set up nuclear-weapon-free zones.

International efforts designed to ensure disarmament and arms control must concentrate on weapons of mass destruction in particular. Whereas, in the field of A and B weapons it has been possible to give effect to the relevant conventions, there are still no comparable arrangements covering chemical weapons. Although this year's discussions in the CCD have not produced any visible progress towards a prohibition agreement, we do not think that they have been altogether futile. Five countries have submitted concrete proposals regarding the still unresolved definition and verification problems. The Federal Republic of Germany, which as early as 1954 undertook not to manufacture ABC weapons, also presented a working paper in the CCD regarding the definition and classification of chemical warfare agents. The paper attempts to develop a practicable method of distinction between warfare agents and other toxic substances on the basis of objective criteria. There is a growing realization among CCD member states that a comprehensive convention can only be achieved step by step. But only after the United States and the Soviet Union have realized the intention they stated in 1974, " . . . to consider a joint initiative in CCD with respect to the conclusion, as a first step, of an international convention dealing with the most dangerous, lethal means of chemical warfare" only then will an international prohibitive agreement be within reach. Like other CCD members, we are waiting somewhat impatiently for a concrete proposal to be made. In the meantime, government experts should continue to seek practicable solutions and wider agreement regarding the complex problems of definition and verification.

The outstanding result of the last CCD session is the presentation of identical drafts by the United States and the Soviet Union for a treaty on the prohibition of environmental warfare. The draft is a step forward as compared with previous proposals, and its basic concept seems acceptable to us. But before the text of the treaty can be finally formulated it will have to be thoroughly examined at the national level and negotiated in the Conference of the Committee on Disarmament. As in previous cases, the draft provided for verification by a complaints procedure to be set in motion in the Security Council. This is certainly not an ideal solution. At any rate, it should be ensured that decisions cannot be blocked by a veto. In its comments on the proposal for a ban on environmental warfare last year, the Federal Government emphasized that efforts to ensure disarmament and arms control should not only cover present instruments of combat but should be forward-looking and designed to prevent disastrous future developments of military technologies.

It is with this positive basic attitude that we shall also examine the new Soviet proposal for a ban on the development of new mass destruction weapons. However, the present draft treaty is much more vague in substance than is the draft on environmental warfare, though the latter also gives rise to questions. It is clear already that verification of a ban on future developments will be most problematic. Perhaps, to begin with, an international panel of scientists should look into the problems and evolve methods whereby the trend of new scientific findings and their possible application for future weapons technologies can be calculated. Before this question is clarified it would hardly seem possible to formulate concrete definitions of what is to be prohibited.

In conclusion I would briefly touch upon the institutional aspect of disarmament The CCD, which not only commands vast expertise but also embodies a representative cross-section of all groupings of states, should continue to be the main forum for negotiating world-wide arms control arrangements.

I hope that the deliberations of the First Committee will lead to constructive draft resolutions. But to achieve this, it will be necessary for all concerned to show a readiness for compromise and to realize that it is not the number of resolutions that ensures concrete progress in the field of disarmament and arms control but rather the will for international co-operation and the conviction that no arrangement can strengthen peace unless it enhances the security of all countries, or at least maintains it undiminished. If we bear this in mind, we have good reason to hope that our resolutions will, even to a greater extent than last year, be adopted by consensus or with a convincing majority and will thus lead to genuine progress.

18. The Federal Minister for Foreign Affairs, Herr Hans-Dietrich Genscher, on the Election of the Federal Republic of Germany to the UN Security Council

The Federal Minister for Foreign Affairs gave the following interview to "Express am Sonntag" for its 18 April 1976 edition:

Question: In 1977 the Federal Republic is due to be elected on to the United Nations Security Council. It will hardly be able to play an international role on that body, yet it will have to adopt positions in conflict situations of world-wide significance and bear part of responsibility for Security Council decisions. Will this not be a heavy burden?

Answer: The Security Council is the principal organ of the United Nations responsible for the preservation of world peace and international security. Even though it has no panacea for difficult conflicts, it has over the years, and in recent years in particular, repeatedly played a major part in easing tensions and halting conflicts. Work as a non-permanent member of the Security Council is part of the moral duty of a Member, but it also involves more responsibility for world affairs, which of course means heavier demands. But at the same time we will be able to have a bigger say in what goes on. We will exercise that responsibility in accordance with the principles of our foreign policy, the foremost aim of which is to safeguard world peace. On the Security Council we shall also be conscious of the additional weight of the Federal Republic in international affairs and the resultant additional responsibility. This greater importance in the field of international relations is the result on the one hand of the exemplary economic and political stability of our country, and on the other the freedom of movement achieved by abandoning the Halstein Doctrine. Within the framework of our peace policy we shall remain in the Security Council an advocate of independence and the right to self-determination for the nations of the Third World. The clearer and the more credibly we do this, the more can we rely on support for our demand for self-determination of the German people, as clearly expressed once again in the Letter on German Unity. Both in the General Assembly and in the Security Council, the right of self-determination and human rights for all will be the maxims of our policy.

19. Speech by Herr Hans-Dietrich Genscher,
Federal Minister for Foreign Affairs,
before the Thirty-first Session
of the General Assembly of the United Nations,
New York, 28 September 1976

Mr. President,

I. Policy of Peace and Co-operation

This General Assembly of the United Nations, like the previous one, must continue to promote the idea of co-operation between all states.

Co-operation means combining all our efforts in the search for peaceful solutions to the problems that make it so difficult for the peoples of this globe to live peacefully together.

Let us not forget: at the end of this century the world will have twice as many people to feed and twice as many jobs to find.

In the year that has passed since the Thirtieth General Assembly it has been possible to lead the world economy out of the deepest recession since 1930—but the world is still far away from lasting, stable growth and continuing acceleration.

In the past year international peace has been maintained—but the conflicts in the Middle East, in Cyprus and elsewhere continue to smoulder, and in southern Africa the task is to avoid a racial war.

At the same time, new forms of illegal force, such as the seizing of hostages, are developing into a world-wide plague.

Whereas old conflicts basically remain unresolved and new ones are already pushing their way to the surface, the potential of destructive weapons in all parts of the world is growing and so is the capability of manufacturing nuclear weapons. The year 1975 brough no progress towards accomplishing so urgent a task as reducing military expenditure.

On the contrary, we are faced with the threat of another build-up in the arms race. This year the human rights covenants entered into force—but in many parts of the world the individual is still denied the most elementary human rights: his right to life and to personal safety, his right to equality without regard to race, his right to move freely, his right to free expression, and his economic and social rights.

In a world threatend in this way it is our duty to create durable foundations for peace and co-operation.

The one needs the other: We cannot achieve peace without the will to co-operate beyond frontiers, and co-operation will remain ineffectual without peace. Thus the future of this planet really does depend on whether we achieve a breakthrough to that co-operation.

Awareness of this began to dawn following the crises of recent years, and this gives us good reason to be hopeful. It is significant that the Conference of Non-aligned States in Colombo, and similarly the Conference of the Group of 77 in Mexico, have so unequivocally supplemented the principle of national sovereignty and independence by the principle of international co-operation "as the basis of a secure word order".

My Government has made this view the guideline for its action in international relations.

II. Foundations of Our Policy

The Federal Government will therefore continue at this General Assembly, as at previous ones, to pursue a policy aimed at safeguarding peace and securing international co-operation.

The foundations and the objectives of our policy remain unchanged: European union, our firmly-rooted position within the Atlantic Alliance, which ensures the balance of power and is thus the prerequisite for peace in Europe, the policy of détente towards the states of Eastern Europe, and partnership and an equitable reconciliation of interests with the Third World.

1. European unification

The members of the European Communtiy have made encouraging progress towards creating stable structures for co-operation in a spirit of solidarity.

For centuries the history of Western Europe was a series of wars.

Even in this century it has been the source of two world wars. Today, however, the people in the European Community see their future as a common future.

So thoroughly has the situation changed within the span of a single generation.

Outside Europe this may not seem an earthshaking event, but all, I am sure, should be able to judge from it what can be achieved through good will in relations between peoples.

The members of the Community have set themselves the task of together putting into practice the great historic concept of freedom and human dignity. We adhere to the aim of European Union.

Yet the Community ist not inwardlooking. It is not a closed community whose responsibility stops at its own front door.

It actively supports efforts towards peace and justice and towards a world economy that is open for trade and investment. It is the biggest trading partner in the world. And it is in particular a partner of the Third World as well: As the most important source of investment capital and technology, as the most important trading partner, and as a pioneer in the creation of equal, balanced relations between industrial and developing countries.

The previous speaker, the Netherlands Foreign Minister, who spoke on behalf of all nine member states of the European Community, has been able to show how far our common aims extend in foreign policy as well.

2. The Atlantic Alliance

The Federal Republic of Germany is a member of the North Atlantic Alliance.

It understands this Alliance and its role in it as a contribution to the safeguarding of peace in its region.

NATO is a pact for peace and it is in line with this understanding of its role that it renders an active contribution of its own to détente. This Alliance testifies to the close and manifold ties between Western Europe and the United States and Canada.

3. The policy of détente

On the basis of the European Community and the Atlantic Alliance a policy of realistic détente towards the East became possible for Western Europe.

That policy starts from the following consideration:

If we cannot remove the ideological division and the basic differences between political and social systems in Europe then it is all the more urgent to resolve conflicts by negotiation or at least mitigate them, and to discover areas where co-operation between East and West is possible to their mutual advantage and for the benefit of the people on both sides.

The policy pursued by the Federal Republic of Germany in concluding treaties with the Soviet Union, the Polish People's Republic, Czechoslovakia, and the other members of the Warsaw Pact serves this aim. We attach special importance to the further development of the relationship between the two German states on the basis of treaty arrangements. The policy of détente pursued by the Federal Government is a long-term policy. It consistently continues the policy initiated by Willy Brandt and Walter Scheel.

The nations of Europe, the United States and Canada held the Conference on Security and Co-operation in Europe. They have laid down principles for peaceful relations and agreed on a whole series of specific arrangements.

Among other things, these are intended to foster economic and scientific co-operation, regulate humanitarian questions, and facilitate contacts between people in East and West and the exchange of ideas and information; in the military field they are intended to build up confidence.

All of these arrangements must now be put into practice. The more co-operation across the ideological barrier becomes possible and the less energy will be wasted in sterile confrontation, the more will the nations of Europe be able to contribute to an equitable reconciliation of interests between the industrialized countries and the countries of the Third World.

In this year, too, we have resolutely pursued our treaty policy.

The agreements concluded with the Polish People's Republic have removed burdens of the past and opened up a hopeful perspective for relations between the two countries.

The relaxation of tension in Europe brought about since 1970 would not have been possible without an improvement of relations between the Federal Republic of Germany and the USSR. Relations between the Federal Republic of Germany and the Soviet Union will also in future be of particular importance for the process of détente. For this reason great significance attaches to the visit of Secretary-General Brezhnev to the Federal Republic of Germany which is planned to take place in the course of this year.

No nation can be more interested in co-operation across the frontiers of different systems than the German people that is compelled to live in two states.

Through Germany runs the frontier which divides Europe. Our negotiations with the GDR have also been, and will continue to be, concerned with easing conditions for the people and with further developing co-operation.

To pursue a policy of détente in a divided country and for a divided country is a great and at the same time difficult task. But we Germans know that there is no acceptable alternative to it.

A great deal has been made possible by negotiation between the two German states, much has been achieved in the way of practical improvements; human suffering could be alleviated; human contacts between Germans became increasingly possible. But by far not all objectives have been attained. As before, the aim of our policy is to overcome the painful consequences of the division of Germany by patient negotiation.

The Federal Government does not resign in the face of the reality of a frontier where only recently shots were still fired on the other side. This must at last be stopped.

The Federal Government will not tire in its efforts to achieve this as well, by means of its policy of détente.

In the heart of Germany lies also the city which for better or worse has been a touchstone of détente: Berlin.

The Federal Government will not relax its efforts to promote the viability of West Berlin. For Berlin, the strict observance and full application of the Quadripartite Agreement is of essential importance. The Federal Government will, as before, ensure that West Berlin continues to be included in international co-operation.

The more we succeed in this the less will be the danger of the city again becoming a source of international crises.

The Federal Republic of Germany whose foreign policy has been a policy of and for peace from the very first day of its existence, will unflinchingly continue its policy of détente and thus contribute to the safeguarding of peace. It remains its political objective to work for a state of peace in Europe in which the German nation will regain its unity through free self-determination. For us, history has not yet passed its final verdict on the division of the German nation.

4. International disarmament

It will be of decisive importance for the progress of détente whether the current negotiations on a second SALT agreement and on the balanced reduction of ground forces in central Europe prove successful.

For nothing could constitute a greater threat to détente than another arms race.

The Federal Government will make special efforts in talks with the United States, the Soviet Union and other countries concerned, to get the stagnant expert discussions on MBFR in Vienna going again. This was announced by Chancellor Schmidt last week.

Peace itself and efforts to safeguard it by means of more stable structures are jeopardized by unrelenting efforts in nearly all parts of the world to build up arms strengths. Exports of conventional weapons in particular have increased rapidly.

The monstrous waste of scarce resources in the industrial countries as in the developing countries works to the detriment of the people.

We must not give up hope because of the disappointing results in the field of arms control and disarmament so far. In the process of détente efforts must be redoubled to halt the arms race and, both world-wide and regionally, to translate into reality effective measures of arms control and arms limitation.

Balanced and controlled disarmament remains one of the most urgent tasks.

But it is high time words were followed by deeds.

The world needs plough and workbench more urgently than rifle and missile.

In Europe, within the framework of the negotiations in Vienna, the Federal Government will continue to seek the establishment of an equal and hence stable relationship of power in central Europe.

The Federal Government welcomes the request made by the non-aligned states in Colombo calling for a special session of the General Assembly to deal with questions of world-wide disarmament and is ready to play a constructive part in it. But we still live in a heavily armed world. All the more urgent, therefore, is the one principal task of international politics, to ward off dangers for peace in time, and that means resolving conflicts without war.

III. Safeguarding Peace

1. The Middle East

Consequently, we look with anxiety towards a region whose unresolved problems are a constant threat to world peace: the Middle East.

The guidelines for a solution to the Middle East conflict were mapped out long ago.

They are based on resolutions of the Security Council, complemented by a large consensus of international opinion that the national rights of the Palestinian people must also be taken into consideration. Thus, at the 1974 Session of the General Assembly, the Federal Republic of Germany stated that a peace settlement, apart from providing for the termination of the territorial occupation, should make allowance for the right of self-determination of the Palestinian people, including the right to establish a state authority, and for Israel's right to live within secure and recognized boundaries.

It is not a question of keeping on repeating the principles governing a solution. It is a question of putting them into practice. The Federal Republic of Germany, together with its partners in the European Community, has a vital interest in a peaceful solution to the conflict in its neighbouring region to the south, and today it is more than ever convinced that a solution is possible.

Our special interest in this region also finds expression in the Euro-Arab dialogue. No one can today speak of the Middle East problem without including the tragic developments in the Lebanon.

Efforts have been of no avail to stop hostilities that have taken a heavy toll of human life and are destroying a country in which the seed of violence has sprung up.

We appeal to all concerned to stop the terrible bloodshed.

2. Southern Africa

A second source of danger for international relations has developed in Southern Africa.

It is impossible to imagine the consequences a racial war embracing the whole region would have. All countries in that region are aware of this. The Federal Republic of Germany has, therefore, not abandoned hope of a peaceful solution being achieved.

But it knows:

Only where no one attempts to hold up a historically necessary change can we expect peaceful developments, can we feel that peace is secure.

Everyone must realize, also in Southern Africa, that racism and colonialism no longer have a place in this world. The sands have run out.

Southern Africa too must determine its own destiny. There is only one way to attain this:

Blacks and whites must develop some form of co-operation based on equality which will prove a sound foundation also in future: majority rule, but at the same time safeguards for the rights of the minority.

In Rhodesia, as we hope, the first and decisive step in this direction has now been taken. This could be the beginning of an era of people of all races in Southern Africa living peacefully together.

Recent developments confirm in an impressive manner the correctness of the position we have always taken:

Only the renunciation of force prevents the catastrophe of a racial war which would otherwise be unavoidable. The urgently required changes in southern Africa can be brought about only by peaceful means and by negotiation. A turn of events is foreshadowed for which all concerned deserve thanks and appreciation, the Secretary of State of the United States, the British Government as well as those African statesmen who are working with perseverance for a peaceful solution of this pressing problem.

As regards the problem of Namibia, we re-affirm the demand:

— that the rule of South Africa should end and the earliest possible date for independence be fixed in a binding manner;

— that the competence of the United Nations should be recognized to lead the former mandated territory to independence;

— that in exercising the right of self-determination under the supervision of the United Nations all political groups in the country should participate in the preparations for independence.

Only the speedy fulfilment of all these demands will prevent any further aggravation of the situation.

The Federal Government will assist a free Namibia as far as possible in building up its economy.

We appeal again to the Government of the Republic of South Africa to give up the policy of apartheid and not to oppose necessary reforms any longer. Only those who are prepared to carry out the necessary changes can preserve the heritage of the past.

We support the appeal of President Kenneth Kaunda of Zambia to the whites in Southern Africa to join with the other parts of Africa in creating a new society which is not based on colour.

Only then will it be possible for a new society of black and white Africans with equal rights to master together the great task of developing the continent.

3. Convention against the taking of hostages

The efforts made by the community of nations to control the use of force must now also include the new illegal forms of force which in recent years have come to be a problem assuming more and more menacing proportions.

The most widespread of these new forms of violence, and one of the most murderous, is the taking of hostages.

The growing number of acts involving the taking of hostages has spotlighted the extent of the threat.

None of the 500 million passengers travelling on airlines every year can be sure not be among the next victims.

Acts involving the taking of hostages are not the problem of just one state or another or of any group of states, it is a problem concerning us all. The United Nations bears special responsibility. The Secretary-General in his annual report rightly pointed that out.

What is at stake is the protection of human beings, the sovereignty of states, the safety of international traffic, and an international order free from violence.

The taking of hostages is a particularly cruel act of violence which indiscriminately claims or threatens the lives of helpless people, of women and children.

For this reason the Geneva Convention of 1949 prohibits this act even as a means of warfare.

It is an act offending the dignity, safety and fundamental rights of the individual person, basic values the protection of which the United Nations Declaration of Human Rights and the International Covenant on Civil and Political Rights proclaim.

Those taking hostages attempt to blackmail sovereign states and to confront them with the unbearable choice of either yielding to their demands or risking the lives of the hostages taken.

Acts involving the taking of hostages are a threat to international relations. The efforts made by all states to settle international conflicts peacefully, and also the endeavours of this world organization to make peace more secure are placed in jeopardy by criminal acts of violence committed by a few.

International conferences, diplomatic exchanges are thus threatened. In exploiting the particular vulnerability of aeroplanes the taking of hostages above all imperils international air traffic.

Our peoples expect the United Nations to exhaust all possibilities of checking this method of using brute force. We must face up to this danger affecting us all and initiate an objective discussion on possible steps. After the bitter experiences of recent months the Governments of all countries should unite in condemning the act of taking hostages as a particularly abhorrent crime and to introduce world-wide measures against it.

The Government of the Federal Republic of Germany deems it necessary that the United Nations should draft a Convention banning the taking of hostages and making sure that the perpetrators are either extradited or brought before court in the country in which they were seized. We are convinced that it should be possible soon to arrive at such a convention within the framework of the United Nations. The Government of the Federal Republic of Germany will therefore request that an item on International Action against the Taking of Hostages be included in the Agenda of this General Assembly as an important and urgent matter.

IV. Measures to Safeguard Human Rights

General acceptance of, and respect for human rights is an inalienable element of any order of peace and world-wide co-operation.

This is one of the noblest aims of the United Nations. The concept of human rights has played a decisive role in the United Nations' emergence.

The year 1976 is a historical year for human rights and for the United Nations.

It is the year in which the international covenants on human rights — the Covenant on Economic, Social and Cultural Rights and the Covenant on Civil and Political Rights — have entered into force. Both Covenants guide our action. The Federal Republic of Germany orients its policy towards the developing countries to the demands embodied in the Covenant on Economic, Social and Cultural Rights.

We advocate in the strongest possible terms respect for the basic human rights, not only in Germany, but all over the world.

Our policy serves the individual human being — only the realization of his rights and his dignity lends ultimate meaning and purpose to all our efforts to ensure political and economic co-operation.

And this includes that all men can live under conditions which are really consistent with human digntiy.

The year 1976 with its important events in the field of human rights now faces us with the task of translating into reality the principles of law we have worked out.

In this new phase the United Nations must remain the champion of human rights.

An institution should therefore be established, which should ensure comprehensive and world-wide protection of human rights. What we need is an independent, international authority passing objective judgements to ensure that human rights are safeguarded in all parts of the world. Such an authority would not be directed against anybody, it would be there for somebody, namely the indivdiual human being and his rights.

The phase of codifying human rights was long and difficult. It lasted 30 years.

The implementing phase will perhaps be even more difficult, but this should not lead us to believe that we can take that much time again.

Much patient negotiating will be necessary.

Our aim must be to guarantee the application of human rights world-wide by means of an institution which would prevent the human rights question from being abused for political purposes.

The Government of the Federal Republic of Germany is aware that this is a difficult task. But it is convinced that the aim of establishing an international court for human rights can be attained.

Its belief is strengthened by its experience with the protective system of the European Convention on Human Rights which has proved its value for more than two decades and which will not lose anything on its importance if the United Nations establishes an institution along Its lines.

V. World-wide Economic Co-operation

I have already pointed out that it is also the application of human rights that makes it incumbent on us to reduce the economic gap between the rich and the poor countries. The difference in prosperity between North and South is a threat to peace and stability throughout the world. The Government of the Federal Republic of Germany notes with great satisfaction that the will for co-operation which is prerequisite to any effective action in this field has grown in all parts of the world and today is actually unchallenged.

The Seventh Special Session of the General Assembly last year, the Conference on International Economic Co-operation in Paris, the UNCTAD Conference in Nairobi and also the Conference of the Non-aligned States in Colombo have confirmed this principle.

It is a positive sign that complicated problems such as raw materials and energy and the re-organization of the Law of the Sea are negotiated at international conferences.

But now it is essential to achieve rapid and concrete results.

Solemn declarations of intent are not enough to feed the people in the poorest countries.

A hard year lies behind us.

In 1975, the year of the nadir of recession, the national products of the free-market industrialized countries fell and although the developing countries' national products continued to rise, their growth rate declined and dropped in many developing countries below the growth rate of the population.

The gap between industrialized and developing countries had decreased for the first time — but it had decreased because the world as a whole became poorer.

The world became all of a sudden aware of the magnitude of the threat. We had to realize that development as such can be accelerated only within an international economy which, as a whole, is expanding.

It was this experience that increased the awareness of the need for co-operation and made 1975 the year of a common departure.

The Federal Government realizes without any illusion that up to now we have come only a short way together, but even along this short distance we certainly have scored results:

1) In 1975 there was a sharp rise in the flow of capital into the developing countries:

   — The OECD countries increased their official and private capital transfers to the unprecedented amount of 39 thousand million dollars which is an increase of 40 per cent.

   This means that for the first time ever the target of the capital transfer amounting to 1 percent of the gross national product was reached.

   The Federal Republic of Germany exceeded that target by having attained 1.18 percent.

   — At the same time there was an increase in the capital influx from the OPEC countries.

2) Progress was made in the efforts to stabilize the developing countries export earnings:

   — The International Monetary Fund considerably widened the possibilities of taking up compensatory credits in the event of a decline in export earnings.

   — The European Community in the Lomé Convention set up the world's first stabilizing system for commodity exports from developing countries.

3) Progress was also made in the opening of markets to Third World exports:

   — The multilateral trade negotiations in Geneva have made this objective a focal subject for talks.

   — This year, too, the European Community plans to increase essentially the possibilities for tariff-free imports of industrial goods from developing countries.

   — In 1975 the Federal Republic of Germany increased its imports of manufactures from developing countries by one quarter — and that in a year of heavy recession.

4) Finally, to promote the development of agriculture in the Third World, it was decided to set up a fund which will make available considerable funds to increase agricultural production.

To speed up the development ofthe Third World is the common task of all countries.

It requires the developing countries themselves to concentrate their strength on the development goal.

It also requires them to assist one another. The Government of the Federal Republic of Germany therefore appreciates it that the Colombo Conference strongly emphasized the idea of collective self-help.

Already now, the oil-producing countries substantially contribute to the transfer of resources to developing countries in want of capital. At the latest OPEC conference they also showed their readiness to share in the responsibility for world economy as a whole.

But undoubtedly the largest external contribution to development has to come from the industrialized countries; in the past the free-market industrialized countries have already been a motor of Third World development.

The power of that motor must grow even stronger.

The integration of the countries with a centrally controlled economy into the world-economic system, which began in recent years, now opens up the possibility that they, too, will finally become a motor of development.

This possibility should, however, be used.

Trade between free-market industrialized countries and centrally planning industrialized countries has almost quadrupled during the past four years.

It is necessary now to increase trade between centrally planning industrialized countries and developing countries with similar speed.

The potential is enormous:

Whereas free-market industrialized countries absorb three quarters of the developing countries' exports, the share of the centrally planning industrialized countries in these exports is no more than 4 per cent.

Looking ahead, the question Is:

What can and what must we do together now in order to promote the equitable reconciliation of interests between industrialized and developing countries?

1) In the four commissions of the CIEC, in the fields of energy, commodities, finance and development, we must quickly find concrete solutions to the problems defined in the initial phase of the conference.

2) At the meetings and conferences on commodity problems decided on commodity problems decided on by UNCTAD IV we must achieve rapid and appropriate results.

3) We would like to see all industrialized countries, whatever their economic system, make greater efforts with regard to the transfer of capital and technology

to developing countries. The developing countries, for their part, should create the prerequisites for these efforts to be successful.

4) We regard an intensified industrialization of the developing countries as an urgent requirement.

We therefore participate in all efforts contributing to this goal and are prepared to open our markets still more.

We are aware of the adjustment problems ensuing in our own economy and shall be prepared for this.

5) The solution of the problems of indebtedness becomes a more and more pressing requirement. Like other countries, the Federal Republic of Germany gives the solution of this problem priority attention.

In the spirit which has imbued the Federal Republic of Germany in rendering its financial assistance and in continuing to render such assistance, it will, together with other donor countries, use its full energies to help solve the problem of indebtedness.

We do so, because we have full confidence in the future of the developing countries and their peoples.

The success of our endeavours to build a co-operative world will decisively be influenced by the outcome of the conference on the Law of the Sea.

We have declared the sea the common heritage of mankind. It is now essential to translate this principle into reality, and that means establishing a legal system governing the seas which will take into account the interests of all states in a well-balanced manner.

The Government of the Federal Republic of Germany will actively participate in the work on these problems because it is convinced that the problems of the developing countries are the problems of the industrialized countries as well.

This is a new piece of knowledge which not yet all of our citizens find easy to accept.

In our countries many people still have to learn that their own destiny is connected with that of all others.

In all industrialized countries a great deal of information and education is still necessary to make it understood that the North-South dialogue is not concerned with the giving and taking of alms, but that it is concerned with our common future.

VI. Role of the United Nations

The Secretary-General, in the introduction to his report to the General Assembly, correctly defined the role of the United Nations when he characterized our time as a period of transition in which we must overcome the antagonism between the principle of national sovereignty and the regulatory principles governing an interdependent world.

Only co-operation can help us steer this development in such a way that it will benefit mankind as a whole.

In this co-operation, a central role falls to the United Nations as the only world-embracing organization, a role which no one and nothing else can play.

According to the mandate of the Charter, our Organization is to be the centre in which the nations of the world will harmonize their actions to attain the common objectives of peace and progress.

Let us at this Thirty-first Session of the General Assembly fulfil this mandate which the Charter gives us.

Let us continue to work on the great task of building a world to conform to the vision of our Charter: a world of peace, a world of economic and social progress, and a world in which the freedom and dignity of man are a reality.

My country today is more than ever convinced that, in creating the United Nations, mankind has endowed itself with a great opportunity.

We understand only too well the impatience of many who are waiting for their most elementary rights to come true.

Nor do we underrate the difficulties which the United Nations is having in trying to close the big gap between demands and reality.

We do not close our eyes to the obstacles besetting the road to an equitable and peaceful world-wide order.

Only the spirit of co-operation on a partnership basis can help us on.
Let us therefore use the opportunity we have.

20. Election of the Federal Republic of Germany to the Security Council

On 21 October 1976, the thirty-first General Assembly of the United Nations voted to fill the seats on the Security Council which were due to become vacant. It confirmed the unanimous recommendation of the Security Council that the Federal Republic of Germany be elected a non-permanent member of the Security Council for two years as from 1 January 1977. 119 of the 138 votes cast were in favour.

Part V

Statistics

1. Financial Contributions of the Federal Republic of Germany within the entire range of the United Nations System in the period 1968 to 1975 in 1,000 DM¹)

Title	1968	1969	1970	1971	1972	1973	1974	1975	1976
a) UN incl. Subsidiary Organs									
– UN contribution (incl. Middle East peace-keeping force)	–	–	–	–	–	17,403	57,555	66,962	75,102
– Economic Commission for Europe (ECE)	1,483	1,401	1,625	1,514	1,650	1,631	1,018	–²)	–
– UN Conference on Trade and Development (UNCTAD)	1,961	2,279	2,043	2,043	2,238	2,192	1,669	–²)	–
– Commission on Narcotic Drugs	289	303	309	310	352	324	502	–²)	–
– UN Industrial Development Organization (UNIDO)	–	–	2,407	2,464	2,670	2,470	1,863	–²)	–
– UN Environment Programme Fund (UNEP)	–	–	–	–	–	–	6,000	5,000	5,000
Total a)	3,733	3,983	6,384	6,331	6,910	24,020	68,607	71,962	
b) Special programmes, relief operations, conventions and activities of the UN outside the UN's ordinary budget									
– UN Children's Fund (UNICEF)	6,000	7,248	9,726	7,500	7,500	8,000	8,000	8,000	8,000
– UN High Commissioner for Refugees (UNHCR)	1,300	1,300	1,500	1,700	2,000	2,000	2,000	2,000	2,000
– UN Relief and Works Agency for Palestine Refugees (UNRWA)	4,000	2,000	–	–	2,000	2,000	2,000	2,000	2,000
– Convention on the Elimination of all Forms of Racial Discrimination (CERD)	–	–	26	–	17	10	10	10	19
– UN peace-keeping force on Cyprus	–	–	–	–	–	2,627	2,532	2,597	2,620
– Cost of transport of forces for UN Middle East peace-keeping force (Federal Ministry of Defence)	–	–	–	–	–	–	1,800	–	–
– Special German aid for alleviating the plight of refugees in the Middle East in co-operation with UNRWA	4,900	10,000	11,857	11,686	10,994	10,116	4,977	4,994	5,000
– UNESCO Institute for Pedagogics, Hamburg	540	540	540	720	720	720	720	800	800

Title	1968	1969	1970	1971	1972	1973	1974	1975	1976
– Saving of the Temple in Borobodur, Indonesia (UNESCO Project)	–	–	–	–	–	1,000	1,000	–	–
– Contribution to the International Study Centre for the Preservation and Restoration of Cultural Treasures in Rome (UNESCO)	83	93	86	94	81	95	90	127	144
– Preservation of the Temple in Moenjodaro, Pakistan (UNESCO Project)	–	–	–	–	–	–	–	1,000	–
– UN Trust Fund for South Africa	–	–	–	–	–	–	–	136	136
– Education and Training Programme for Southern Africa	–	184	–	–	275	–	145	136	136
– UNIDROIT	–	–	–	–	–	43	46	49	38
– UN Study Group on Lead and Zinc	–	–	–	–	–	9	12	10	15
– International Woman's Year	–	–	–	–	–	–	50	3,053	2,998
– Contribution to Narcotic Drugs Control	–	–	–	–	–	310	206	–	–
– UN Fund for Drug Abuse Control	–	–	–	1,000	–	–	500	–	–
– UN Development Programme (UNDP)	36,000	41,000	41,000	48,000	48,000	55,000	62,400	79,000	79,000
– UN Fund for Population Activities (UNFPA)	–	–	5,500	5,500	7,500	10,500	15,000	18,000	18,000
– UN World Food Programme (WFP)	10,600	12,000	21,923	28,960	34,127	17,923	19,841	24,250	26,000
– German Share of EC Joint Programme:									
– UN Emergency Programme (Cheyson Fund) (1st and 2nd issue)	–	–	–	–	–	–	60,000	155,000	–
– UN Relief and Works Agency for Palestine Refugees in the Middle East	–	–	–	–	–	–	3,752	2,637	3,200
– UN World Food Programme (WFP)	–	–	–	–	–	–	3,908	5,136	7,100
– UNRWA (separate)	–	–	–	–	–	–	2,084	2,054	3,500

Title	1968	1969	1970	1971	1972	1973	1974	1975	1976
– UNHCR Special Operation/Refugees South Viet Nam	–	–	–	–	–	–	–	–	–
– Saving of the Temples in Philae (UNESCO Project)	–	–	–	–	–	–	–	5,000	–
– UN Force in Cyprus (UNFICYP)	4,000	4,000	3,666	3,369	3,220	–	–	–	–
– UN Relief Operations in Dacca (UNROD)	–	–	–	15,000	3,300	–	–	–	–
– UN Fund for Uganda refugees					703				
– UN Fund for Southern Sudan	–	–	–	–	1,800	–			
– Operation 'Pure Water' for Bangladesh	–	–	–	–	1,500	–			
– Other purpose-tied voluntary contributions of the Federal Republic of Germany to UN or Specialized Agencies for individual projects or special programmes (incl. World Bank activities)	–	–	41,000	48,000	51,395	9,668	8,577	15,161	13,300
– Participation of the Federal Republic of Germany in development projects of regional economic commissions (except ECE) and regional development banks	–	–	1,570	1,656	2,017	2,422	2,221	1,934	2,000
Total b)	67,423	78,365	138,394	174,185	178,149	122,443	201,871	333,084	

c) UN Specialized Agencies incl. International Atomic Energy Agency[3])

Title	1968	1969	1970	1971	1972	1973	1974	1975	1976
– UN Educational, Scientific and Cultural Organization (UNESCO)	8,315	9,351	8,562	9,043	8,335	9,792	10,829	13,776	14,367
– UN Food and Agriculture Organization (FAO)	10,438	10,598	10,142	10,115	10,780	8,566	12,919	11,379	17,657
– International Labour Organization (ILO)	4,419	4,878	5,349	5,594	5,334	5,252	6,987	7,377	14,330
– World Meteorological Organization (WMO)	648	680	783	754	870	820	1,053	933	1,100
– Inter-Governmental Maritime Consultative Organization (IMCO)	126	151	149	169	225	177	235	175	235
– WHO International Reference Centres	–	–	–	–	–	–	266	447	503
– WHO National Reference Centres	–	–	–	–	–	127	178	237	239

Title	1968	1969	1970	1971	1972	1973	1974	1975	1976
– World Health Organization (WHO)	15,275	16,660	16,940	17,926	16,759	14,956	17,160	18,904	24,917
– Voluntary contribution to WHO	–	–	–	–	–	190	180	200	200
– WHO Consulting Centre	–	–	–	–	–	–	–	199	287
– World Bank – capital increase	–	–	–	–	–	7,024	–	–	–
– International Development Association (IDA) share of subscribed capital incl. increases	156,000	142,000	142,740	237,200	235,953	301,804	381,400	423,000	–⁴)
– World Health Organization – voluntary contributions	–	–	–	–	–	348	–	140	–
– International Labour Organization – voluntary contributions	–	–	–	–	1,062	456	232	3,064	–
– World Intellectual Property Organization (WIPO) – voluntary contributions	–	–	–	–	70	70	38	120	–
– UNESCO – voluntary contributions	–	–	–	–	–	659	471	2,345	–
– FAO – voluntary contributions	–	–	–	–	–	4,500	1,080	–	–
– Universal Postal Union (UPU)⁵)	136	174	174	153	160	195	203	244	272
– International Telecommunication Union (ITU)⁵)	841	819	996	1,100	1,200	1,350	1,750	2,000	2,200
– WMO – voluntary contribution	–	–	–	–	–	–	57	–	–
– International Atomic Energy Agency (IAEA)	3,620	3,410	3,702	4,791	4,799	5,026	5,969	7,601	7,000
– FAO European Commission for the Control of Foot-and-Mouth Disease	–	–	–	–	–	15	21	18	21
Total c)	199,818	188,721	189,537	286,845	285,547	361,327	441,028	492,159	
Total a) to c)	270,974	271,069	334,315	467,361	470,606	507,790	711,506	897,205	

¹) Contributions in foreign exchange are stated at medium exchange rates; amounts stated in other statistics may therefore slightly vary;
²) From 1974, part of the regular UN contribution;
³) Excl. International Civil Aviation Organization (ICAO);
⁴) Under sect. 17, Budget Law 1976, The Federal Government is authorized to raise the 3rd instalment of 438.4 mill. DM to IDA, due in 1976, by means of interest-free bonds redeemable at any time; a separate decision on this procedure will be taken in 1977–79.
⁵) Contributions to the regular UPU and ITO budgets are paid from the special budget of the Ministry of Posts and Telecommunications.

2. Overall Survey of the Net Payments of the Federal Republic of Germany to Developing Countries and Multilateral Agencies — 1950 to 1975 (in mill. DM)

Form of Assistance	1950-1972	1973	1974	1975	1950-1975[3]
I. Official Development Aid[1]	27,609.1	2,941.1	3,715.2	4,165.2	38,430.6
1. Bilateral	22,446.8	2,112.3	2,628.5	2,859.3	30,046.9
a) grants (non-repayable)	10,524.1	1,079.7	1,211.2	1,369.4	14,184.4
– technical assistance	5,690.9	798.7	985.6	1,156.3	8,631.5
– other grants (incl. Indus Basin)	4,833.2	281.0	225.6	213.1	5,552.9
b) credits covering a period of more than 1 year (bilateral financial assistance incl. debt rescheduling and shares in the DEG – German Development Company –)	11,922.7	1,032.6	1,417.3	1,489.9	15,862.5
2. Multilateral grants and credits	5,162.3	828.8	1,086.7	1,305.9	8,383.7
a) contributions to multilateral organizations	2,883.0	442.7	623.5	787.6	4,736.8
b) payments of subscribed capital	2,056.5	348.5	440.9	512.1	3,358.0
c) financial assistance	222.8	37.6	22.3	6.2	288.9
II. Misc. Official Payments	6,609.2	611.6	248.6	22.4	7,491.8
1. Bilateral	4,032.6	596.8	244.7	– 30.3	4,843.8
– credits of the Development Loan Corp. (KW) incl. debt rescheduling	3,291.1	487.2	58.1	83.5	3,919.9
– refinancing of the Federal Ministry of Finance	721.9	109.5	177.8	– 149.4	859.8
– DEG loans	19.6	0.1	8.8	35.6	64.1
2. Multilateral (credits of the Federal Bank)	2,576.6	14.8	3.9	52.7	2,648.0
III. Private Development Aid[2]	1,061.1	419.5	459.5	505.0	2,445.1

Form of Assistance	1950-1972	1973	1974	1975	1950-1975
IV. Payments by the Economy	33,630.0	849.9	3,804.9	7,534.1	45,818.9
1. Bilateral	28,899.4	525.9	3,880.9	6,664.1	39,970.3
– direct investments and other forms of investment	16,612.7	1,358.7	2,544.1	4,187.3	24,702.8
– guaranteed export credits (100 %)	12,286.7	– 832.8	1,336.8	2,476.8	15,267.5
2. Multilateral	4,730.6	324.0	– 76.0	870.0	5,848.6
V. Total Payments (net)	68,909.4	4,822.1	8,228.2	12,226.7	94,186.4
of which: official	34,218.3	3,552.7	3,963.8	4,187.6	45,922.4
private	34,691.1	1,269.4	4,264.4	8,039.1	48,264.0

¹) Bilateral und multilateral grants as well as credits on easy terms;
²) Payments of non-governmental institutions (Churches, trade unions, associations, foundations etc.) from their own funds;
³) From 1975 incl. Portugal.

225

3. Payments and Contributions of the Federal Republic of Germany to Developing Countries and Multilateral Agencies – 1971 to 1975 (in mill. DM)

Object of expenditure	1971 Net	1972 Net	1974 Gross	1974 Returns	1974 Net	1975 Gross	1975 Returns	1975 Net
I. Official Development Aid*)	2,563.2	2,604.7	4,315.8	600.6	3,715.2	4,968.1	802.9	4,165.2
1. Bilateral	1,848.7	1,938.2	3,225.8	597.3	2,628.5	3,658.1	798.8	2,859.3
a) Grants (nonrepayable)	973.0	980.3	1,211.2	–	1,211.2	1,369.4	–	1,369.4
– Technical assistance	721.1	774.1	985.6	–	985.6	1,156.3	–	1,156.3
– Misc. grants (incl. Indus Basin)	251.9	206.2	225.6	–	225.6	213.1	–	213.1
b) Credits over 1 year	875.7	957.9	2,014.6	597.3	1,417.3	2,288.7	798.8	1,489.9
– Bilateral capital assistance (incl. debt conversions and German Development Company [DEG]-holdings)								
2. Multilateral grants and credits	714.5	666.5	1,090.0	3.3	1,086.7	1,310.0	4.1	1,305.9
a) Contributions to multilateral agencies	408.9	383.4	623.5	–	623.5	787.6	–	787.6
b) Payments to subscribed capital	273.9	266.8	440.9	–	440.9	512.1	–	512.1
c) Credits	31.7	16.3	25.6	3.3	22.3	10.3	4.1	6.2
II. Misc. Official Payments	573.0	478.5	1,640.9	1,392.3	248.6	1,538.3	1,515.9	22.4
1. Bilateral	504.0	373.5	881.8	637.1	244.7	870.7	901.0	– 30.3
– Credits of the Development Loan Corporation (incl. debt conversions)	455.2	391.0	605.8	547.7	58.1	778.5	695.0	83.5
– Refinancing of the Federal Ministry of Finance	33.4	21.7	263.2	85.4	177.8	52.7	202.1	– 149.4
– DEG loans	15.4	4.2	12.8	4.0	8.8	39.5	3.9	35.6
2. Multilateral (Credits of the Federal Bank)	69.0	105.0	759.1	755.2	3.9	667.6	614.9	52.7
III. Private Development Aid†)	378.1	398.4	459.5	–	459.5	505.0	–	505.0

Object of expenditure	1971 Net	1972 Net	1974 Gross	1974 Returns	1974 Net	1975 Gross	1975 Returns	1975 Net
IV. Payments by the Economy								
1. Bilateral	3,171.5	2,041.1	13,038.1	9,233.2	3,804.9	18,178.1	10,644.0	7,534.1
	2,766.5	1,334.1	13,038.1	9,157.2	3,880.9	17,178.1	10,514.0	6,664.1
– direct investments and other forms of investments	1,335.5	1,532.7	7,437.6	4,893.5	2,544.1	9,339.2	5,151.9	4,187.3[2]
– guaranteed export credits (100 %)	1,439.1	198.6	5,600.5	4,263.7	1,336.8	7,838.9	5,362.1	2,476.8
2. Multilateral[3]	405.0	707.0	—	76.0	− 76.0	1,000.0	130.0	870.0
V. Total Payments	6,685.8	5,522.7	19,454.3	11,226.1	8,228.2	25,189.5	12,962.8	12,226.7
of which: official	3,136.2	3,083.2	5,956.7	1,992.9	3,963.8	6,506.4	2,318.8	4,187.6
private	3,549.6	2,439.5	13,497.6	9,233.2	4,264.4	18,683.1	10,644.0	8,039.1

Year	Gross national product DM mill.	Total payments Absolute DM mill.	Total payments % share of GNP	Official dev. aid Share of GNP as %
1968	540.0	6,653.7	1.23	0.41
1969	605.2	7,951.0	1.31	0.38
1970	685.6	5,453.1	0.80	0.32
1971	761.9	6,685.8	0.88	0.34
1972	833.9	5,659.4	0.68	0.31
1973	926.9	4,822.1	0.52	0.32
1974	995.7	8,228.2	0.83	0.37
1975	1,040.4	12,226.7	1.18	0.40

*) Out of this 88 % from Federal Budget (item 23 = 70 %, other items = 18 %), 12 % from other sources (ERP, Development Loan Corporation, Federal Länder and the DEG).

1) Payments of non-governmental institutions (Churches, trade unions, associations, foundations etc.) from their own funds.

2) This includes: 1,310 mill. DM direct investments, 700 mill. DM re-investments, a balance of 17 mill. DM from the purchase and sale of securities.

3) Loans of the World Bank and other multilateral institutions from the German capital market.

4. Official Grant and Credit Commitments to Developing Countries and Multilateral Agencies — 1973 to 1975

Type of Commitment	1973		1974		1975	
	Total mill. DM	Share %	Total mill. DM	Share %	Total mill. DM	Share %
Bilateral Commitments	3,262	76.0	4,920	79.0	3,924	73.3
Grants	1,318	30.7	1,768	28.4	1,609	30.1
of which: technical assistance	1,004	23.4	1,518	24.4	1,357	25.4
misc. grants	314	7.3	250	4.0	252	4.7
Credits (incl. debt rescheduling*)	1,944	45.3	3,152	50.6	2,315	43.2
Multilateral Commitments	1,031	24.0	1,307	21.0	1,427	26.7
Payments of subscribed capital	482	11.2	505	8.1	502	9.4
Misc. grants	499	11.6	752	12.1	875	16.4
Credits	50	1.2	50	0.8	50	0.9
Official Development Aid Commitments	4,293	100	6,227	100	5,351	100

*) Debt rescheduling commitments totalled 334 mill. DM in 1973, 247 mill. DM in 1974, and 452 mill. DM in 1975.

5. Members of the United Nations and its Related Agencies

Countries	UN	IAEA	ILO	FAO	UNESCO[1]	WHO[2]	IMF	BANK	IDA	IFC	ICAO	UPU[3]	ITU[4]	WMO[5]	IMCO[6]	UNCTAD[7]	GATT Parties[8]	WIPO
I. AFRICA																		
Algeria	×	×	×	×	×	×	×	×	×	—	×	×	×	×	×	×	×[10]	×
Benin	×	—	×	×	×	×	×	×	×	—	×	×	×	×	—	×	×	×
Botswana	×	—	—	×	—	×	×	×	×	—	—	×	×	×	—	×	×[10]	—
Burundi	×	—	×	×	×	×	×	×	×	—	×	×	×	×	—	×	×	—
Cameroon	×	×	×	×	×	×	×	×	×	×	×	×	×	×	—	×	×	×
Central African Republic	×	×	—	×	×	×	×	×	×	—	×	×	×	×	—	×	×	×
Chad	×	—	×	×	×	×	×	×	×	—	×	×	×	×	—	×	×	×
Congo	×	—	×	×	×	×	×	×	×	—	×	×	×	×	×	×	×	×
Egypt, Arab Republic of	×	×	×	×	×	×	×	×	×	×	×	×	×	×	×	×	×	×
Equatorial Guinea	×	—	—	—	—	—	×	×	×	—	×	×	×	—	×	×	×[10]	—
Ethiopia	×	×	×	×	×	×	×	×	×	×	×	×	×	×	×	×	—	—
Gabon	×	×	×	×	×	×	×	×	×	×	×	×	×	×	—	×	×	×
Gambia	×	—	×	×	×	×	×	×	×	×	×	×	×	×	×	×	×	—
Ghana	×	×	×	×	×	×	×	×	×	×	×	×	×	×	×	×	×	×
Guinea	×	—	×	×	×	×	×	×	×	×	×	×	×	×	×	×	—	—
Guinea-Bissau	×	—	—	×	×	×	—	—	—	—	—	×	—	—	—	—	—	—
Ivory Coast	×	×	×	×	×	×	×	×	×	×	×	×	×	×	×	×	×	×
Kenya	×	×	×	×	×	×	×	×	×	×	×	×	×	×	×	×	×	×
Lesotho	×	—	×	×	×	×	×	×	×	×	×	×	×	×	×	×	×[10]	—
Liberia	×	×	×	×	×	×	×	×	×	×	×	×	×	×	×	×	—	—
Libya	×	×	×	×	×	×	×	×	×	×	×	×	×	×	×	×	—	—
Madagascar	×	×	×	×	×	×	×	×	×	×	×	×	×	×	×	×	×	—
Malawi	×	—	×	×	×	×	×	×	×	×	×	×	×	×	×	×	×	×
Mali	×	×	×	×	×	×	×	×	×	—	×	×	×	×	—	×	×[10]	—
Mauritania	×	—	×	×	×	×	×	×	×	×	×	×	×	×	×	×	×	—
Morocco	×	×	×	×	×	×	×	×	×	×	×	×	×	×	×	×	—	×
Niger	×	×	×	×	×	×	×	×	×	—	×	×	×	×	—	×	×	×
Nigeria	×	×	×	×	×	×	×	×	×	×	×	×	×	×	×	×	×	×
Rhodesia	—	—	—	—	—	—	—	—	—	—	—	—	×	×	—	—	×	—
Rwanda	×	—	×	×	×	×	×	×	×	—	×	×	×	×	—	×	×	—
Senegal	×	×	×	×	×	×	×	×	×	×	×	×	×	×	×	×	×	×
Seychelles	×	—	—	—	—	—	—	—	—	—	—	—	—	—	—	—	—	—
Sierra Leone	×	×	×	×	×	×	×	×	×	×	×	×	×	×	×	×	×	—
Somalia	×	—	×	×	×	×	×	×	×	×	×	×	×	×	×	—	×	—
South Africa	×	×	—	—	—	×	×	×	×	×	×	×	×	×	×	—	×	×
Sudan	×	×	×	×	×	×	×	×	×	×	×	×	×	×	×	×	—	×
Swaziland	×	—	×	×	—	×	×	×	×	×	×	×	×	×	×	—	×[10]	—
Togo	×	—	×	×	×	×	×	×	×	×	×	×	×	×	—	×	×	×
Tunisia	×	×	×	×	×	×	×	×	×	×	×	×	×	×	×	×	×	×
Uganda	×	×	×	×	×	×	×	×	×	×	×	×	×	×	×	—	×	×
Tanzania	×	—	×	×	×	×	×	×	×	×	×	×	×	×	×	×	×	—

Countries	UN	IAEA	ILO	FAO	UNESCO[1]	WHO[2]	IMF	BANK	IDA	IFC	ICAO	UPU[3]	ITU[4]	WMO[5]	IMCO[6]	UNCTAD[7]	GATT Parties[8]	WIPO
Upper Volta	×	−	×	×	×	×	×	×	×	−	×	×	×	×	−	×	×	−
Zaire, Republic of	×	×	×	×	×	×	×	×	×	×	×	×	×	×	×	×	×	×
Zambia	×	×	×	×	×	×	×	×	×	×	×	×	×	×	×	−	× 10)	−
II. AMERICA																		
Argentina	×	×	×	×	×	×	×	×	×	×	×	×	×	×	×	×	×	−
Bahamas	×	−	−	−	−	×	×	×	−	−	−	×	×	×	−	−	−	−
Barbados	×	−	×	×	×	×	×	×	−	−	×	×	×	×	×	×	×	−
Bolivia	×	×	×	×	×	×	×	×	×	×	×	×	×	×	−	×	−	−
Brazil	×	×	×	×	×	×	×	×	×	×	×	×	×	×	×	×	×	×
Canada	×	×	×	×	×	×	×	×	×	×	×	×	×	×	×	×	×	×
Chile	×	×	×	×	×	×	×	×	×	×	×	×	×	×	×	×	×	×
Colombia	×	×	×	×	×	×	×	×	×	×	×	×	×	×	×	−	−	−
Costa Rica	×	×	×	×	×	×	×	×	×	×	×	×	×	×	×	−	−	−
Cuba	×	×	×	×	×	×	−	−	−	−	−	×	×	×	×	×	×	×
Dominican Republic	×	×	×	×	×	×	×	×	×	×	×	×	×	×	×	×	×	−
Ecuador	×	×	×	×	×	×	×	×	×	×	×	×	×	×	×	×	−	−
El Salvador	×	×	×	×	×	×	×	×	×	×	×	×	×	×	−	×	−	−
Grenada	×	−	−	−	×	×	−	−	−	−	−	−	−	×	−	−	−	−
Guatemala	×	×	×	×	×	×	×	×	×	×	×	×	×	×	−	×	−	−
Guyana	×	−	×	×	×	×	×	×	×	×	×	×	×	×	−	×	×	−
Haiti	×	×	×	×	×	×	×	×	×	×	×	×	×	×	−	×	×	−
Honduras	×	×	×	×	×	×	×	×	×	×	×	×	×	×	×	−	−	−
Jamaica	×	×	×	×	×	×	×	×	−	×	×	×	×	×	−	×	×	−
Mexico	×	×	×	×	×	×	×	×	×	×	×	×	×	×	×	×	−	×
Nicaragua	×	−	×	×	×	×	×	×	×	×	×	×	×	×	−	×	×	−
Panama	×	×	×	×	×	×	×	×	×	×	×	×	×	×	×	×	−	−
Paraguay	×	×	×	×	×	×	×	×	×	×	×	×	×	×	−	×	−	−
Peru	×	×	×	×	×	×	×	×	×	×	×	×	×	×	×	×	×	−
Surinam	×	−	−	−	−	−	−	−	−	−	−	×	−	×	−	−	−	−
Trinidad and Tobago	×	−	×	×	×	×	×	×	×	×	×	×	×	×	×	×	×	−
United States	×	×	×	×	×	×	×	×	×	×	×	×	×	×	×	×	×	×
Uruguay	×	×	×	×	×	×	×	×	−	×	×	×	×	×	×	×	×	−
Venezuela	×	×	×	×	×	×	×	×	−	×	×	×	×	×	−	×	−	−
III. ASIA																		
Afghanistan	×	×	×	×	×	×	×	×	×	×	×	×	×	×	−	×	−	−
Bahrain	×	−	−	×	×	×	×	×	−	−	×	×	×	−	−	−	× 10)	−
Bangladesh	×	×	×	×	×	×	×	×	×	−	×	×	×	×	−	−	×	−
Bhutan	×	−	−	−	−	−	−	−	−	−	−	×	−	−	−	−	−	−
Burma	×	×	×	×	×	×	×	×	×	×	×	×	×	×	×	×	×	−
China (People's Republic)	×	−	×	×	×	×	−	−	−	−	−	×	×	×	×	×	−	−
China/Taiwan	−	−	−	−	−	−	×	×	×	×	×	×	×	×	×	×	−	−
India	×	×	×	×	×	×	×	×	×	×	×	×	×	×	×	×	×	×

Countries	UN	IAEA	ILO	FAO	UNESCO[1]	WHO[2]	IMF	BANK	IDA	IFC	ICAO	UPU[3]	ITU[4]	WMO[5]	IMCO[6]	UNCTAD[7]	GATT Parties[8]	WIPO
Indonesia	×	×	×	×	×	×	×	×	×	×	×	×	×	×	×	×	×	×
Iran	×	×	×	×	×	×	×	×	×	×	×	×	×	×	×	×	−	−
Iraq	×	×	×	×	×	×	×	×	×	×	×	×	×	×	×	×	−	×
Israel	×	×	×	×	×	×	×	×	×	×	×	×	×	×	×	×	×	−
Japan	×	×	×	×	×	×	×	×	×	×	×	×	×	×	×	×	×	×
Jordan	×	×	×	×	×	×	×	×	×	×	×	×	×	×	×	×	−	×
Khmer Republic (Cambodia)	×	−	×	×	×	×	×	×	×	−	×	×	×	×	×	×	×	−
Korea (North)	○	×			×	×					×			×	−	−	−	×
Korea (South)	○	×	−	×	×	×	×	×	×	×	×	×	×	×	×	×	×	−
Kuwait	×	×	×	×	×	×	×	×	×	×	×	×	×	×	×	×	×	−
Laos	×	−	×	×	×	×	×	×	×	×	×	×	×	×	×	×	×	−
Lebanon	×	×	×	×	×	×	×	×	×	×	×	×	×	×	×	×	×	−
Malaysia	×	×	×	×	×	×	×	×	×	×	×	×	×	×	×	×	×	−
Maldives	×	−	−	×	−	×	−	−	−	−	×	×	×	−	×	×	10)	−
Mauritius	×	×	×	×	×	×	×	×	×	×	×	×	×	×	−	×	×	−
Mongolia (People's Republic)	×	×	×	−	×	×	−	−	−	−	×	×	×	×	−	×	−	−
Nepal	×	−	×	×	×	×	×	×	×	×	×	×	×	×	×	×	×	−
Oman	×	−	−	×	×	×	×	×	×	×	×	×	×	×	×	×	−	−
Pakistan	×	×	×	×	×	×	×	×	×	×	×	×	×	×	×	×	×	−
Philippines	×	×	×	×	×	×	×	×	×	×	×	×	×	×	×	×	×	−
Qatar	×	−	×	×	×	×	×	×	−	−	×	×	×	×	−	×	10)	×
Saudi Arabia	×	×	−	×	×	×	×	×	×	×	×	×	×	×	×	×	−	−
Singapore	×	×	×	×	×	×	×	×	−	×	×	×	×	−	×	×	×	−
Sri Lanka (Ceylon)	×	×	×	×	×	×	×	×	×	×	×	×	×	×	×	×	×	−
Syria	×	×	×	×	×	×	×	×	×	×	×	×	×	×	×	×	−	−
Thailand	×	×	×	×	×	×	×	×	×	×	×	×	×	×	×	×	−	−
Turkey	×	×	×	×	×	×	×	×	×	×	×	×	×	×	×	×	×	−
United Arab Emirates	×	−	×	×	×	×	×	×	−	−	×	×	×	−	−	−	−	×
Vietnam[9]	−	×	×	×	×	×	×	×	×	×	×	×	×	×	×	−	×	−	×
Yemen (Arab Republic)	×	−	×	×	×	×	×	×	×	×	×	×	×	×	×	−	×	−
Yemen (People's Democratic Republic)	×	×	×	−	×	×	×	×	−	×	×	×	×	×	−	×	10)	−

IV. EUROPE

Countries	UN	IAEA	ILO	FAO	UNESCO[1]	WHO[2]	IMF	BANK	IDA	IFC	ICAO	UPU[3]	ITU[4]	WMO[5]	IMCO[6]	UNCTAD[7]	GATT Parties[8]	WIPO
Albania	×	×	−	×	×	×	−	−	−	−	−	×	×	×	−	×	−	−
Austria	×	×	×	×	×	×	×	×	×	×	×	×	×	×	×	×	−	×
Belgium	×	×	×	×	×	×	×	×	×	×	×	×	×	×	×	×	×	×
Bulgaria	×	×	×	×	×	×	−	−	−	−	×	×	×	×	×	×	○	×
Byelorussian S.S.R.	×	×	×	−	×	×	−	−	−	−	−	×	×	×	−	×	−	×
Cyprus	×	×	×	×	×	×	×	×	×	×	×	×	×	×	×	×	×	−
Czechoslovakia	×	×	×	×	×	×	−	−	−	−	×	×	×	×	×	×	×	×
Denmark	×	×	×	×	×	×	×	×	×	×	×	×	×	×	×	×	×	×

231

Countries	UN	IAEA	ILO	FAO	UNESCO[1]	WHO[2]	IMF	BANK	IDA	IFC	ICAO	UPU[3]	ITU[4]	WMO[5]	IMCO[6]	UNCTAD[7]	GATT Parties[8]	WIPO
Finland	X	X	X	X	X	X	X	X	X	X	X	X	X	X	X	X	X	X
France	X	X	X	X	X	X	X	X	X	X	X	X	X	X	X	X	X	X
German Democratic Republic	X	X	X	—	X	X	—	—	—	—	—	X	X	X	X	X	—	X
Germany (Federal Republic of)	X	X	X	X	X	X	X	X	X	X	X	X	X	X	X	X	X	X
Greece	X	X	X	X	X	X	X	X	X	X	X	X	X	X	X	X	X	X
Holy See	O	X	—	—	—	—	—	—	—	—	—	X	X	—	—	X	—	X
Hungary	X	X	X	X	X	X	—	—	—	—	—	X	X	X	X	X	X	X
Iceland	X	X	X	X	X	X	X	X	X	X	X	X	X	X	X	X	X	—
Ireland	X	X	X	X	X	X	X	X	X	X	X	X	X	X	X	X	X	X
Italy	X	X	X	X	X	X	X	X	X	X	X	X	X	X	X	X	X	—
Liechtenstein	O	X	—	—	—	—	—	—	—	—	—	X	X	X	—	X	X	X
Luxembourg	X	X	X	X	X	X	X	X	X	X	X	X	X	X	X	—	X	X
Malta	X	—	X	X	X	X	X	X	X	X	X	X	X	X	X	X	X	—
Monaco	O	X	—	—	X	X	—	—	—	—	—	X	X	—	—	X	—	X
Netherlands	X	X	X	X	X	X	X	X	X	X	X	X	X	X	X	X	X	X
Norway	X	X	X	X	X	X	X	X	X	X	X	X	X	X	X	X	X	X
Poland	X	X	X	X	X	X	X	—	—	—	X	X	X	X	X	X	X	X
Portugal	X	X	X	X	X	X	X	X	—	X	X	X	X	X	—	X	X	X
Romania	X	X	X	X	X	X	X	—	—	X	X	X	X	X	X	X	X	X
San Marino	O	—	—	—	X	—	—	—	—	—	—	X	—	—	—	X	—	—
Sweden	X	X	X	X	X	X	X	X	X	X	X	X	X	X	X	X	X	X
Switzerland	O	X	X	X	X	X	—	—	—	—	X	X	X	X	X	X	X	X
Spain	X	X	X	X	X	X	X	X	X	X	X	X	X	X	X	X	X	X
Ukrainian S.S.R.	X	X	X	—	X	X	—	—	—	—	—	X	X	X	—	X	—	X
U.S.S.R.	X	X	X	—	X	X	—	—	—	—	—	X	X	X	X	—	X	X
United Kingdom	X	X	X	X	X	X	X	X	X	X	X	X	X	X	X	X	X	X

V. OCEANIA

Countries	UN	IAEA	ILO	FAO	UNESCO[1]	WHO[2]	IMF	BANK	IDA	IFC	ICAO	UPU[3]	ITU[4]	WMO[5]	IMCO[6]	UNCTAD[7]	GATT Parties[8]	WIPO
Australia	X	X	X	X	X	X	X	X	X	X	X	X	X	X	X	X	X	X
Fiji	X	—	X	X	X	X	X	X	X	—	X	X	X	X	—	—	[10]	X
Nauru	—	—	—	—	—	—	—	—	—	—	—	X	X	—	—	—	—	—
New Zealand	X	X	X	X	X	X	X	X	X	X	X	X	X	X	X	X	X	—
Papua-New Guinea	X	—	—	—	—	X	—	—	—	—	—	—	—	—	—	—	—	—
Tonga	—	—	X	X	X	X	—	—	—	—	X	X	X	X	X	[10]	—	—
Western Samoa	X	—	—	—	—	X	X	X	X	X	—	—	—	—	—	—	X	—
Total	148	107	127	130	137	143	126	125	113	104	134	148	143	138	95	137	87	66

Notes:

Source: United Nations Handbook 1975, New Zealand, Ministry of Foreign Affairs; hits 1975 Membership (138 UN Full Members); there is no UN publication of membership of a later date, membership to the UN Charter has been updated according to the resolutions passed by the General Assembly, membership of the individual Specialized Agencies according to available information, in particular on the basis of the Federal Law Gazette, Part II; membership was not indicated where no reliable information, in particular on newly admitted countries, was available.

1) UNESCO has 3 Associate Member States: the British Antilles, Papua-New Guinea and Namibia.

2) WHO has 1 Associate Member: Rhodesia.

3) The 148 Members of UPU include the following Territories not contained in the list: the Netherlands Antilles; Macao; all the British Oversea Territories, including the Colonies, Protectorates and Trust Territories administered by the United Kingdom; all the Territories represented by the French PTT; all the Territories of the United States, including the Trust Territory of the Pacific Islands.

4) The 143 Members of ITU include the following Territories not contained in the list: all the Territories represented by the French PTT; Macao; Territories of the United States; Oversea Territories administered by the United Kingdom; Papua-New Guinea is an Associate Member.

5) Of the 138 Members of WMO, the following have maintained their meteorological services: French Polynesia; French Territories of the Afars and Issas; the Islands of the former West Indies Federation and other British Territories in the Caribbean area; Rhodesia.

6) IMCO has 1 Associate Member: Hong Kong.

7) The UNCTAD Members are all Members of the UN; the controlling organ is the Trade and Development Board, its 55 Members being represented on a geographical basis; the Member States represented in the four main Committees are elected primarily on the basis of their economic structure; the Committees are: (a) the Committee on Commodities, with 48 Members; (b) the Committee on Manufactures, with 45 Members; (c) the Committee on Invisibles and Financing relating to Trade, with 45 Members and (d) the Committee on Shipping, with 37 Members.

8) Apart from the 87 GATT Contracting Parties there are the 11 States distinguished by 10) in the Table; these maintain "special relations" with GATT in various forms and observe the GATT rules and regulations without being a Member.

9) The Republic of South Vietnam was a Member to those Specialized Agencies where marked correspondingly, the Democratic Republic of Vietnam was a Member of WHO and WMO; after reunification as the Socialist Republic of Vietnam, Membership, according to the respective rules of procedure of the Agency, is either considered as being in abeyance or as represented by the representatives of the Socialist Republic of Vietnam, who in a way succeeded to Membership or have been recognized as a new Member.

× indicates Membership;   O indicates Observer.

Although they are not UN agencies, GATT and IAEA have been included because in their operations they are closely connected with UN and its various bodies.